P9-DXT-691

VOLUNTEER VACATIONS

Tenth Edition

VOLUNTEER VACATIONS

Tenth Edition

SHORT-TERM ADVENTURES THAT WILL BENEFIT YOU AND OTHERS

Bill McMillon, Doug Cutchins, and Anne Geissinger

Cover and interior design: Scott Rattray
Typesetting: Jonathan Hahn
Cover photos: (top) Digital Vision Photography/Veer; (bottom) Abigail Chance; (back)
i-to-i Meaningful Travel

Many of the personal vignettes included in this edition were provided courtesy of the
sponsoring organizations and permissions are their responsibility.

The authors have made every effort to ensure that all the listing information is correct
and current at the time of publication.

© 2009 by Bill McMillon, Doug Cutchins, and Anne Geissinger
All rights reserved
Published by Chicago Review Press, Incorporated
814 North Franklin Street
Chicago, Illinois 60610
ISBN-13: 978-1-55652-784-5
Printed in the United States of America

For the Saramaccan people of Ligolio, Suriname

Contents

Foreword

Ed Asner

IT'S BEEN SAID that "man would rather spend himself for a cause than live idly in prosperity." I'm sure upon uttering that axiom in a group, you'd see everyone nodding wisely—agreeing that hard work for a cause is preferable to the good life unfulfilled. It's a noble thought during a philosophical discussion. When everyone's in accord on that point, pull out some airline tickets to Perryville, Arkansas, and ask who's willing to give up their Bermuda vacation in order to work with livestock. Any takers?

It's a hard sell. Public service is an antiquity in today's society. In the thirties the Civilian Conservation Corps instilled in the minds of young men and women the notion that national service is an obligation, indeed, a privilege: putting something back into the country in exchange for all the benefits derived from living in a free and democratic society. It was a wonderful setup and one that should have been perpetuated.

Since that time, however, our country's military bent has made national service an anathema—national service has come to mean the draft, the military, risk of life and limb on some foreign shore. Some states, to supplement low budget allocations, use public service as punishment for misdemeanors. In Oregon, for instance, DWI offenders can be seen picking up highway litter.

In short, the notion of a "volunteer vacation" sounds like a disciplinary measure akin to assigning extra household chores to a balky teenager.

Happily, there are people like Bill McMillon, Doug Cutchins, and Anne Gessinger (along with the hundreds of people who have taken volunteer vacations) to set us straight: volunteering for a worthy cause can be fun, fulfilling, and an adventure you'll anticipate year after year. Maybe working with livestock isn't your thing, but there's plenty of variety: go on archaeological expeditions, assist with health care in remote villages, maintain trails in beautiful mountain climes, or build homes for the homeless. Some programs encourage you to bring the kids; some pay part of your expenses.

Best of all, you'll be helping people who need you. These days our local, state, and federal government budgets (and many government budgets around the world) have cut "people programs" in favor of big business and the military. More and more, our nation and our world must look to volunteers to fill the gaps that governments are unwilling or unable to fill—in health care, education, and programs for the disabled and underprivileged.

Read this book . . . try a volunteer vacation. The world will be a better place and so will you.

Preface

YOUR COMMUNITY IS growing. Whether or not you want it to, whether or not you are aware of it, the bounds of where you can go, what you can do, and who you can meet grow almost every day. As technology improves, communities and countries that were once geographically and culturally isolated are coming into close contact with other cities and nations. We recall walking into a village in the middle of the rainforest of Suriname, commenting on how remote the village was and how little contact it had with the outside world, and then noticing a Nike swoosh shaved into the back of a villager's haircut. The fact that this icon of American corporate culture had made its way to a village that lacked roads, running water, and electricity demonstrated what we already knew but had forgotten: there are very few communities left on Earth that you can't reach, and we are all quickly becoming interconnected.

This process of globalization has had both positive and negative aspects. More people have access to better health care. More children are being educated. More communities are getting basic services, such as clean drinking water and electricity. But these same communities are under attack from outside influences both cultural and economic. Is it a good thing when a child learns to read . . . but not in the language of her parents? What happens to a rural family who finally gets electricity . . . but the husband has to work—and live—in the nearest city in order to afford it? And why do so many people around the world seem to love American products, sports, and popular culture, but profess a disdain for our country?

There are no easy answers to these questions. But, as the definition of your community changes and more people become your "neighbors," you have a level of responsibility to try to figure these and other questions out.

We would argue that volunteering is one of the best ways to start to find these answers. As a volunteer, you can begin to halt the tide of the nastier effects of globalization, and instead promote the benefits of international understanding and cooperation. Through personal, one-on-one exchanges and dialogues, individuals around the world—including people from different communities in the United States—will better understand and appreciate the people in their national and global neighborhoods.

Why turn a vacation into a volunteer vacation? After researching this book, we're hard-pressed to see why you wouldn't! First, the opportunities presented here are amazing. We challenge you to read this book and not find organizations that make you want to get on the next plane to Nepal, France, or California. Second, your help is desperately needed. The 150 organizations listed in this book exist for a reason—there is a lot of need in the world, and the skills that you have can be put to tremendously good use in helping to fulfill that need.

We hope that you'll take advantage of the chance that you have to turn a regular vacation into an experience that will truly benefit yourself, others, and your community. Almost everyone who undertakes these projects returns home proclaiming that their vacations benefited them at least as much as they did the people being served. And when this happens to you, we hope that you'll then take the next step: share the experience. Invite friends over to see pictures of your trip. (They'll be more interested in these pictures than those of your last trip to the beach, we promise!) Talk to a group at your place of worship about what you did. Write a column for the local newspaper. Call an elementary school and ask if you can come speak to a class. The medium isn't crucial; what's most important is that you share the lessons that you learned with a wider audience, because then your understanding of a new community is spread to more people.

And keep your mind open—you may even find that a volunteer vacation is so rewarding that you want to take on a longer-term commitment. If that happens to you, turn to the end of this book, because we've included a special section with information on some long-term volunteer programs.

Volunteer vacations can change your perspective on the world, teach you new skills, and greatly affect the lives of others. We hope that you are inspired to make an ordinary vacation extraordinary, and to use your talents to better yourself and your community.

—Doug Cutchins and Anne Geissinger

Acknowledgments

for Doug Cutchins and Anne Geissinger

OUR FIRST THANKS have to go to the organizations that form the heart of this book. For months, they put up with our requests, reminders, and questions, spending time and resources on e-mails and phone conversations. Each organization was truly outstanding to work with. In addition to their cooperation, though, we are also thankful for the work they do, the opportunities they create, and the assistance they give to volunteers, all in order to help improve the planet and the human condition.

We are also thankful for the help and cooperation of the authors and photographers whose work appears in this book to help bring volunteer experiences to life. None of these artists received compensation; all agreed to have their work published as a way to help promote the volunteer organizations and to inspire others. We are indebted to them for their kindness and generosity.

It is one of the greatest oddities of our lives that we have never met Bill McMillon, or even talked to him on the phone. Yet we are deeply impressed and inspired by the years of work he put into the early editions of this book. There are many people about whom we can say, "This book would not be what it is without you." Without Bill, though, this book simply would not be at all.

We sometimes wonder what we did to deserve the faith that our friends at Chicago Review Press have shown in us. Cynthia Sherry recruited us out of the blue to take over authorship of this book, and she has always been there to answer our questions and give helpful, timely advice. Lisa Rosenthal, Brooke Kush, and

Michelle Schoob, our editors, have improved the book and our writing in innumerable ways, always asking good questions and pushing us to produce the best book possible. Our publicists— Catherine Bosin, Elisabeth Malzahn, and Jen Wisnowski—have surprised us with their incredible resourcefulness and tenacity in finding new audiences and media outlets for the book, and delighted us with their marvelous senses of humor. We are indebted to and thank them all.

On more personal notes, we would like to thank our dear friends and mentors, Steve Langerud and George Drake, for inspiring us and pushing us; the "Rockababy" families for giving us the idea to explicitly include information on family volunteer opportunities; and Erik and Carolyn for the emergency use of the laptop that goes "ping!"

Emma and Bea, our daughters, have been our ongoing sources of inspiration and joy throughout the three editions of this book that we've written. It's hard to imagine a seven-year-old and five-year-old with more patience, whether with the book or with their parents.

Lastly, writing this book gives us a daily excuse to think about the Saramaccan people of Ligolio, Suriname, who generously opened their village and lives to two young, recently married American Peace Corps volunteers for two years. Our time in Ligolio helped create us as we are today, changed how we see the world, and gave us the confidence that we could make an impact. We dedicate this book to them.

Introduction

SEE A NEW part of the United States or a completely different country.

Help other people.

Relax.

Make new friends.

Learn a few words in a new language or resurrect the Spanish that you haven't used since high school.

Change your perspective on what it means to be rich or poor, first world or third world, developed or underdeveloped.

How? Take a volunteer vacation.

"A volunteer vacation?" you might say. "Doesn't that imply work? But isn't that why I'm going on vacation, to get away from work?"

Yes and no. If you take advantage of one of the opportunities in this book, you'll certainly work. You'll build bridges and blaze trails (both real and metaphorical), teach people how to read, take care of injured wildlife, play with kids in an orphanage, or do any of a hundred other jobs that will make a real difference on our planet. That's work—hard work.

But it's completely different than what most of us do to bring home a paycheck every week.

You'll be in a new place, surrounded by people you don't know. You'll be using parts of your brain and body that haven't gotten good workouts in years. You're likely to experience some kind of paradigm shift and to look at yourself, your country, or the world in a new way. Not only will you come home refreshed and rejuvenated, as you would after any vacation, but you'll also have the knowledge that you've made a difference in someone's life or in the world.

Sounds good—what's next?

There are two ways to go about using this guide. The first is to open it up and begin to dream, to allow yourself to exclaim, "That's it, honey—pack your bags for the Northern Mariana Islands! I hear it's beautiful this time of year." If you're open to new places to go and things to do, this is the approach for you; start reading and dreaming. Some people, though, need to be a little more intentional in their planning. If you know that you want to go to Europe, for example, or that you really want to work with kids, or that you can't spend more than five hundred dollars, then you need to be more selective in your reading. Make good use of the indexes in the back of this book and frequently check the Web sites of the organizations you're considering, since information can and does change over time. This is especially true of program costs, which can change quickly with shifts in the global economy.

What This Guide Does and Doesn't Do

This is a resource guide; it is not a review book. We provide basic information about select organizations that we have carefully vetted and that we feel good about recommending in order to allow you to begin to make decisions about what organizations are right for you and the experience that you want to have. Given that well over a hundred organizations run thousands of programs in scores of countries, we wouldn't want to try and make a judgment call for you as an individual; what is perfect for some people is horrible for others. Instead, we give you excellent information that you need to know about these organizations so that you can begin to make an informed decision. We've made a trade-off in doing so: instead of focusing on giving you a little bit of information on as many organizations as possible, we've been very selective and pared down our list, but have given you in-depth information about each organization. Even with this additional information, though, we hope that nobody goes on a volunteer vacation without first talking with a staff member of the organization and, if at all possible, with people who have volunteered with the organization in the past. Every organization's listing in this book has extensive contact information, including e-mail addresses and Web site URLs. Use the recent explosion in blogging to help your research—a quick Google blog search might turn up several journals from volunteers who traveled with an organization you are considering. Research and evaluate organizations the same way you would go about making any other decision about how to use your time and money. (Speaking of money, it's important for you to know that none of the organizations listed in this book had to pay anything to be included. This book is free publicity for them, and they deserve it. We hope that their inclusion in *Volunteer Vacations* helps them to recruit volunteers like you.)

We've given you another valuable tool to start with in addition to this expanded information. Sprinkled throughout this book you'll find volunteer vignettes, stories written by past volunteers about their experiences with some of these organizations, as well as photos of volunteers in action. These more personal glimpses into the daily lives of volunteers will give you a better sense of what your experience might be like, and they can help you to imagine yourself in the volunteers' places.

How Do I Evaluate an Organization to See If It Is Right for Me?

Here are ten questions you should get answers to before signing on with a volunteer organization.

1. Does the work involved mesh with what I want to do on my vacation? Will it allow me to develop or use skills that are important to me?
2. Will the project take me to a place that I want to go?
3. Do I have the same goals and values as those of the organization? (This is especially important for organizations that have overt political or religious goals; you don't want to end up promoting a cause, directly or

indirectly, that you don't believe in. Read the mission statement carefully in each entry.)

4. What do past volunteers say about their experiences with this organization?
5. What are living conditions at the site like?
6. What will my exact job responsibilities be? How much scut work (cooking, cleaning, filing, and so on) will I be expected to do? Keep in mind that someone has to do this work, and it is often divided among all of the employees and volunteers, from top to bottom.
7. How much does it cost to participate? What exactly is included in a program fee?
8. When does the project take place, how long does it last, and does it fit with my schedule?
9. Will I be working in a group? What is the profile of the average volunteer? Age range? What are the motivations of the other people in the group?
10. What kind of training or orientation is offered? (This information is crucial for international organizations, where you might be working in a culture very different from your own.)

Always check the U.S. State Department's lists of countries under travel warnings and public announcements to better understand the security situation in the places that you might be traveling. We would strongly discourage anyone from volunteering in a country that is under a travel warning, and we would caution you to do more research before volunteering in a country under a public announcement.

Getting the Most Out of This Book

Each listing in this book contains up to twelve sections:

- *General contact information:* including (as available) postal address, phone and fax numbers, e-mail addresses, and Web site URLs.

- *Project Type:* We asked each organization to place itself in one of approximately twenty-five categories, so that you can tell at a glance what an organization does, broadly speaking. You can use this section (in addition to the indexes) if you are glancing casually through the book looking for, say, opportunities to volunteer with orphans, or another specific type of opportunity.
- *Mission Statement Excerpt:* This statement gives you an idea of how each organization defines itself.
- *Year Founded* and *Number of Volunteers Last Year:* Though numbers can certainly be misleading, you can get a sense of the scope of an organization's work by looking at how long it has been in existence and how many people they are used to serving. That said, don't reject small or recently founded organizations out of hand; some of our favorite organizations are young, but they have passionate, go-getter administrators behind them.
- *Funding Sources:* To borrow the old dictum from the movie *All the President's Men,* "Follow the money." This step is important, as knowing where an organization's funding comes from helps you know more about its reason for being and who supports its work. Luckily, most organizations are very up-front about this information; they don't want disaffected volunteers who don't share their mission. Assume that the funding sources that are listed here are in addition to the program fees that organizations charge to volunteer with them.
- *The Work They Do:* Here's where we get into the meat of the description. This part describes in broad terms what the work of the organization is, as well as how volunteers help with that work. Look for specifics on volunteer jobs and examples of how you'll be spending your time with this organization.
- *Project Location:* The location can be incredibly specific for some of our smaller organizations, or "worldwide" for organizations that operate a large number of ever-

changing global operations. Also included in this section are details, as we know them, about lodging accommodations so that you can be sure you'll be comfortable with the arrangements.

- *Time Line:* Information here includes when applications are accepted, when volunteer positions begin, and how long positions last (minimum, maximum, and average time lengths).
- *Cost:* Yes, virtually all of these opportunities cost money (the few that do not usually require very specialized skills or a long-term commitment). This section tries to detail as best it can what those costs will be, as well as what is included in the organizations' fees and what additional expenses you will need to bear. Pay close attention to insurance coverage; if the organization does not provide insurance, check with your insurance provider before departure to make sure that you will be covered overseas. If not, please consider purchasing a short-term supplemental policy.
- *Getting Started:* This section gives information about how to best contact the organization or obtain an application, whether or not an interview is required, as well as details on training and orientation programs.
- *Needed Skills and Specific Populations:* If an organization requires that you have mastered specific skills before volunteering with them, that information will be noted here. Also found here is information regarding age minimums and maximums, as well as information for volunteers with disabilities and families.

Toward the end of the book you will find our short section on long-term volunteer opportunities. We hope that you will seriously consider these as well as, or perhaps after undertaking, a shorter-term volunteer vacation. The long-term opportunities listed here all have the added bonus of providing funding for your experience; you won't have to foot the bill for one of these long-term stints. Taking a volunteer vacation will change your perspective; a long-term volunteer commitment will change your life.

Expectations: What Is Reasonable and What Is Unreasonable

Be nice to the organizations that offer these opportunities. Remember that many of them operate on extremely lean budgets with underpaid and overworked staff. Please don't request printed information from a group unless you are seriously considering volunteering with them. Make ample use of the vast resources of the Internet—all of the organizations in this book have Web sites that you can access for basic information. Be polite and understand that your request is one of many that the organization is dealing with at any given time. Act as a partner, not as a consumer. Consider sending a small check along with each request for information, and if the organization is based overseas, send them an international reply coupon (available at your local post office) to help defray the cost of postage. Remember: the more money these organizations spend on administration, the less they have left to spend on what they're working to achieve.

That said, organizations have a responsibility to their volunteers as well. Organizations should live up to their promises and advertising. They should answer your questions fully, honestly, and in a timely manner. To some extent, there is also the aspect that "you get what you pay for." In other words, if you are paying thousands of dollars for an experience, you have a right (within limits) to expect more service than someone whose experience is wholly sponsored by the organization.

Last, don't expect to change the world overnight. Have reasonable expectations of the organization, yourself, and your ability to create long-term change. Recognize that the work you do is important, but that it is just one piece of the larger puzzle of improving global conditions. Let the process, not the product, be your measure of success.

VOLUNTEER VACATIONS

Tenth Edition

ACDI/VOCA

50 F Street NW, Suite 1075
Washington, DC 20001
(800) 929-8622; Fax: (202) 626-8726
E-mail: volunteer@acdivoca.org
Web site: www.acdivoca.org; volunteer-specific information
at www.vocafoundation.org

Project Type: Agriculture; Community Development; Economic
Development; Professional/Technical Assistance; Rural
Development; Women's Issues
Mission Statement Excerpt: "ACDI/VOCA's worldwide mission
is to promote economic opportunities for cooperatives, busi-
nesses, and communities through the innovative application
of sound business practices."
Year Founded: 1963
Number of Volunteers Last Year: Approximately 300
Funding Sources: ACDI/VOCA receives government funding
from the U.S. Agency for International Development and the
U.S. Department of Agriculture, as well as gifts, grants, and
donations from private sources.
The Work They Do: ACDI/VOCA creates volunteer opportunities for experts in agriculture, business, finance, cooperative
development, and natural resource management.
ACDI/VOCA volunteers are typically mid- to late-career
professionals with significant experience who provide
expertise to host organizations in economically developing
countries. Many volunteers are members of teams, and
many conduct repeat assignments. ACDI/VOCA is driven by
the needs of its host countries, not by the desires of volunteers; as such, they only place volunteers after receiving
requests from their offices around the world.
Project Location: Projects are located around the world,
including the Middle East, Africa, Latin America, Eastern
Europe and the former Soviet Union, and Southeast Asia.
Accommodations vary from country to country; in urban
areas, volunteers are typically housed in moderate-quality

Azerbaijani farmer Ismail Aslanov speaks with ACDI/VOCA staff while in his strawberry field. The ACDI/VOCA's volunteer program connected Ismail with expert volunteer specialists who introduced new varieties of strawberries and provided training in the best practices for strawberry farming. The end result of Ismail's experiences with ACDI/VOCA staff and volunteers was an impressive 25 percent increase in his income. *Photo courtesy of ACDI/VOCA- Heather Luca*

hotels, guesthouses, or apartments that the project leases. In rural areas, volunteers may be asked to stay with the host or in more rustic settings.

Time Line: Volunteers are placed year-round. Placements are typically two to six weeks in length.

Cost: ACDI/VOCA pays and arranges for all assignment-related expenses, including round-trip coach airfare, passport, visas, lodging, meals and incidentals, required immunizations, emergency medical evacuation, and supplemental health insurance.

Getting Started: Applications are accepted year-round via the ACDI/VOCA Web site. Volunteers are interviewed at the time of selection for an assignment, and briefings are provided before volunteers travel to their assignment.

Needed Skills and Specific Populations: ACDI/VOCA volunteers are typically mid- to late-career and senior professionals with a minimum of ten years of experience in one of the following areas: accounting; agricultural extension and education; banking and finance; business management; community development; cooperative and association development; domestic and international marketing; enterprise development; entrepreneurship; farm management; food and meat processing; food storage and handling; fruit, vegetable, and plant production and protection; grain and commodity inspection and storage, information technology and e-commerce; livestock production and disease control; ecotourism and agrotourism; policy reform; post-harvest handling; rural credit; sustainable agriculture; trade associations; and training of trainers. Many retired experts have volunteered with ACDI/VOCA. Because some work sites are in rural areas in economically developing countries, ACDI/VOCA may have problems accommodating volunteers with disabilities. Some programs require U.S. citizenship. ACDI/VOCA does not recruit families.

Strawberry Farming Increases Incomes in Azerbaijan

By Erin Gamble

ACDI/VOCA

In Gelilabad, Azerbaijan, ACDI/VOCA taught farmers how to grow strawberries as a way to supplement their incomes. Although demand was high for fresh berries, they were not widely grown in the region. To introduce strawberry production to the local farmers, ACDI/VOCA sent Cliff Hatch, a volunteer from Massachusetts with over twenty years experience in organic agriculture production. Mr. Hatch visited Gelilabad and conducted training seminars in farm management. He also brought two thousand strawberry plants to launch the new program. The variety he brought, the Tribute-Tristar type, has a distinct advantage over other local types in that they produce three fruitings a year, allowing farmers to sell their harvests throughout the year rather than just in one season.

One project participant, Ismail Aslanov, had never grown strawberries before, but he was eager to take part in the project. He received 150 strawberry plants and began tending them using the techniques Mr. Hatch had taught him. Mr. Aslanov was able to propagate the new plants, and from his original 150 plants, he was able to grow 20,000. He now maintains eight thousand strawberry plants and gives the rest to nearby farmers to share the new techniques he has learned.

Multiple harvests have allowed Mr. Aslanov to increase his profits. "Before now we didn't have varieties with more than one fruiting and harvest," he notes, "which meant that the market was flooded . . . and prices dropped." Now, he can get $1.30 per kilogram for his berries out of season, as opposed to just 40 cents in May and June, prime harvest time. In 2000, ACDI/VOCA sent a second volunteer, Margaret Morse, to Azerbaijan to check on the farmers' progress. Mrs. Morse, a production agriculture expert from Virginia, brought samples from the Chandler variety of strawberry, which yields a sweeter, larger fruit. Due to his success with growing and propagating the plants, Mr. Aslanov received 650 Chandler strawberry plants. Mrs. Morse provided training in spacing and land contouring techniques, conducted soil tests, and made recommendations on soil preparation and irrigation. Mr. Aslanov has implemented all of Mrs. Morse's suggestions, commenting that "the more information we have, the better off we will be."

Ismail Aslanov continues to farm potatoes and other vegetables, but he has realized a 25 percent increase in his income due to his strawberry operation. He has plans to expand his farm to four times its current size. His success is due to the knowledge, and plants, provided by ACDI/VOCA volunteers.

African Conservation Trust (ACT)

P.O. Box 310
Link Hills, 3652
South Africa
+27 31-7675044
E-mail: info@projectafrica.com
Web site: www.projectafrica.com

Project Type: Archaeology; Community Development; Historic
   Preservation; Natural Conservation (Land); Scientific
   Research
Mission Statement Excerpt: "The mission of the African
   Conservation Trust (ACT) is to provide a means for conser-
   vation projects to become self-funding through active partic-
   ipation by the public. This gives ordinary people a chance to
   make a positive and real contribution to environmental
   conservation by funding and participating in the research
   effort as volunteers."
Year Founded: 2000
Number of Volunteers Last Year: 53
Funding Sources: ACT receives funding through the United
   Nations, South African National Lottery, and the South
   African National Heritage Council.
The Work They Do: Most of ACT's programs involve long-term
   natural conservation or historic preservation efforts such as
   a hippo project on Lake Malawi and a rock art mapping
   project in South Africa. Examples of specific work carried
   out by volunteers include: radio tracking of various species
   of African mammals, sand trapping at holes dug under the
   perimeter fence to monitor entry and exit species and
   numbers, conducting monthly game counts at water holes
   and perhaps walking transects, clearing the fence line of
   vegetation and eradicating alien invasive plants on the farm,
   exploring the Ukhalhamba-Drakensberg Park in South
   Africa for new, unrecorded rock art painting and archaeological sites of the indigenous San people, or conducting a
   hippo census on Lake Malawi by boat.

Project Location: Projects are carried out in the sub-Saharan countries of South Africa and Malawi. Conditions vary by location. In South Africa, volunteers are based in the mountains at an extensive base camp. The roughest conditions may be found in Malawi, where volunteers camp in expedition conditions. Volunteers usually provide their own camping gear.

Time Line: Volunteers are accepted year-round. Volunteers can commit to as little as a two-week period to as much as a one-year experience; the average stay is about four weeks.

Cost: ACT's program fee is £950 per month. The program fee includes pick up from and drop off at the airport nearest the site, all in-country, project-related transport, accommodation, food, and training. Air transportation to and from the country involved (as well as flights to and from the airport nearest the project site) are not included in the program fee.

Getting Started: Prospective volunteers should contact ACT via e-mail or the organization's Web site. ACT will provide orientation and training if necessary.

Needed Skills and Specific Populations: In South Africa the work is very physical and includes working and walking on steep slopes, so volunteers must have hiking or backpacking experience. Volunteers must be at least eighteen years old; there is no maximum age limit. ACT cannot accommodate volunteers with disabilities.

African Impact

11 Philips Avenue
Belgravia, Harare
Zimbabwe
+(263) (0) 4-702814-7
E-mail: info@africanimpact.com
Web site: www.africanimpact.com

Project Type: Community Development; Education;
 Medical/Health; Natural Conservation (Land); Orphans;
 Rural Development; Youth
Mission Statement Excerpt: "Explore. Inspire. Impact."
Year Founded: 2003
Number of Volunteers Last Year: 1,000
Funding Sources: None outside of volunteer program fees
The Work They Do: African Impact facilitates a wide variety of
 volunteer projects with the goal of assisting conservation
 initiatives and local communities, while providing a life-
 changing experience for international volunteers. African
 Impact works hard to build strong relationships with local
 authorities and in communities. Projects range throughout
 southern and eastern Africa and include offerings such as
 lion rehabilitation in Zimbabwe; wildlife photography and
 conservation education in South Africa; rural preschool and
 community development in Mozambique; and sports
 coaching in Zambia. Volunteers take on a similarly broad
 range of tasks, including assisting in clinics, building
 orphanages, and teaching in primary schools to doing
 conservation education, working with lions, and doing
 elephant and leopard research.
Project Location: African Impact operates in southern and
 eastern Africa, including Zambia, Zimbabwe, Mozambique,
 South Africa, Kenya, and Botswana. While some of their
 projects involve physical work, such as walking through the
 bush, coaching children in soccer, or laying bricks, volunteers are well-informed of this before they sign up. For
 accommodations, volunteers either live at a base camps

adjacent to a game reserve where the volunteer is working, or in volunteer houses in towns and villages. At all sites, volunteers have a communal area, comfortable bathrooms, and bedrooms that they share with no more than four others.

Time Line: Projects run throughout the year, but most projects do have specific start dates each month. While African Impact is flexible on how long volunteers stay, most work between two weeks and three months.

Cost: The project fee varies, but depending on the specific project, volunteers generally pay between $2,000 and $3,000 per month. The fee includes accommodation, three meals each day, airport transfers, transport to and from the projects, and a volunteer manual with information on the projects. The program fee does not include flights and travel insurance.

Getting Started: Volunteers must apply online at least three weeks before they wish to depart; no interview is required. African Impact provides volunteers with an orientation that includes a tour of the surrounding area, an introduction to the local customs and culture, a lesson in the local language, and necessary project-specific training.

Needed Skills and Specific Populations: African Impact does not have any required skills; the only restriction is that, for safety reasons, volunteers with the lion rehabilitation project must be at least five feet tall. Volunteers must be at least eighteen years old, but there is no maximum age limit. African Impact enthusiastically works with volunteers with disabilities, and families are welcome as long as all children meet the minimum age requirement.

AidCamps International

483 Green Lanes
London, N13 4BS
England
+44 (0) 845 652 5412
E-mail: info@aidcamps.org
Web site: www.aidcamps.org

Project Type: Community Development; Construction; Education; Medical/Health; Orphans; Rural Development; Youth

Mission Statement Excerpt: "Providing development aid and
support to local communities, primarily but not exclusively
in developing countries, for the furtherance of the relief of
poverty, the advancement of education and health care, and
other purposes beneficial to the community."

Year Founded: 2002

Number of Volunteers Last Year: 120

Funding Sources: Individuals

The Work They Do: AidCamps mostly builds community gathering spots for children, such as schools, orphanages, and
resource centers. Volunteer groups typically work on
building these community buildings, while individual volunteers take part in community-focused projects that might
include teaching, conservation work, research, or other
opportunities. Individual volunteer placements are based on
the volunteer's skills and interests and the community's
needs.

Project Location: AidCamps places volunteers in Cameroon,
India, Nepal, and Sri Lanka. All volunteers reside in
AidCamps accommodations near the community; conditions
vary by country and are usually fairly simple, but AidCamps
makes every attempt to make volunteers as comfortable as
possible given the local environment. Individual volunteers
may choose to stay with a host family.

Time Line: Group volunteer projects have fixed start and end
dates, usually lasting three weeks. Individual volunteers are
welcomed throughout the year for a minimum of one week,

and a maximum as allowed by visa constraints. Most individual volunteers participate for between three weeks and three months.

Cost: Group volunteer projects have a per-person registration fee of £180 and a minimum donation of £415, which covers most of the volunteer's in-country costs. Individual volunteers have a £45 registration fee and a minimum donation of £300 to £500, though this does not cover any of the in-country costs.

Getting Started: Volunteers may access application materials on AidCamps' Web site. The group volunteer programs are first-come, first-served, so prospective volunteers should apply well before their intended departure date. In addition, AidCamps requires criminal record checks for all volunteers; for US citizens, this means obtaining a record check from the FBI, which can take five to six months. Otherwise, individual volunteers should apply at least three months before they would like to depart, and need to complete a phone interview. AidCamps provides in-county orientation and training.

Needed Skills and Specific Populations: Volunteers with groups simply need good health, enthusiasm, and cultural sensitivity. Individual volunteers will need skills that match their unique placement. The minimum age for volunteers is eighteen, unless a family is volunteering together, in which case there is no minimum age. AidCamps does not have a maximum age limit, and works quite a bit with senior volunteers. In general, the situation at AidCamps' work locations are not suitable for volunteers with disabilities.

Ambassadors for Children (AFC)

1201 North Central Avenue
Indianapolis, IN 46202
(866) 338-3468; Fax: (317) 536-0258
E-mail: contact@ambassadorsforchildren.org
Web site: www.ambassadorsforchildren.org

Project Type: Construction; Education; Medical/Health;
Orphans; Social Justice; Youth
Mission Statement Excerpt: "Ambassadors for Children is a
not-for-profit organization dedicated to serving children
around the world through short-term humanitarian service
trips and sustainable projects."
Year Founded: 1998
Number of Volunteers Last Year: Approximately 500
Funding Sources: Private donors, corporate sponsors, and grants
The Work They Do: Ambassadors for Children supports children in approximately twenty locations around the world
by identifying and supporting sustainable programs. Examples of these programs include developing small businesses
to aid socioeconomically disadvantaged families in Belize
and El Salvador; building and supporting an orphanage in
India; and supplying and shipping medical equipment to
Serbia, El Salvador, Malawi, and Jordan. Ambassadors for
Children also provides a large variety of activities for AFC
volunteers traveling on short-term humanitarian trips to
implement in orphanages, schools, and communities. These
projects include opportunities such as teaching English as a
second language, supervising sporting and recreational
activities at orphanages, schools, and communities; and
assisting with medical and dental assessments of children.
Project Location: AFC currently operates humanitarian trips to
Jamaica, Mexico, El Salvador, Belize, Guatemala, Costa
Rica, Peru, Serbia, Jordan, India, Nepal, Malawi, South
Africa, Kenya, Uganda, and South Dakota. Housing for
most of AFC's trips is in unique guesthouses, boutique
hotels, moderate hotels, and eco-lodges.

An AFC volunteer gets joyfully messy with children in an orphanage outside of Cape Town as together they mix up the batter for steam bread. Steam bread is a South African specialty; therefore this is not only a fun, engaging, and tasty activity, but also an opportunity to pass along a strong tradition. *Photo courtesy of Ambassadors for Children*

Time Line: AFC operates at least one trip almost every month of the year, and usually offers more than thirty volunteer programs per year. Trips vary in length from five days to three weeks, with most falling in the seven to ten day range. AFC offers multiple trips and destinations over spring breaks, summer vacation, and at Christmas.

Cost: Ground packages including transfers, accommodations, orientation, welcome dinner, farewell dinner, some meals, a tour, and donation to the volunteer sites start at $699 for domestic programs and range to approximately $1999 for overseas programs, depending on the length of the trip. Airfare is not included in AFC's pricing. AFC has fund-raisers throughout the year to cover its administrative costs, so virtually all program fees are used to offset the program costs.

Getting Started: Prospective volunteers should contact AFC via e-mail or phone. AFC requires a volunteer profile and waiver of liability to be filled out before the volunteer can officially join an AFC trip. Beginning two months before the trip, AFC provides both an orientation guide and the services of a trip leader. AFC also offers an on-site orientation during the first day of the trip, which includes basic information on AFC, the history, culture, and food of the destination, an overview of the itinerary, and an introduction to the volunteer work and global partners.

Needed Skills and Specific Populations: No specific skills are required, but AFC always encourages teachers, students, doctors, dentists, carpenters, and other skilled professionals to volunteer. There is no minimum age limit, but volunteers under age eighteen must be accompanied by an adult. Senior volunteers are welcomed. Volunteers with disabilities are also welcomed, provided that they have someone accompanying them who can provide help as needed. AFC has been working with families since its inception, and strongly encourages family volunteers.

The Little Girl Who Stole My Heart

By Kelly Campbell

Ambassadors for Children

Two-week Malawi trips in September 2006 and June 2007

Her name is Janet Banda. When I first met her she was two years old. She had been found severely malnourished under a bridge in Malawi with several of her brothers and sisters. Her mother had recently passed away from AIDS and the kids were left to fend for themselves. By some stroke of luck, this little girl was rescued and taken to an orphanage where she was nursed back to health.

In September, when I first came to this orphanage with Ambassadors for Children, she immediately caught my eye. She was dressed in a little red and white plaid dress, tiny as can be, with big, gorgeous brown eyes, and a shyness to her that made you want to scoop her up and never let go. This little girl had suffered through more pain and loss at the age of two than most people endure in a lifetime. Yet, here she was, eating a cookie and slowly sipping away at some juice, cautious of her surroundings, yet eager to observe the strange people in her home. Throughout the two weeks I was in Malawi observing Janet, she rarely spoke. She remained to herself, yet she had an innocence and independence that captivated me.

The following year, I returned to Malawi and there she was, in the same red and white plaid dress. The minute I walked into the orphanage, my eyes were once again immediately drawn to her. Somehow I managed to find her amongst the 150 other children in the room within seconds. I felt an immense sense of relief to know that she was still alive and doing well. She looked at me and did a double take—she recognized me and stared at me for some time, trying to remember where she had seen this familiar face. While still shy, I noticed that she seemed healthier and more active. She was playing with the other small children in the room, and she was more responsive when I approached her, though still very reserved.

Within two days of being at the orphanage and interacting with Janet, she finally opened up to me and trusted me enough to speak. Her first and only words to me were, "Janet Banda, Janet Banda!" She wanted me to know her name. The significance behind her name is truly moving. She was given a Western name by the founders of the orphanage and adopted the last name of Banda since her background was virtually unknown. President Banda is known as the father of Malawi, and now Janet is known as a child of Malawi. She is a product of her country and the gracious people who rescued her.

I and the other volunteers put on an activity day for the orphans one day, and Janet was out in full force. She was running wild, excited at all the strange new toys and games, and egging me on to chase her around the room. I had never seen her so full of life and so happy to be interacting with other people. It was as if she completely broke down her wall and allowed herself be a real child for a day. She must have pushed aside the horrible images and memories in her head and decided that she was going to have fun like the other children—what strength that must have taken for this tiny, shy little girl.

Janet will probably never realize the impact she made on me. She changed my entire perspective on life and what is important. She showed me that life is worth fighting for and that sometimes you have to make the best of the situation you find yourself in, no matter how discouraging it might seem. If this little girl can survive the loss of her parents, starvation, disease, and violence, then I can survive just about anything. Janet Banda is truly one of the most inspiring people I have ever met, and she is only three years old—imagine what she can accomplish in the years to come.

American Hiking Society

1422 Fenwick Lane
Silver Spring, MD 20910
(301) 565-6704; Fax: (301) 565-6714
E-mail: volunteer@americanhiking.org
Web site: www.americanhiking.org

Project Type: Natural Conservation (Land); Trail
Building/Maintenance
Mission Statement Excerpt: "As the national voice for America's
hikers, American Hiking Society promotes and protects foot
trails and the hiking experience."
Year Founded: 1976
Number of Volunteers Last Year: 650
Funding Sources: Government, private, and corporate donors as
well as individual and group memberships
The Work They Do: The American Hiking Society offers a
series of weeklong trail building, maintenance, and restoration projects on America's public lands. Each crew consists
of six to fifteen volunteers accompanied by a crew leader;
crew leaders are also volunteer positions, for which experienced volunteers may also apply.
Project Location: The American Hiking Society has volunteer
projects in more than thirty states, including Alaska and
Hawaii. Projects are rated from easy to extremely strenuous
based on the type of work or amount of hiking required.
Lodging is normally a tent site in either a campground or a
backcountry location. Participants must provide their own
tents, sleeping bags, pads, and all personal gear. A few projects each year do feature cabin accommodations, the spots
for which fill up quickly. Tools and supervision are provided
by the host agency or organization.
Time Line: American Hiking Society's volunteer projects are
available from early January through the first week in
November. Most of its projects are one week in length, but
it occasionally has two-week projects.

Cost: A volunteer's first trip with the American Hiking Society costs $275, which includes a one year membership in the organization. Each subsequent trip in the calendar year is $175. Food and lodging is provided, but volunteers must pay their own travel expenses.

Getting Started: Prospective volunteers can search for available opportunities on the American Hiking Society Web site, or they can call the number listed to request a printed version of the schedule. The host of each project provides on-site training.

Needed Skills and Specific Populations: Previous trail-building experience is not necessary, but volunteers do need to be in good physical condition. The American Hiking Society offers "family-friendly" projects, open to families with children between the ages of thirteen to eighteen. The American Hiking Society does not have a maximum age for volunteers, and welcomes volunteers with disabilities; all projects are rated on a scale from easy to very strenuous, giving volunteers the opportunity to select projects that best suit their abilities.

American Jewish World Service (AJWS)

45 West 36th Street, 11th Floor
New York, NY 10018
(800) 889-7146; Fax: (212) 792-2930
E-mail: volunteer@ajws.org
Web site: www.ajws.org

Project Type: Community Development; Economic
Development; Education; Human Rights; Social Justice;
Women's Issues; Youth

Mission Statement Excerpt: "Through grants to grassroots
organizations, volunteer service, advocacy and education,
AJWS fosters civil society, sustainable development and
human rights for all people, while promoting the values and
responsibilities of global citizenship within the Jewish
community."

Year Founded: 1985

Number of Volunteers Last Year: 560

Funding Sources: Private donors, foundations

The Work They Do: AJWS offers a number of various
programs, including seven-week summer projects (Volunteer
Summer) for young adults; weeklong programs (Alternative
Breaks) to college students; the World Partners Fellowship
for recent college graduates and young professionals; and
Volunteer Corps for people ranging from young
professionals to retirees.

Project Location: Depending on the program, participants can
volunteer in: Uganda, Ghana, South Africa, Senegal,
Guatemala, Nicaragua, Honduras, El Salvador, Peru,
Mexico, the Dominican Republic, India, Thailand, and
Cambodia.

Time Line: AJWS's Volunteer Summer lasts for seven weeks;
Alternative Breaks last for one week to ten days; World
Partners Fellowship lasts for nine months; Volunteer Corps
placements range in length from two months to one year,
with the average being three to four months. AJWS Study
Tours are approximately ten days to two weeks.

Cost: Because of the range of programs, AJWS has a number of different program fees. The program fee for Alternative Breaks is $550 per participant. Program fees cover all costs of food and lodging while in the field, tools and supplies for the group's work project, basic staff costs, and financial support for the host organization in their primary work. The program fee for Volunteer Summer begins at $3,600, which includes roundtrip airfare to New York for orientation, international transportation, housing and meals while in the field, and international medical assistance. Acceptance to Volunteer Summer is need-blind, and financial aid and scholarships are available. AJWS supplies each World Partners Fellow with a modest stipend, lowest reasonable roundtrip airfare, and living accommodations. Fellows are expected to raise a minimum of $1,000 to support AJWS. There is no program fee to participate in AJWS Volunteer Corps. AJWS pays for volunteers' airfare and provides emergency evacuation assistance. Volunteers are financially responsible for health insurance and in-country cost-of-living, including housing, food, and local transportation. These costs vary greatly based on location of service.

Getting Started: AJWS programs require a written application, and many also require a phone or in-person interview. Applications are available online at the AJWS Web site. AJWS provides training and orientation for all of its programs; orientations for Alternative Breaks, Volunteer Summer, and Volunteer Corps are conducted in the United States before departure, while World Partners Fellowships' orientation takes place in the country of service. Orientation provides skills training in the volunteer experience, cross-cultural communication, and, when necessary, language training. All AJWS programs allow participants to discuss, and learn more about, the intersection of Judaism, international development, and social justice.

Needed Skills and Specific Populations: AJWS Volunteer Summer is open to high school and college-aged students, ages sixteen to twenty-four; Alternative Breaks are open to college students; World Partners Fellowship is open to recent college graduates and young professionals. Participants in these programs must be Jewish. For Volunteer Corps, there is no minimum age to participate, but volunteers should have at least several years of professional experience; senior volunteers are welcome. Participants in Volunteer Corps must be Jewish or part of an interfaith couple. AJWS Study Tours are available to anyone of any age. Volunteers with disabilities are welcomed, though all volunteers must be able to manage the challenges of living in an economically developing country for an extended period of time. AJWS does not currently have volunteer opportunities for families.

AmeriSpan

117 South 17th Street, Suite 1401
Philadelphia, PA 19103
(800) 879-6640 or (215) 751-1100;
Fax: (215) 751-1986
E-mail: info@amerispan.com
Web site: www.amerispan.com

Project Type: Community Development; Education;
Medical/Health; Natural Conservation (Land); Orphans;
Trail Building/Maintenance; Women's Issues

Mission Statement Excerpt: "AmeriSpan . . . aims to facilitate
second-language acquisition combined with temporary
volunteer opportunities throughout Latin America."

Year Founded: 1993

Number of Volunteers Last Year: More than 300

Funding Sources: None; self-funded

The Work They Do: AmeriSpan represents more than 165
different host organizations in Latin America. Most of these
organizations are small, local, nonprofit initiatives, but
some, such as Common Hope and Habitat for Humanity,
are worldwide organizations. Others, particularly those that
host internship opportunities in Argentina, are for-profit
organizations. Volunteer work varies depending on the host
organizations, but it can range from highly professional
projects to caring for orphans, and from teaching English to
trail maintenance. Customized internship and volunteer
placements are available.

Project Location: AmeriSpan offers volunteer sites throughout
Latin America. The work site is most often a direct reflection of the type of volunteer work and the economic development of the host country. For example, volunteers at an
underfunded orphanage in Bolivia should expect extremely
basic living and work conditions and little supervision due
to a lack of staffing. Conversely, a volunteer at a law firm in
Buenos Aires will find work conditions similar to those in
the United States. Volunteers stay with host families during

the initial language part of the program, which lasts for two to six weeks, then stay in lodging just for volunteers, with shared rooms (two people per room), and shared kitchen facilities during the volunteer experience.

Time Line: Volunteers are accepted year-round, but usually arrive on the first Monday of every month. Volunteers must commit to a four-week volunteer experience plus, in most cases, a one- to six-week language training program. The average volunteer stays for an eight-week volunteer stint, plus two weeks of language training. There is no limit to how long one may volunteer with AmeriSpan.

Cost: Program fees range from $350 to $3,500, depending on location, project, and length of the volunteer experience. Fees include language instruction, lodging, full or partial board, and emergency medical service. Volunteers must provide for their own airfare, in-country transportation, and meals while at the volunteer placement. AmeriSpan makes direct donations to host organizations, including more than $250,000 worth of medical supplies reaching needy communities in Latin America in a single year.

Getting Started: AmeriSpan's application process includes an application, essay, resume, two reference letters, and a telephone interview. AmeriSpan's partner organizations conduct an in-country volunteer meeting before the work starts, covering details of the organization, the volunteers' duties, and cultural issues. If the placement is close to the language school, the volunteer coordinator will visit the placement with the volunteer before starting work. The training a volunteer receives at the placement varies by organization.

Needed Skills and Specific Populations: Some host organizations require proficiency in Spanish or Portuguese; some require education or experience related to the volunteer placement. Most host organizations will accept volunteers who are at least eighteen years old, but some have a minimum age of twenty-one or twenty-three. Senior volunteers are welcomed by AmeriSpan. AmeriSpan has had several families volunteer through them; these are accepted on a case-by-case basis, and only if parents accompany youth volunteers. Volunteers with disabilities are welcomed, but prospective volunteers should contact AmeriSpan before applying, as not all countries and projects can make accommodations for them.

Amigos de las Américas

5618 Star Lane
Houston, TX 77057
(800) 231-7796; Fax: (713) 782-9267
E-mail: info@amigoslink.org
Web site: www.amigoslink.org

Project Type: Community Development; Education;
Medical/Health; Rural Development; Youth
Mission Statement Excerpt: "Amigos de las Américas builds
partnerships to empower young leaders, advance community development, and strengthen multicultural
understanding in the Americas."
Year Founded: 1965
Number of Volunteers last year: 744
Funding Sources Include: Support from corporations and
foundations
The Work They Do: Amigos de las Américas provides students
an opportunity to experience hands-on, cross-cultural understanding and leadership by volunteering in teams of two or
three as public health, education, and community development workers in rural communities or semi-urban neighborhoods. Collaborating with local sponsoring agencies and
community members, volunteers usually help identify local
resources, then implement community improvement projects
in their community's schools, health clinics, or residences.
Programs include, but are not limited to: community-based
initiatives; sanitation and development; environmental
education; family nutrition; health education; school renovations; home improvement; youth group formation and
collaboration; education; and leadership development.
Examples of past volunteer projects include teaching nutrition classes, forming local women's groups, and facilitating
creative expression workshops for youth. Amigos de las
Américas also offers several projects, open to college or
post-college students, that focus on indigenous culture,
community nutrition, child health promotion, and other

Volunteers work together with local villagers to construct an outdoor covered area to use as a meeting place for the local youth group, who was not allowed to use the adult facilities. They also built a clay basketball court. The volunteers started by working with local kids to come up with a plan, then they worked with two municipal engineers on an almost daily basis to design and build the area and court. The project overcame substantial adversity in the form of skepticism from the adults as well as religious distrust between Catholics and Pentecostals in the town. In the end, the project had both support and supplies provided by local adults and was successfully completed. *Photo courtesy of Aaron Bray*

themes. Since its inception, more than twenty thousand Amigos de las Américas volunteers have lived and worked in fifteen Latin American and Caribbean countries.

Project Location: Amigos de las Américas currently offers twelve summer projects located in seven countries: Costa Rica, the Dominican Republic, Honduras, Mexico, Nicaragua, Panama, and Paraguay. Volunteers live with host families along with one or two project partners who are also Amigos de las Américas volunteers. In many of the rural communities, electricity (and, sometimes, running water) is not available. Many of the communities are located in mountainous regions that require hiking and walking.

Time Line: Exact dates vary by year, but almost all projects take place during the summer. Projects are four, six, or eight weeks in length, and all have set start and end dates; most end in early to mid-August. The exception is a one-month program in Costa Rica, which takes place in January.

Cost: The program fee is $4,200, which includes international airfare from Houston or Miami, insurance, training, all room and board, and in-country transportation.

Getting Started: Prospective volunteers can download an application from the Web site or contact Amigos de las Américas by phone or e-mail to request one. The application deadline is in early April. Qualified applicants complete a phone interview with Amigos. Volunteer training includes Spanish language instruction, Latin American history and cultural awareness, health and safety, first aid, positive development approaches, human relations, leadership, management, and presentation skills. Volunteers who live in one of thirty cities in the United States undergo in-person training over an eight-month period, meeting once or twice per month. Volunteers outside of these cities receive their training by correspondence.

Needed Skills and Specific Populations: Volunteers must have taken at least two years of high school Spanish or have an equivalent skill level. Volunteers must be at least sixteen years old and have completed their sophomore year of high school; the maximum age for volunteers is twenty-three. Every effort will be made to successfully place volunteers with disabilities, but those volunteers may be hindered by the conditions present in Latin America.

Lessons from Maté

By Anna Morenz

Amigos de las Américas

As we pick our way along the coastline, shoes squelching in the swampy reeds, the maté (a cup used specifically for drinking hot tea in a communal fashion) is passed from person to person with seamless adherence to tradition. The server holds the thermos and pours a steaming trickle of water over the small tea leaves firmly packed into the maté, or gourd. When it is my turn to drink, I wrap my hands around the warm maté, feeling the delicate tickle of the leather stitching around the gourd. Sipping cautiously from the straw-like *bombilla,* the potent bitterness of the tea thrills my senses. Much to the Uruguayans' surprise and delight, I praise the exotic flavor and pass the maté back to the server, who promptly begins the ritual of pushing the yerba leaves into a neat, compressed mound to make room for the water.

The entire summer in Uruguay with Amigos de las Américas played out like a grand maté ritual: sharing, serving, and trying a myriad of new flavors. Work in La Colorada, a tiny town perched on the scenic coast of Uruguay, depended on collaboration with the youth of the community. Before we arrived, the youth laid out several projects they wanted to complete, including functional and aesthetic improvement of the local soccer field, swing sets, and bus stops. My partner and I cannot say that we completed these projects—that honor belongs to the community—but we did act as catalysts in the completion. For example, when we painted over the graffiti scribbles on the bus stops, so many teenagers showed up to help that we did not have enough paintbrushes for everyone.

After painting a vibrant base coat, we accented the bus stop with our handprints, an explicit symbol of our collaborative effort.

We shared more than paintbrushes with community members. Cooped up inside on gray, rainy afternoons, we swapped card games, learning *chancho* in exchange for teaching Go Fish. With the teenagers, we avidly compared cultures, discussing dating customs, job opportunities, and family life in Uruguay and the United States. We struck upon shocking similarities, from a mutual interest in Green Day to an abiding love of hot cocoa, which caused that distant corner of the world to radiate a tender coziness I associate with home. Food was one of the best ways to exchange cultures, especially since cultures have many idiosyncrasies when it comes to nourishing the body. One evening the teens taught us how to make *tortas fritas,* or fry bread, which we then smothered in *dulce de leche,* a variety of caramel that is ubiquitous in Uruguay. In turn, we prepared a batch of brownies, which the teens eagerly sampled and approved.

Through this constant cultural exchange, I came to consider the teens as true friends and my host family as a genuine second family. Snapping sticks into the fireplace, my host mother told us humorous anecdotes from her year in Italy as a nanny, as well as tragic stories that cast seemingly implacable shadows over her amber eyes. We listened quietly to the gentle flow of her Spanish and to the empathetic crackle and sigh of the fire. The relationships that we forged with community members enabled our volunteer work to be more effective and meaningful.

In training for our Amigos experience, we read a provocative article criticizing the intentions of U.S. volunteers in Latin America. The article accused volunteers of inadvertently imposing their economic, social, and cultural value systems on Latin American people and of being powerless to instigate any kind of significant change outside the United States. As a volunteer embarking for five weeks of community service in a Latin American country, I was determined not to commit the same mistake of insensitive volunteerism that had fueled the arguments behind the article. I realized that I was not traveling thousands of miles to clutch to my value systems as if they were a shield against the unknown; I was traveling to rediscover the common ground of humanity, which has been stained crimson by war and intolerance. I wanted to reach out to a community, no matter how small, and remind them not to sleepwalk through the day, feeling powerless to change or understand the disparities in life. I also wanted them to know, as Uruguayan author Eduardo Galeano once wrote, *"Tengo mucho que aprender de la gente"*—"I have a lot to learn from the people."

Amizade Global Service-Learning

P.O. Box 110107
Pittsburgh, PA 15232
(412) 441-6655; Fax: (412) 441-6655
E-mail: volunteer@amizade.org
Web site: www.amizade.org or
www.globalservicelearning.org

Project Type: Community Development; Education; Historic
Preservation; Human Rights; Rural Development; Women's
Issues; Youth
Mission Statement Excerpt: "Amizade empowers individuals
and communities through worldwide service and learning."
Year Founded: 1994
Number of Volunteers Last Year: 350
Funding Sources: Grants and donations
The Work They Do: Amizade carries out a number of projects
in the areas of community empowerment, education, the
environment, health care, housing, infrastructure, building
of peaceful relationships, and creation of responsible individuals. Current projects open to volunteers include
constructing school classrooms and working with physically
challenged youth in Bolivia; working with street children in
Brazil; volunteering with a community organization in rural
Jamaica; supporting women's rights in Tanzania;
participating in historic preservation activities at concentra-
tion camps in Poland; constructing primary and secondary
schools, roads, and hospitals in Ghana; working with
organizations that are addressing social, religious, and political divisions in Northern Ireland; participating in historic
preservation and environmental cleanup at the OTO Ranch
near Yellowstone National Park; tutoring elementary children at the Navajo Nation in Arizona; and feeding the
hungry and homeless in Washington, D.C.
Project Location: Amizade carries out projects in Santarém,
Brazil; Cochabamba, Bolivia; Petersfield, Jamaica; Belfast
and Ballycastle, Northern Ireland; Berlin, Germany;

Two Amizade volunteers help local masons, Pechino and Raimundo, plaster cement on the outer wall of a community center for at-risk youths in Santarém, Brazil. The community center is where students go either before or after school. In Brazil, school is only half the day, so any students who do not have a parent at home are likely to roam the streets the other half of the day. At the center, the students get to do activities, such as sports, education, or professional training. The centers are a great place for kids and teenagers to learn key skills and values in an effort to keep them from the temptations of street life. *Photo courtesy of Matt Clements*

Auschwitz-Birkenau, Poland; Tanzania; Puerto Morelos, Mexico; Gardiner, Montana; the Navajo Nation, Arizona; and Washington, D.C. Given the huge differences between these places, the work sites and accommodations vary, from the heart of Belfast to a coastal village in Mexico, and from the Navajo reservation to a Tanzanian village. However, at all sites, Amizade provides lodging and meals. Lodging varies by site and ranges from home stays to dorms to hotels. Meals incorporate locally available food and are cooked and served by local Amizade staff.

Time Line: Opportunities exist year-round. Projects run for a minimum of one week and a maximum of six months; the average volunteer stint is around three weeks.

Cost: Program fees range from about $700 for a single program week to $8,240 for an entire semester. This fee covers lodging, meals, educational activities, recreational activities, and, in most cases, local transportation. Fees for the courses include university tuition and the course instruction. Participants are responsible for transportation to the work site, immunizations, travel insurance, and departure taxes.

Getting Started: Prospective volunteers can download an application and other documents from Amizade's Web site or call the office. Once in-country, volunteers receive an orientation from local site directors, which typically includes information on local safety and security, intercultural communication specific to that site, as well as local history and geography.

Needed Skills and Specific Populations: No specific skills are required. Volunteers must be at least eighteen years old to work on their own; a parent or guardian must accompany volunteers aged twelve to seventeen. Only the Montana site accepts volunteers under age twelve. Senior volunteers are welcomed at all sites. Volunteers with disabilities are encouraged and welcomed to participate in Amizade's programs, though some community conditions are better suited to volunteers with disabilities than others.

My Life Changing Experiences in the Amazon

By Matt Clements

Amizade Global Service-Learning

On June 6, 2007, I arrived in Santarém, Brazil, venturing outside of the United States for the first time. That day was the beginning of a volunteer experience that resulted in a change in my self-awareness, my outlook, and my career path.

During my three weeks in Santarém, my Amizade group spent our mornings at the construction site of a community center for at-risk youths. When we arrived at the work site on the first day, I felt intimidated because I didn't know what to expect. Within minutes, my fears had faded as we met our collaborators and began to work. Working closely with Brazilian masons and local children, I developed an amazing bond with the people and the community.

Our mornings were dedicated to the work site, but our afternoons were filled with exploration and adventure. Whether it was going to the local beaches, exploring the downtown market, going to the former home of rubber production for the Ford motor company in Belterra, or taking an overnight boat trip to see the picturesque waterfalls of nearby Alenquer, our days were full of amazing adventures. The vibrant culture, full of parties and cultural gatherings, swept me off my feet and I fell in love with the city, the land, the people, and the culture. Getting to see, experience, and understand the culture of Brazil through both meaningful community service and travel was a truly unforgettable experience that made this trip so valuable to me.

My outlook on life and my career goals have changed drastically because of my experiences in Brazil. I now realize how privileged I am in comparison to others in countries around the world. Before I embarked on my journey to Brazil, I was a college student with no true aims or career goals in front of me. After I returned, I discovered a newfound dedication to development and global service that has encouraged me to pursue a degree in international development. In the future I plan to spend time abroad with Amizade, volunteering while I attempt to understand and appreciate more foreign cultures.

Appalachian Mountain Club (AMC)

P.O. Box 298
Gorham, NH 03581
(603) 466-2721 x192; Fax: (603) 466-2822
E-mail: amcvolunteers@outdoors.org
Web site: www.outdoors.org

Project Type: Trail Building/Maintenance

Mission Statement Excerpt: "We promote the protection, enjoyment, and wise use of the mountains, rivers, and trails of the Appalachian region."

Year Founded: 1876

Number of Volunteers Last Year: 729

Funding Sources: Government, foundation, and individual donors

The Work They Do: AMC is the nation's oldest nonprofit conservation and recreation organization. Its twelve Northeast chapters maintain more than 1,700 miles of trail, including 350 miles of the Appalachian Trail. Previous projects include the construction of new trails in Acadia National Park, Maine; a canoe portage trail in Baxter State Park, Maine; a loop trail to the Appalachian Trail in Grafton Notch, Maine; the construction of bog bridges in the New Hampshire White Mountains; reconstruction of the Appalachian Trail in the Berkshire region of western Massachusetts; and rock work on alpine trails near the peak of Mount Washington in New Hampshire. Volunteers build, maintain, and repair trails, all of which involve moderate to strenuous physical manual labor.

Project Location: AMC offers trail crews and skills workshops in the White Mountain National Forest of New Hampshire and Maine, in Acadia National Park and Baxter State Park in Maine, in the Berkshire Mountains of Massachusetts, and in other locations in the Appalachian region. A variety of projects are offered at roadside and remote locations. Volunteers should be prepared to work outside in all weather conditions and sometimes in steep terrain. Accommodations are provided in the form of tents or bunkhouses, and they are, necessarily, quite basic.

Time Line: Openings for work crews are usually offered from March through November. Most programs last from one to twelve days. A twenty-one-day Teen Trails Leadership program is also available.

Cost: Most program fees range from free to $500, with the average being about $170; the Teen Trails Leadership program is $825. Included in the program fee are training, tools, lodging in a tent or bunkhouse, safety equipment, food, cooking and eating equipment, and first aid supplies. Volunteers must supply their own personal gear and transportation to and from the start location of the program.

Getting Started: Information about the coming year is posted each January on AMC's Web site. Prospective volunteers can apply through the Web site or by calling the Chapter Trails Chair at the phone number listed. AMC members receive *AMC Outdoors* magazine, which also lists all volunteer opportunities. (Membership is not required in order to participate in volunteer programs, however.) Volunteers are not required to interview with AMC before beginning their project. All training and orientation is done on the trail.

Needed Skills and Specific Populations: Volunteers should be in good physical condition and have an enthusiastic willingness to work. Some backpacking experience is helpful, as is previous experience in trail building. Training in the use and maintenance of tools is given at each project site. The minimum age of volunteers is generally fifteen, but this varies by program. Senior volunteers are welcomed, as are volunteers with disabilities and families. Specialty crews are often scheduled for groups of teens, adults, and women.

Appalachian Trail Conservancy (ATC)

P.O. Box 224
Blacksburg, VA 24063
(540) 961-5551; Fax: (540) 961-5554
E-mail: crews@appalachiantrail.org
Web site: www.appalachiantrail.org

Project Type: Historic Preservation; Natural Conservation (Land); Trail Building/Maintenance

Mission Statement Excerpt: "The Appalachian Trail Conservancy (ATC) is a volunteer-based organization dedicated to the preservation and management of the natural, scenic, historic, and cultural resources associated with the Appalachian Trail, in order to provide primitive outdoor-recreation and educational opportunities for Trail visitors."

Year Founded: 1925

Number of Volunteers Last Year: Over 500

Funding Sources: Government and private donors. The USDA Forest Service and the National Park Service cosponsor the ATC volunteer trail crews.

The Work They Do: The Appalachian National Scenic Trail is the longest continuously marked footpath in the world and America's first national scenic trail. It follows the crest of the Appalachian Mountains for more than 2,100 miles along ridges and through rural farm valleys and rugged high country. ATC Maintaining clubs are assigned a section or sections of the Appalachian Trail to maintain. Clubs are assisted by the ATC volunteer trail crews to complete large-scale projects. ATC organizes and supports the volunteer efforts to maintain and build the Appalachian Trail. Trail work is hard, physical labor. Volunteer work assignments include new trail construction, rock work, log work, shelter construction, and other physically demanding tasks. Trail crews of six to ten volunteers work under the supervision of skilled leaders. Trail construction involves working with hand tools, and getting dirty is guaranteed. The crews work eight-hour days, rain or shine, hot or cold, regardless of black flies, mosquitoes, and other insects.

Project Location: Volunteers can work anywhere along the length of the Appalachian Trail. Crew base camps are located in northern Maine, central Vermont, Pennsylvania, southwestern Virginia, and the Great Smoky Mountains in Tennessee. Volunteer crew members may backpack into a backcountry campsite and set up a primitive tent camp near the project site. Crews may also work from car camps or developed campgrounds. During the course of the crew season, the weather can vary from sweaty, summertime heat to freezing, winter-like cold.

Time Line: The Maine Trail Crew operates from June through mid-August. The Vermont Volunteer Long Trail Patrol operates mid-July through mid-September. The Mid-Atlantic Trail Crew works during September and October. The Virginia-based Konnarock Trail Crew operates from mid-May through August. Based in the Great Smoky Mountains, the Rocky Top Volunteer Trail Crew works in September and October. Prospective participants in any of these crews' programs may volunteer for one to six weeks; the average volunteer stint is five to ten days.

Cost: There is no program fee, though volunteers are responsible for their own transportation to and from their base camp. Once volunteers reach the base camp, most expenses are covered, including shelter, food, transportation to and from work projects, tools, safety equipment, and group camping gear (as available). Crew members need to bring work clothing, sturdy boots, and their own basic camping gear.

Getting Started: On the ATC Web site, prospective volunteers can find additional information on ATC trail crews, apply, or download a print-and-mail application. Prospective volunteers may also contact ATC's office to request an application. ATC does not require an interview, but does require two references. Volunteers receive training in "leave no trace" camping techniques and trail crew safety the evening before their project starts. All skills training is provided in the field during the course of the project.

Needed Skills and Specific Populations: Good health, willingness to cooperate, community spirit, and enthusiasm are more important than previous trail experience. Participants should be comfortable living and working in a primitive outdoor setting. Volunteers must be at least eighteen years old; senior volunteers are "welcome and encouraged!" ATC will work with volunteers with disabilities to accommodate individual needs. ATC also welcomes international volunteers, but it cannot assist them in obtaining entry to the United States.

ARCHELON, the Sea Turtle Protection Society of Greece

3rd Marina of Glyfada, 166 75
Glyfada, Athens
Greece
+(30) 210 8982600
E-mail: volunteers@archelon.gr
Web site: www.archelon.gr

Project Type: Natural Conservation (Sea)

Mission Statement Excerpt: ARCHELON "protect[s] the sea turtles in Greece through monitoring and research, developing and implementing management plans, raising public awareness, and rehabilitating sick and injured turtles."

Year Founded: 1983

Number of Volunteers Last Year: 400

Funding Sources: Government, faith-based, and private sources

The Work They Do: ARCHELON helps to protect Greece's three major turtle nesting areas, which cover about sixty miles of shoreline. They accomplish this mission by protecting more than twenty-five hundred nests from human and animal threats, tagging turtles for monitoring purposes, treating injured and sick turtles (more than fifty per year, on average), teaching more than eighteen thousand students in environmental education programs, and maintaining a public education campaign that reaches tens of thousands of visitors. Volunteers assist with nest management and habitat protection by conducting morning and night surveys via beach patrols and excavations, and they also provide protection to turtles and their nests. Volunteers can also help with the public awareness campaign by staffing information stations and presenting slide shows. There are also opportunities to assist with the daily treatment of injured sea turtles.

Project Location: Volunteers work at one of the three turtle nesting areas, located in Zakynthos, Peloponnesus, and

Crete, or at the Sea Turtle Rescue Center in Athens. In Zakynthos, where the first national marine park for sea turtles in the Mediterranean was established in 1999, volunteers assist in protecting the nesting beaches. In Peloponnesus, volunteers protect nests from foxes and other mammals, help with sand dune restoration and the maintenance of nature trails, and assist in the newly established Nature Information Centres. On the island of Crete, volunteers help manage nesting areas. Volunteers stay free, in campsites that are restricted to ARCHELON volunteers, with very basic outdoor sanitary and cooking facilities that feature cold-water showers, gas stoves, and refrigerators. Volunteers must provide their own camping gear, including a tent and a sleeping bag, as well as their own food to cook.

Time Line: Volunteers are welcomed year-round at the Sea Turtle Rescue Center. At the other three sites, volunteers are accepted between May and October. Volunteers must commit to a minimum of twenty-eight days.

Cost: ARCHELON's program fee ranges from €150 to €250, depending on the time of year. The program fee does not include international travel costs or room and board expenses, the latter of which ARCHELON estimates will cost about €15 per day.

Getting Started: Contact the organization via e-mail, phone, or its Web site. ARCHELON provides training upon arrival, as well as direct supervision during the first week.

Needed Skills and Specific Populations: The only needed skill is the ability to communicate in both spoken and written English. Volunteers must be at least eighteen years old and speak English; there is no maximum age limit. Volunteers with disabilities will find it difficult at best to work with ARCHELON, given the nature of the work and the basic sanitary facilities at the camp.

ArtCorps

8 Enon Street, #2B
Beverly, MA 01915
(978) 927-2404; Fax: (978) 998-6837
E-mail: artcorps@nebf.org
Web site: www.artcorp.org

Project Type: Community Development; Education;
Medical/Health; Natural Conservation (Land); Social
Justice; Women's Issues; Youth

Mission Statement Excerpt: "To advance social change
initiatives by promoting arts and culture as powerful tools
to generate cooperative and sustainable work between
development organizations and the communities they
serve."

Year Founded: 1998

Number of Volunteers Last Year: 8

Funding Sources: ArtCorps has seed funding from the New
England Biolabs Foundation, and receives additional
support from other foundations and individual donors.

The Work They Do: Through creative arts and cultural projects,
ArtCorps artists help community members reflect upon
important local issues, voice their opinions, and take action.
ArtCorps was created to bridge the communication gap
between grassroots organizations and their constituents by
using art as an outreach tool. Through community arts projects, artists educate and inspire people to participate actively
in improving the environmental, health, and social
conditions in their communities. Working in collaboration
with a local nonprofit organization, ArtCorps volunteers
help their host communities tackle public health, environmental, and women's and children's rights issues. Artists
may come from a variety of backgrounds, including theater,
painting, sculpting, and others.

Project Location: ArtCorps volunteers work in communities
across Guatemala, El Salvador, and Honduras. The climate
varies—from the heat of El Salvador and the northern

Guatemalan rainforest to the chilly mountains in Guatemala's altiplano—as do the communities and living conditions. Host organizations provide each volunteer with basic accommodations that include a bed, shelves, table, and chair. Most volunteers live in rural communities but a few live in more urban environments; most have electricity but a few do not. Some communities have strong Mayan cultures and others are predominately Ladino. Placements in 2008 included Ciudad Romero, Bajo Lempa, El Salvador; San Salvador, El Salvador; Paso Caballos and Carmelita, Petén, Guatemala; Purulha, Guatemala; Río Blanco, Guatemala; Chiché, Guatemala; and Lago Atitlan, Guatemala.

Time Line: ArtCorps only accepts volunteers for eleven-month placements. Volunteer assignments begin annually in January.

Cost: ArtCorps and the overseas host organization provide international transportation, room and board, a stipend for project expenses, a small personal stipend, medical insurance, training, a mid-year retreat, Internet access (where available), and local transportation. Volunteers are expected to bring approximately $2,000 in personal funds to supplement their food and communications as well as travel outside of the country every ninety days to get their passport stamped, as required by local immigration law.

Getting Started: ArtCorps has a brief, initial screening application available on their Web site that must be submitted in order to receive the full written application. Volunteers who meet the basic eligibility requirements will be asked to complete a full written application along with a resume and samples of their art pieces or performances no later than May each year. Finalists will be interviewed by telephone, and must provide contact information for three references. All applicants receive notice of the final decision on their application by August prior to their departure.

Needed Skills and Specific Populations: ArtCorps volunteers must be professional artists, fluent in Spanish, passionate about social or environmental issues, mature, and have community arts experience. ArtCorps has found that its best volunteers are enthusiastic, adaptable, creative, organized, team players, assertive, and flexible. ArtCorps prefers candidates with substantial work experience; there is no maximum age limit. Volunteers may be of any nationality but will be responsible for handling their own visa needs. Volunteers must obtain a doctor's signature indicating they are healthy enough to meet the demands of living in a rural community in a developing country; volunteers with disabilities should contact the office to discuss their specific needs. Spouses are welcome to travel with the artists as long as they are able to cover all expenses.

Asociación Centro de Estudios de Español Pop Wuj ("Pop Wuj")

Primera Calle 17-72 Zona 1
Quetzaltenango
Guatemala
+(502) 7761-8286
E-mail: info@pop-wuj.org
Web site: www.pop-wuj.org or www.popwujclinic.org

Project Type: Community Development; Construction; Education; Medical/Health; Natural Conservation (Land); Rural Development

Mission Statement Excerpt: "To aliviate poverty and bring opportunities of development to some rural communities in Highlands Guatemala."

Year Founded: 1992

Number of Volunteers Last Year: 550

Funding Sources: Foundations, individuals, former students and teachers

The Work They Do: Pop Wuj creates sustainable, community-organized projects that include a greenhouse, reforestation, a day care center, social services that include a health-care clinic, a brick stove building project, a scholarship program, and fund-raising. Volunteers assist in the administration and daily operation of all of these programs. Pop Wuj also offers an intensive Spanish language course that volunteers can undertake either before or during the volunteer experience.

Project Location: Pop Wuj's projects are located in rural, highland Guatemala, near the city of Quetzaltenango. Volunteers live in the city with Guatemalan host families, and travel daily to the community projects. Volunteers also have the option of arranging their own lodging if they prefer not to live with a host family.

Time Line: Volunteers can start at any time, but are requested to begin on the first Monday of the month when possible. Pop Wuj requests that volunteers commit to at least three months, but accepts volunteers for any length of time.

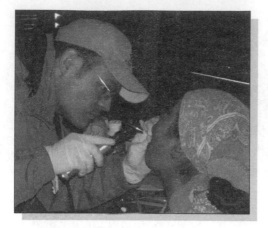

A Pop Wuj volunteer cares for a woman at the medical clinic after Hurricane Stan, which brought a lot of damage and forced this woman's community to relocate. The new community is called Xeabaj II and now is located in the western highlands of Guatemala. *Photo courtesy of Asociación Centro de Estudios de Español Pop Wuj*

Cost: There is no cost to volunteer with Pop Wuj. Volunteers can choose to add language instruction and homestays for $160 to $250 per week; the time of year also impacts the program fee. The program fee does not include transportation to the volunteer sites on a daily basis or airfare to Guatemala.

Getting Started: Prospective volunteers should contact Pop Wuj to discuss a time line, skills the volunteer has, and any dietary needs. Volunteers who wish to add the optional language instruction need to also complete an application and submit it at least two weeks in advance. Experienced volunteers provide orientation and training to new volunteers.

Needed Skills and Specific Populations: While volunteers with agricultural and construction skills are always needed, Pop Wuj welcomes all volunteers. There is no minimum or maximum age for volunteers; volunteers with disabilities are welcome, though many rural communities are not well-equipped to serve special needs. Families are welcomed and can be housed together or separately if the family members wish a full language immersion experience.

Never Superfluous

By Kayti Mills

Asociación Centro de Estudios de Español Pop Wuj

I hadn't intended on volunteering when I came to Xela. In the past I have had experiences volunteering in organizations where I felt unnecessary and sometimes even in the way of the good work that was already getting done by the organizations. Pop Wuj is not like this; never was the work superfluous. I worked with both the social work program and the medical program. With their social work program I worked very closely with one special woman, Carmen, whose clear Spanish is only matched by her clearly open heart and dedication to children and families. She manages a program that provides scholarships to over 160 children so there is more than enough work for one woman, no matter how dedicated. I was able to assist Carmen significantly by lowering a barrier between the padrinos (donors of the scholarships) and the recipients, sending them the children's letters and grades. I also traveled with Carmen to four different communities around Xela where we did reinforcement activities with the children and caught up on each individual family's case. Within the medical program, I served as a translator between the other volunteer doctors and the patients—but don't worry, knowing Spanish is a big help with Pop Wuj, but is not required. I had only three weeks of Spanish under my belt and learned most of what I know just by listening to Carmen! In short, working with Pop Wuj was both challenging and rewarding.

Association of International Development and Exchange (AIDE)

1221 South Mopac Expressway, Suite 100
Austin, TX 78746
(512) 457-8062 or (866) 6ABROAD; Fax: (413) 460-3502
E-mail: volunteer@aideabroad.org
Web site: www.aideusa.org

Project Type: Community Development; Education;
Medical/Health; Natural Conservation (Land); Orphans;
Trail Building/Maintenance; Youth
Mission Statement Excerpt: "AIDE will be a catalyst for change
in the world by building bridges between individuals from
diverse cultures."
Year Founded: 2007, though it grew out of a previous organiza-
tion, Alliance Abroad Group, which was founded in 1992
Number of Volunteers Last Year: 300
Funding Sources: None; AIDE is self-funded.
The Work They Do: AIDE offers a variety of volunteer projects
tailored to the wishes of the individual volunteer or group.
Volunteers can teach English, assist at a sustainable living
center, work on an organic farm, protect sea turtles habitats,
help at an orphanage, assist in hospitals, health clinics, or
pharmacies, work in an animal rehabilitation center, participate in an archaeological dig, aid community development
initiatives, and much more.
Project Location: Volunteers are placed in Argentina, Chile,
Costa Rica, Thailand, Ecuador, Peru, and Spain. Accommodations and meals vary by project site, but in most cases
volunteers are provided a home stay and food.
Time Line: Volunteers are accepted year-round for a minimum
of two weeks and a maximum of twelve months.
Cost: Program fees range from $950 to $3,000. Fees include a
predeparture and post-arrival orientation, volunteer placement, airport transfer in the host country, accommodation,
all meals, and insurance. Volunteers must pay for their own
airfare.

Getting Started: Prospective volunteers should download an application from the AIDE Web site, complete it, and send it to AIDE by postal mail, fax, or e-mail. A phone interview is required. Orientation is provided both before departure and after arrival; on-site training is offered for some programs.

Needed Skills and Specific Populations: Volunteers must be at least eighteen years old, and senior volunteers are welcomed. Most volunteer sites cannot accommodate volunteers with disabilities. For some programs, it is necessary to have a basic to intermediate level of Spanish, a Bachelor's degree, experience working with children, good physical and mental health, and/or a criminal background check. Volunteers from outside the United States are welcomed as long as a visa for the host country can be obtained.

Australian Tropical Research Foundation (ATRF)

PMB 5 Cape Tribulation
Queensland, 4873
Australia
+61 7 4098 0063
E-mail: hugh@austrop.org.au or hugh@ledanet.com.au
Web site: www.austrop.org.au

Project Type: Natural Conservation (Land); Scientific Research;
  Social Justice
Mission Statement Excerpt: "To conduct and facilitate research
  into terrestrial and aquatic ecosystems in Australia and elsewhere; to research human impact on the Australian tropics
  and develop and promote sound management practices for
  the tropics."
Year Founded: 1988
Number of Volunteers Last Year: 61
Funding Sources: Specific project-based funding for research,
  plus some private donations for station operation
The Work They Do: Previous and current ATRF research projects include: the development of techniques for assisted
  regeneration of rain forests; the development of appropriate
  technology (particularly energy conservation and renewable
  energy) for living in the wet tropics; research on the produc-
  tivity, phenology, and pollination of cluster figs, on the
  ecology of flying foxes (fruit bats) and their relatives, on the
  conservation biology of flying foxes (particularly on the
  development of nonlethal deterrent systems), and weed
  control techniques; and the chemical analysis of plant and
  insect materials. Volunteers assist in many research and
  station activities, including radio-tracking bats, counting
  figs, stomping grass for forest regeneration, constructing
  buildings, digging holes for tree planting, weed control, and
  running the Bat House (ATRF's visitor's center). The ATRF
  is part of Al Gore's Climate Project.
Project Location: The station is located in the Daintree tropical
  lowlands. Considered the jewel of the Australian Wet

Tropics World Heritage Area, the lowlands are sandwiched between the coastal fringe and the coastal mountain range. The area features a wide variety of habitats, from coastal reefs to tropical rain forest, though it claims to be "one of the most benign tropical rain forest environments anywhere in the world . . . there are no seriously nasty things here." The station is based on twenty-five acres of old revegetated pasture less than half a mile from the coast. Accommodation is in light and airy bunkhouse-style buildings. Breakfast and lunch are self-catered, whereas dinner is taken as a group. Food tends to be plentiful, which has led to the site's tongue-in-cheek nickname, "the Cape Tribulation Cooking Camp."

Time Line: Volunteers are accepted year-round. Volunteers must stay at least two weeks; the maximum length of stay is open for negotiation. The record length of stay is about one year.

Cost: The program fee for volunteers is A$35 per day, which covers all food and accommodations. Volunteers who stay for more than three months may be able to negotiate a lower fee. The program fee does not include transportation to Australia or to the work site. Volunteers have very few on-site expenses, since there are few places there to spend money.

Getting Started: Prospective volunteers should contact the station by e-mail and inquire about potential dates. No formal orientation or training is offered, but the station will provide these as needed.

Needed Skills and Specific Populations: Volunteers must be at least nineteen years old; there is no maximum age limit. Those who use wheelchairs will find that the station is not accessible; prospective volunteers with other physical disabilities will probably be able to be accommodated, though they must discuss this with the organization well in advance of their planned trip. Families are welcome to volunteer at ATRF.

AVIVA

P.O. Box 60573
Table View, 7439
South Africa
+27 21 557 4312; Fax: +27 86 634 2063
E-mail: info@aviva-sa.com
Web site: www.aviva-sa.com

Project Type: Community Development; Construction; Education; Natural Conservation (Land); Natural Conservation (Sea); Orphans; Youth

Mission Statement Excerpt: "AVIVA is dedicated to providing value for money volunteering experiences in South Africa with carefully researched projects throughout the country."

Year Founded: 2001

Number of Volunteers Last Year: 300

Funding Sources: None

The Work They Do: Volunteers can choose from over a dozen wildlife, conservation, and community based projects. Examples of these projects include volunteering with the African Penguin Conservation to help feed and care for penguins; environmental education; and working with orphans by assisting with child development, baby feeding, homework, nursing, food collection, and a variety of other tasks.

Project Location: Many of AVIVA's projects are situated in and around Cape Town, South Africa. Accommodation and self-service breakfasts are provided for all volunteers staying at the AVIVA House in Cape Town. All meals are provided for volunteers who participate at Balule, Amapondo, Wild Coast schools, Zeekoevlei, Inkwenkwezi, Tamboti, whale and dolphin research, and Wild Coast horses projects.

Time Line: Projects are available year-round, though not all projects are available at all times of year. Most projects have set start dates, which are updated regularly on AVIVA's Web site. The minimum period for volunteer projects varies from two to six weeks, with longer stays possible. Visas are required for those who wish to stay more than ninety days; AVIVA can assist with the application process. Volunteers normally stay an average of eight weeks, though volunteers have stayed for periods ranging from two weeks to ten months.

Cost: Program fees range from $960 to more than $2,500, with most in the $1,500 range. Some programs' fees include all meals, as well as any required domestic flights. Volunteers who stay on for a second project or more receive reduced program fees for these subsequent projects. All program fees include airport transfers, orientation, a comprehensive welcome pack, accommodations, some or all meals, transportation to the volunteer site, and an AVIVA fleece. Most Cape Town–based projects include a variety of guided tours. For volunteers joining projects further afield, an optional Cape Town week can be added to their stay, with these tours included. Volunteers must provide their own airfare to Cape Town.

Getting Started: Prospective volunteers can apply via the online application form found on the AVIVA Web site. Each volunteer receives a thorough welcome brief from a member of the AVIVA team, and orientation activities are included with most projects to introduce volunteers to Cape Town's cultural and natural attractions. When volunteers join a project, they are given relevant training and supervision.

Needed Skills and Specific Populations: No special skills are needed, though volunteers should be able to speak English reasonably well. Volunteers should indicate any previous experience or qualifications on their application form. Volunteers must be at least sixteen years old, and all projects are open to senior volunteers. People with disabilities are welcome to apply, though the nature of the disability may dictate whether or not a project is suitable for them. Due to the nature of the work and location of many projects, facilities for disabled people may be limited or nonexistent.

Azafady

Studio 7, 1a Beethoven Street
London, W10 4LG
United Kingdom
+44 (0) 20 8960 6629; Fax: +44 (0) 20 8962 0126
E-mail: info@azafady.org
Web site: www.madagascar.co.uk

Project Type: Community Development; Construction; Education; Medical/Health; Natural Conservation (Land); Rural Development; Scientific Research

Mission Statement Excerpt: "Azafady is a registered UK charity and Malagasy NGO working to alleviate poverty, improve well-being, and preserve beautiful, unique environments in southeast Madagascar."

Year Founded: 1994

Number of Volunteers Last Year: 80

Funding Sources: Private sources

The Work They Do: Azafady operates two volunteer programs in Madagascar to help support its work on humanitarian and conservation initiatives. Working with local communities, volunteers on the Pioneer Program assist with projects addressing needs such as cleaner water, improved sanitation, and better basic health care and education, and volunteers on the Lemur Venture project help conserve wild lemurs and their natural habitat. Examples of recent volunteer projects in Madagascar include: providing access to clean drinking water for ten thousand people in rural areas; building fully equipped schools allowing access to education for more than eighteen hundred children who previously had no educational opportunities; cultivating ten thousand seedlings of two critically endangered tree species; and collecting valuable data on endangered lemur species.

Project Location: All of Azafady's volunteers work in southeast Madagascar, in the town of Fort Dauphin and surrounding rural areas. Camping facilities are provided for volunteers throughout the programs, although volunteers do need to bring their own tent. Facilities are basic, but there will always be latrine and private washing amenities. Electricity and piped water are available when in Fort Dauphin. In the field, however, water is collected and then treated from rivers and wells. Volunteers should be prepared for physical work, adventurous road journeys, and long walks to reach remote project sites. Simple, nutritionally balanced food is provided by Azafady.

Time Line: Volunteer projects start in January, April, July, and October each year. Lemur Venture is available as a four- or eight-week placement, and the Pioneer Program lasts for ten weeks.

Cost: Azafady's program fee is £2,000 for the Pioneer Program, and £1,400 or £2,200 for Lemur Venture, depending on the length of stay. The program fee covers all in-country travel costs, training and orientation, all meals, and use of campsites. Not included in the program fee are airfare to Madagascar, or visa, vaccination, and travel insurance costs.

Getting Started: Prospective volunteers should download an application form from the Azafady Web site or phone or write to request a form; interviews are not required. On arrival in Madagascar, a comprehensive one-week orientation is provided to give volunteers lessons in the Malagasy language as well as a background on local culture, the region, practicalities of living in Madagascar, medical information, and the history of Azafady.

Needed Skills and Specific Populations: No special skills are needed, as all required skills are learned while working; Azafady requires only enthusiasm and sensitivity. Volunteers must be at least eighteen years old; there is no maximum age limit as long as volunteers are able-bodied and capable of dealing with the sometimes basic conditions. Azafady is limited in the types of disabilities it can accommodate; prospective volunteers with disabilities are asked to contact Azafady for further information.

Bangladesh Work Camps Association (BWCA)

289/2 Workcamp Road
North Shajahanpur, Dhaka-1217
Bangladesh
+88 2 935-8206
E-mail: bwca@bangla.net
Web site: www.mybwca.org

Project Type: Agriculture; Developmental Disabilities;
   Education; Natural Conservation (Land); Orphans; Rural
   Development; Youth
Mission Statement Excerpt: "Let's work together to have a
   better world through promoting peace and solidarity in the
   spirit of 'learning while working and living together,' which
   is aimed at the young generation around the world."
Year Founded: 1958
Number of Volunteers Last Year: 23
Funding Sources: None
The Work They Do: Bangladesh Work Camps Association
   (BWCA) short-term volunteers can become involved in a
   number of types of work, such as building renovations,
   community development work, health care, helping to
   prepare for festivals, social and environmental work, and
   relief and rehabilitation work after natural disasters. Volunteers who work with BWCA for two months or more can
   assist on more involved projects such as working with
   people with disabilities, teaching, or assisting with agricultural projects. Specific examples of volunteer work with
   BWCA include installing low-cost latrines, planting trees,
   and giving "Greening Asia" presentations in local schools
   and communities. BWCA also organizes temporary eye
   clinics for cataract patients at the work site, and volunteers
   can assist volunteer surgeons and doctors both inside and
   outside the operating theater.
Project Location: Work camps and projects are situated in rural
   villages that do not have access to modern conveniences.
   The work conditions and accommodations are therefore

quite basic in nature. Volunteers usually stay in dormitory-like settings, and cooking is done communally. Since BWCA tends to attract volunteers from all over the world, it asks that volunteers come prepared to cook food that is native to their homeland to share with others.

Time Line: Short-term work camps operate between October and March for a maximum of two weeks. Medium-term volunteers can stay for two months up to one year and can start anytime.

Cost: Short-term volunteers pay a program fee of $250. Medium-term volunteers also pay $250 plus a per-day fee of $2.50 for the first three months. After these first three months, volunteers pay $50 per month plus $2.50 per day. The program fee includes lodging, food, and in-country transportation, but not travel to Bangladesh.

Getting Started: Prospective volunteers must apply at least one month before they wish to start; interviews are not required. Applications may be obtained by e-mailing BWCA at the address listed. BWCA holds an orientation session one day before each program begins, which includes an overview of program activities, basic language training, and information on the social, cultural, and economic condition of Bangladesh.

Needed Skills and Specific Populations: Short-term volunteers do not need any special qualifications or experience. Medium-term volunteers should have some proven skills in the area in which they wish to volunteer. Volunteers must be eighteen to thirty-five years old. BWCA is unable to accommodate volunteers with disabilities.

Bike-Aid

2017 Mission Street, Suite 303
San Francisco, CA 94110
(800) RIDE-808; Fax: (415) 255-7498
E-mail: bikeaid@globalexchange.org
Web site: www.globalexchange.org/getInvolved/bikeaid

Project Type: Community Development; Human Rights;
Natural Conservation (Land); Rural Development; Social
Justice; Women's Issues

Mission Statement Excerpt: "Global Exchange is an
international human rights organization dedicated to
promoting political, social, and environmental justice glob-
ally. . . . We [work] to increase global awareness among the
U.S. public while building partnerships around the world
through programs like Bike-Aid."

Year Founded: 1988

Number of Volunteers Last Year: Approximately 35

Funding Sources: Private donors

The Work They Do: Bike-Aid is a cross-country bike trip that
combines service learning, physical challenge, group living,
and political education. While biking across the country,
Bike-Aid volunteers stop once per week in a community
along the route. There they learn more about the challenges
faced by people in these communities and undertake volunteer projects to help with these challenges. Throughout the
summer, riders engage in antiracism trainings and critical
consciousness workshops about the global economy and
current international events. Meeting with community-based
organizations along the route and interacting with International Partner riders, who are affiliated with Global
Exchange's international human rights campaigns, enable
global solidarity and community alliances to be built. Examples of past projects include sending books to women in
prison, painting a house, and cleaning up a park. The
average day starts between 6:00 and 10:00 A.M., depending
on the mood of the group, temperature readings, and

distance to travel for the day. About once a week, volunteers do not pedal at all.

Project Location: The cross-country ride itineraries start from either Seattle or San Francisco. Shorter rides, from San Francisco to Tijuana and around the Hawaiian islands, are also available. Bike-Aid organizes community host stays in towns along the route. Volunteers unroll their sleeping bag in YMCAs, churches, gymnasiums, campgrounds, and people's homes. Frequently, local community members invite riders to potluck suppers, pancake breakfasts, or community activities. Occasionally, riders will have to provide their own food and lodging.

Time Line: Cross-country and West Coast rides take place in the summer, and Hawaiian rides are in December. The shortest rides are two weeks long; the longest rides are ten weeks long.

Cost: Bike-Aid's program fee is $4,000, which includes most lodging expenses and some food. Volunteers must pay for their transportation costs to the start and from the finish of the ride, as well as bicycling equipment needs.

Getting Started: Prospective volunteers can apply on the Web site listed. An orientation is provided before departure, and a bicycling training schedule is sent to volunteers along with a welcome packet of information.

Needed Skills and Specific Populations: Given the nature of Bike-Aid, volunteers must obviously be in good physical condition, but beginning athletes are welcomed. Riders aged sixteen to sixty have completed Bike-Aid rides. All riders must provide a signed medical release form from a physician before the ride. Volunteers with disabilities are not only welcomed, but are strongly encouraged to participate in Bike-Aid rides.

Biosphere Expeditions

P.O. Box 11297
Marina del Rey, CA 90295
(800) 407-5761; Fax: (800) 407-5766
E-mail: northamerica@biosphere-expeditions.org
Web site: www.biosphere-expeditions.org

Project Type: Natural Conservation (Land); Natural Conservation (Sea); Scientific Research

Mission Statement Excerpt: "Biosphere Expeditions promotes sustainable conservation and preservation of the planet's wildlife by forging alliances between scientists and the public. Our goal is to make, through our expedition work, an active contribution toward a sustainable biosphere where each part can thrive and exist. At Biosphere Expeditions we believe in empowering ordinary people by placing them at the centre of scientific study and by actively involving them out in the field where there is conservation work to be done."

Year Founded: 1999

Number of Volunteers Last Year: Over 300

Funding Sources: Corporate partnerships and in-kind donations; donors include Land Rover, Motorola, Silva, Globetrotter, and Cotswold Outdoor

The Work They Do: Biosphere Expeditions allows the general public to have meaningful, hands-on engagement with conservation tasks by partnering them with scientists in the field. Volunteers are involved with all aspects of the scientific field research. Examples of past projects include snow leopard research in the Altai; lion, leopard, and cheetah conservation in Namibia, Botswana, and Zambia; a biodiversity study in the Peruvian Amazon; whale, dolphin, and turtle research in the Azores; elephant-human conflict resolution in Sri Lanka; and wolf and bear research in Slovakia. All data collected during each volunteer vacation are published in a report that includes a review of the expedition and its conservation research. The report is sent to all volunteers within a few months of the end of the expedition, and any suitable material will be published in scientific journals or other publications to make sure as many people as possible know about and benefit from the research performed. Volunteers' names will appear in the acknowledgments of all scientific papers. Volunteers will be sent copies of any publications arising out of their expeditions.

Project Location: Projects can take place anywhere in the world and are constantly changing with the scientific research being conducted. Biosphere Expeditions does not believe adverse conditions need to be a part of this scientific research; instead, it strongly believes that volunteers need to be well fed and comfortable in order to become proficient research assistants. Accommodations are always locally owned and vary from simple bed-and-breakfasts to lodge research centers to tent base camps in a mountain valley. Lodging and food is provided by Biosphere Expeditions.

Time Line: Project dates vary from year to year. The shortest project is one week long; the longest is three months. Most volunteers work for one or two weeks.

Cost: Program fees range from $1,500 to $3,350 per two-week slot, which does not include airfare. Once the expedition starts, all reasonable expenses (excluding personal items and souvenirs) are included in the program fee. On average, two-thirds of the program fee benefits the project directly and locally, while the rest goes toward administrative overhead, research, and the establishment of new expeditions. Each project's expedition report (mentioned above) includes details on how the project's program fees were spent in terms of supporting the research project.

Getting Started: Prospective volunteers should start by thoroughly reading the information found on the Web site listed and by selecting an expedition. Spots on expeditions are reserved with a $600 deposit, which can be sent electronically. Training is part of the expedition.

Needed Skills and Specific Populations: Biosphere Expeditions works hard to allow many people to take a meaningful part

A volunteer bonds with his camel during a Biosphere expedition in canyons in Oman, searching for the presence of Arabian leopards. *Photo courtesy of Dr. Matthias Hammer*

in scientific research. There is no minimum or maximum age limit, and the organization proudly notes that its oldest volunteer to date was eighty-two years old. Families are welcome to volunteer with Biosphere Expeditions, but should contact the organization to discuss their needs. Some degree of fitness is required, but generally good health and an enjoyment of the outdoors are sufficient. Individuals with disabilities are welcomed and they should contact Biosphere Expeditions to find out about the suitability of specific expeditions for their needs.

The Day We Caught Two Cheetahs

By Martyn Roberts

Biosphere Expeditions

Cheetahs galore! Believe it or not, but today we had *two* chee-tahs in the traps, both without collars and part of a completely uncollared group of male juveniles and their adult mother. In order to fit them with collars, we had to tranquillize them. The whole team was there when we darted them, watched them go under, and then carried each to a lab table where we measured, weighed, took a blood sample, and then finally col-lared the cheetahs.

The procedure takes about an hour with four of us work-ing on each animal and the rest of the team on the perimeter of the table, observing and taking photographs. Right at the end of the hour, when they were still sound asleep, everyone was allowed to touch them. How amazing to feel the cats, to touch the world's fastest moving land animal. I will never forget these two weeks of working with cheetahs in Namibia. Working with live cats, experiencing a new country—what a way to vacation!

And then it was over. We carried them back into the bush and laid them down in shaded "waking up" spots. After an injection of anti-sedative, we watched them wake up slowly. They soon staggered off into the distance to rejoin their mother and siblings. It all went off without a hitch, and there were quite a few tears of joy at our success, at the marvelous opportunity that we were afforded today. Wish us luck for the next couple of days when we try to catch more of the same group. We certainly feel like the luckiest people on the planet!

Bob Marshall Wilderness Foundation (BMWF)

P.O. Box 190688
Hungry Horse, MT 59919
(406) 387-3808; Fax: (406) 387-3889
E-mail: trails@bmwf.org
Web site:www.bmwf.org

Project Type: Community Development; Education; Natural
Conservation (Land); Trail Building/Maintenance; Youth

Mission Statement Excerpt: "The Bob Marshall Wilderness
Foundation assists in maintaining and restoring the trail
system of the Bob Marshall Wilderness Complex with
national organizations, youth groups, and individual volunteers. We foster wilderness stewardship skills and education
through volunteer opportunities in Montana's premier
wilderness area and surrounding wild lands."

Year Founded: 1997

Number of Volunteers Last Year: 400

Funding Sources: Government; foundations; private donors

The Work They Do: Working with four different national
forests in Montana's Bob Marshall Wilderness Complex, the
BMWF identifies trail system improvements and then
creates educational, challenging, environmentally minded,
and scenic trail service projects into "The Bob." Most of the
projects are focused on trail maintenance, but the BMWF
also offer campsite restoration, weed eradication, and seed
collection projects. The offered projects vary in difficulty, so
prospective volunteers should review the descriptions on the
BMWF Web site.

Project Location: Many of the BMWF's projects are located in
Montana's wilderness backcountry focused around a base
camp near a creek or river. Work areas may be located up to
three miles from base camp, providing a hike to the project
each morning. Base camps are essentially a group tent site
complete with a kitchen area and primitive latrine or
outhouse; most of the time there is running water nearby
such as a creek or river. Occasionally projects are based out

After a day of work, a Bob Marshall Wilderness Foundation volunteer enjoys some fishing at scenic Sunburst Lake with Swan Peak overhead—complete with a glacier (pictured). During time off on a service project, volunteers are free to explore nearby peaks with stunning views, take a refreshing dip in the creek, observe wildlife in their natural habitat, or just enjoy the solitude of their surroundings (or go fishing!). *Photo courtesy of Bob Marshall Wilderness Foundation*

of forest service cabins with cooking facilities available and crews tent-camping around the cabin. Every project is accompanied by a wilderness crew leader who is certified in backcountry medicine and emergencies and has a breadth of technical trail knowledge and camping experience.

Time Line: The field season begins in June and ends in late September. While projects go on throughout the summer, each has definite start and end dates, which are usually posted on the BMWF's Web site the previous January. The projects range in length from daylong weekend projects to weeklong backpacking trips.

Cost: Overnight projects require a $50 deposit, which is refundable at the end of the project. The BMWF provides all food, and prides itself on creative backcountry meals. Volunteers need to bring all needed personal gear for overnight projects, but the BMWF will provide all tools, group cooking supplies, safety gear, and supervision.

Getting Started: Volunteer registration paperwork is available on the BMWF Web site, or can be mailed to prospective volunteers; interviews are not required. Once volunteers register for a project they are sent a detailed project description including a packing list, directions to the trailhead, and very specific information about the project. Crew leaders provide training on trail maintenance, tool usage, and safety concerns.

Needed Skills and Specific Populations: For many of the projects no prior experience is necessary; volunteers just need to come motivated to work, prepared to have fun, and ready to make the project a success. Trail maintenance and campsite restoration requires physical labor, which involves lifting, bending, and possibly carrying or moving heavy objects, such as rocks or logs. Volunteers signing up for extended trips are expected to be experienced backpackers and will need to provide their own gear and share in camp chore responsibilities. Volunteers under eighteen are encouraged to participate if they are up to the challenge, but will need an accompanying adult on the project. The BMWF welcomes volunteers of all ages, as long as their energy, interest, and experience makes them a good fit. They proudly note that "our oldest volunteer to date was 89 years old and cleared trail with the best of 'em!" Volunteers with disabilities that would require an adjustment on the part of the crew or crew leader to adapt to the backcountry should contact the Bob Marshall Wilderness Foundation to explore possibilities and/or to modify a project based on the volunteer's needs. Families, clubs, groups, and organizations that have between four and eight people may ask the BMWF for a custom-made project.

Interview with Bill Thomas, Volunteer Extraordinaire

By BMWF
Bob Marshall Wilderness Foundation

How many times have you worked with BMWF?
I would say in the last six years I've worked close to twelve weeklong projects plus a few day projects as well.

Why do you volunteer in the backcountry?
I enjoy hiking, backpacking, and camping in the backcountry so volunteering is a way to get to do these activities. Plus I have a desire to help maintain trails, especially those that regular trail crews don't have time for. I've always enjoyed trail work. Also, there is the camaraderie and teambuilding experience when you go out and work with a new group of people. It's always amazing how a diverse group can come together and accomplish so much work in a week's time. It's also about getting back to the basic elements of life. And all of this trail and team building you get to do with the magnificent backcountry as your workplace!

What piece of camping gear is essential for you in the woods?
That's difficult, but I suppose it is a good pair of well-fitting hiking boots. Since your feet are your mode of transport in the backcountry, it is essential that they are well supported, comfortable, and in good condition.

Describe a typical backcountry meal.
We usually start with some kind of packaged rice, pasta, or bean dinner and then add veggies we've dried from the garden such as tomatoes, peppers, beans, peas, and onions. We may

add a little sharp cheese or canned meat such as salmon, turkey, or chicken.

What do you like about the Bob Marshall Wilderness Complex?
I like the fact that nearly whole river systems are intact. It's great to be able to hike a trail along such beautiful stretches of water as the Middle and South Forks of the Flathead, the Spotted Bear River, and the forks of the Teton and Sun Rivers to name just a few. I enjoy the panorama of the whole scene from the valley bottom up to the high peaks.

Bridges for Education (BFE)

8912 Garlinghouse Road
Naples, NY 14512
(585) 534-9344
E-mail: mdodge@frontiernet.net
Web site: www.bridges4edu.org

Project Type: Education

Mission Statement Excerpt: "The purpose of Bridges for Education (BFE) is to promote tolerance and understanding using English as a bridge."

Year Founded: 1994

The Work They Do: BFE offers the opportunity to teach conversational English at an international language camp. Since its founding, students from a total of thirty-nine countries have attended this camp. BFE volunteers teach three hours of classes in the morning, supervise two hours of activities in the afternoon, and spend two to three hours on evening activities with the students. All of the BFE students have had at least one year of English language classes before attending this camp. In the BFE classroom, students are divided into beginning, intermediate, and advanced groups, each of which rotates through each team of teachers. The three-week camp is then followed by a paid one-week vacation in the host country.

Project Location: BFE currently hold camps in Belarus, Turkey, and China. Accommodations for teachers may be basic, depending on the country and school. Teachers stay in dormitories, two to a room, with shared bathrooms down the hall. Dormitories are not air-conditioned. Teachers take their meals in a cafeteria that usually serves local fare; special or restricted diets usually cannot be accommodated.

Time Line: BFE's language camps are usually held during the first three weeks of July, with the group vacation and travel during the last week of that month.

Cost: The program fee to teach with BFE is $950 for Europe and $980 for China. This program fee includes all accommodations and food during both the language camp and the week of travel, as well as weekend activities throughout the month. Airfare to the country of service is not included in the program fee, and it must be arranged through BFE's official travel agent.

Getting Started: Prospective teachers can download an application from BFE's Web site; BFE requires that prospective volunteers complete an interview. A deposit on the program fee is due by the end of March.

Needed Skills and Specific Populations: Volunteer teachers must already have state certification or teaching experience in a private school or college; all subject areas are accepted. BFE also accepts educated adults, student teachers, and college students as teaching assistants. Families with teenagers are welcomed. Native speakers of English are requested, but no other language proficiency is required.

BTCV

Sedum House, Mallard Way, Potteric Carr
Doncaster, DN4 8DB
United Kingdom
+44 (0) 1302 388883; Fax: +44 (0) 1302 311531
E-mail: information@btcv.org.uk
Web site: www.btcv.org

Project Type: Community Development; Natural Conservation
(Land); Trail Building/Maintenance
Mission Statement: "To create a more sustainable future by
inspiring people and improving places."
Year Founded: 1959
Number of Volunteers Last Year: 285,505
Funding Sources: Government and private sources, including
lottery revenue
The Work They Do: BTCV is a huge organization that offers
many, many kinds of volunteer opportunities around the
world, including New Zealand, Kenya, South Africa,
Cameroon, Albania, Italy, Germany, and the United States.
Many of the projects are conducted outdoors and are
conservation-oriented, but many others deal with aspects of
community or rural development. Examples of past projects
include joining workers at an organic farm in Kushiro,
Japan; tree planting in Nepal; enhancing the biodiversity
potential of woodlands in England's Peak District; and
planting living willow riverbank revetments in West York-
shire to provide a habitat for water voles. There are over
two thousand UK-based volunteer options, some of which
are just a day long.
Project Location: Seventy-five percent of BTCV's volunteers
work within the United Kingdom; the remaining 25 percent
are spread across the world at partner organizations. Work
sites and conditions vary widely depending on the
placement. Food and lodging are covered by the program
fee, but the exact arrangments depend on the work site.

Time Line: Placements are available year-round. Day projects tend to run from 10:00 A.M. to 4:30 P.M., with a break for lunch. Other BTCV Holiday programs run for a minimum of two days and a maximum of six weeks, with an average of one week for UK programs and two weeks for non-UK programs.

Cost: In the past, program fees have run the gamut from free (for nonresidential programs in the UK) up to £310 per week in the United Kingdom and £875 for three weeks in Kenya. Program fees for projects in the United Kingdom may also cover some local transportation costs or leisure activities. For nonresidential programs, transportation costs to the volunteer site are the responsibilty of the volunteer. Most of the fees go toward administration expenses, although some community-based non-UK organizations do benefit financially from the program fees.

Getting Started: The entire process is Web-based, from selection of a program to registration to payment of the program fee. Go to the Web site listed and click "Holidays." You may also contact a BTCV office in the United Kingdom to ask about opportunities. Training is provided on-site, and BTCV does not require an interview. You must apply to a program at least six weeks before it begins.

Needed Skills and Specific Populations: Volunteers must speak English sufficiently to understand and follow instructions and safety information. The mimimum age to participate is eighteen. There is no maximum age limit, although BTCV cannot offer insurance to those over eighty-one years old. Volunteers with disabilities are welcomed, but they should discuss their needs with BTCV to find a suitable opportunity. Families with children under age eighteen who reside in the United Kingdom may be able to volunteer with BTCV at a local project.

Camp AmeriKids

88 Hamilton Avenue
Stamford, CT 06902
(800) 486-4357; Fax: (203) 658-9615
E-mail: camp@americares.org
Web site: www.campamerikids.org

Project Type: Medical/Health; Youth

Mission Statement Excerpt: "To enhance the lives of youth in the Tri-State Area who are infected with or affected by HIV/AIDS by providing respite, skill building, and a supported transition into adulthood."

Year Founded: 1995

Number of Volunteers Last Year: 130

Funding Sources: Private funding through foundations, corporations, and individuals

The Work They Do: Camp AmeriKids's program is dedicated to providing two eight-day sessions of a summer experience to inner-city children ages six to seventeen who are living with HIV/AIDS, for whom camp is a chance to leave the city and just be kids. Children participate, under the guidance of counselors and program staff, in swimming, boating, dance, drama, arts and crafts, sports, and nature activities. Volunteers serve as camp counselors on a twenty-four-hour-a-day basis during the camp session. The counselor's role is to fully participate in all of the camp activities so that campers are encouraged and motivated to learn new things and have a memorable camp experience. Camp AmeriKids also utilizes wellness and medical volunteers.

Project Location: Camp AmeriKids is located in Warwick, New York, on 90 acres of countryside that features a freshwater lake, two outdoor swimming pools, a sports field, and arts classrooms. Campers and staff reside in designated cabins, which contain full bathrooms with running water. All meals are served family style in the dining hall.

Time Line: Camp AmeriKids operates in late July and early August. Volunteers commit to nine full days, which includes one and a half days of training. Volunteers can participate in one or both camp sessions.

Cost: There is no program fee to participate in Camp AmeriKids, and accommodations and food are provided to volunteers. Volunteers must pay for their own travel costs to and from the camp site.

Getting Started: Prospective volunteers should visit the Camp AmeriKids Web site or call its office at the toll-free number listed for an application. Potential volunteers are thoroughly screened and must complete a phone interview before being accepted as volunteers. Orientation and training takes place at the camp facility for one and a half days and covers camp policies, HIV education, and information on child development.

Needed Skills and Specific Populations: Volunteers do not need to have any particular previous experience—just enthusiasm, high energy, and a willingness to share their summer with kids. Volunteers must be at least eighteen years old, and families are welcome to volunteer as a group, provided all members of the family meet the minimum age requirement. There is no maximum age limit, and Camp AmeriKids has hosted volunteers over sixty-five years old. In general, Camp AmeriKids welcomes volunteers with disabilities, though the camp is not wheelchair accessible.

Caretta Research Project (CRP)

P.O. Box 9841
Savannah, GA 31412
(912) 447-8655
E-mail: WassawCRP@aol.com
Web site: www.carettaresearchproject.org

Project Type: Natural Conservation (Sea); Scientific Research
Mission Statement Excerpt: "The Caretta Research Project is a highly interactive educational research project that trains participants in the disciplines of fieldwork as they gather data on threatened nesting loggerhead sea turtles on Wassaw National Wildlife Refuge, Georgia."
Year Founded: 1973
Number of Volunteers Last Year: 78
Funding Sources: Private donors and grants
The Work They Do: CRP is a research, education, and conservation project that protects the threatened loggerhead turtles that nest on Wassaw Island. Volunteers help patrol the beaches each night, looking for nesting turtles. When nests are located, the turtles are tagged and nests are protected. Scientific data is also collected for collaborative projects with other organizations.
Project Location: The project is located in the Wassaw National Wildlife Refuge, an island off the coast of Georgia. The work site and available accommodations are basic and rustic, and there is no electricity or hot water.
Time Line: The research project runs from mid-May through early September. Volunteers must commit to at least one week of work, Saturday to Saturday. Volunteers may stay for as many weeks as they wish.
Cost: The program fee is $725. The fee includes food, lodging, and transportation to and from the island on Saturdays. Volunteers should not incur any costs once on the island. Volunteers are responsible for their own transportation to and from Landings Harbor Marina, near Savannah. One

hundred percent of the program fee is used to offset the cost of this program.

Getting Started: To ensure that volunteers can work on the dates they desire, they should check the Web site for available dates and call to make a reservation. After a reservation has been confirmed by phone, volunteers should print the application from the Web site, complete it, and send it in with a check. CRP requires that prospective volunteers complete a phone interview. Training is provided once volunteers arrive on Wassaw Island.

Needed Skills and Specific Populations: Volunteers should be physically fit, as this volunteer position requires a lot of walking. Flexibility and a sense of humor are also important, as volunteers share close living quarters (both with other humans and a lot of bugs!) in the summer heat of the American South. Volunteers must be at least fifteen years old; children aged thirteen and over who are accompanied by their parents are also allowed. Senior volunteers are welcomed as long as they are in good physical condition. Prospective volunteers with disabilities should call first to discuss their specific needs, as Wassaw is a remote island with no medical facilities.

Caribbean Volunteer Expeditions (CVE)

P.O. Box 388
Corning, NY 14830
(607) 962-7846; Fax: (607) 936-1153
E-mail: ahershcve@aol.com
Web site: www.cvexp.org

Project Type: Archaeology; Construction; Historic Preservation
Mission Statement: "CVE provides an opportunity for
volunteers from the U.S. who are interested in historic
preservation to spend time in the Caribbean learning local
history and architecture, while contributing to
preservation."
Year Founded: 1990
Number of Volunteers Last Year: Approximately 40
Funding Sources: None; entirely self-funded
The Work They Do: CVE carries out historic preservation projects such as building surveys, reports, cemetery
inventories, and actual construction on historic projects.
Volunteers help by recording buildings through photography
and drawings, filling out forms, painting, and performing
carpentry work.
Project Location: Projects are located throughout the
Caribbean. Most are in towns, but some are in more rural
locations. Volunteers usually stay in cabins, hotels, or
guesthouses.
Time Line: Projects go on throughout the year, usually for a
week at a time.
Cost: Fees run from $500 to $1,000 for one week. This
program fee does not include airfare, but it does include
lodging and food, which are arranged by CVE, as well as
local transportation.
Getting Started: Prospective volunteers should call or e-mail
CVE and request an application form. In-country training is
provided to volunteers.
Needed Skills and Specific Populations: On some CVE projects
it is helpful to have volunteers with architecture, computer,

or drafting skills. Volunteers under eighteen must be accompanied by a parent or guardian; families have volunteered with CVE in the past. Senior citizens are welcome to apply, and CVE occasionally parters with Elderhostel. CVE cannot accommodate volunteers with disabilities.

Casa Guatemala

5 Avenida 7-22 Zona 10
Guatemala City
Guatemala
+(502) 236-17748; Fax: +(502) 233-19408
E-mail: casaguatemal@guate.net.gt or
hbackpackers@guate.net.gt
Web site: www.casa-guatemala.org

Project Type: Administrative; Agriculture; Developmental
Disabilities; Education; Medical/Health; Orphans; Youth
Mission Statement Excerpt: "Casa Guatemala is an orphanage
that cares for the nurturing, health, and education of over
250 children."
Year Founded: 1977
Number of Volunteers Last Year: 200
Funding Sources: Foundations, individuals, and faith-based
organizations
The Work They Do: Casa Guatemala was built with the
purpose of offering a home, medical care, education, and a
healthy environment to orphaned and homeless children
who are at high risk of abandonment, abuse, and neglect.
Its doors are also open to children who come from
extremely poor families that cannot attend to their basic
needs. Volunteers teach English, computer skills, gym, and
art classes; assist with the health and personal hygiene of
the children; entertain children and coordinate games; assist
the children with their homework; work in the kindergarten
classes, the library, the farm, and read to children; assist in
the kitchen; and help with repairs and repainting when
needed. Long-term volunteers are first assigned to work for
two weeks at a hostel/bar called Hotel Backpackers in El
Relleno that financially supports the orphanage.
Project Location: The orphanage is located in the Guatemalan
jungle near Rio Dulce. It is isolated, and can be quite hot
and humid. Volunteers' housing is fairly basic and is located
next to a pigpen.

Time Line: Volunteers are welcomed throughout the year for a minimum of three months. There is no maximum for volunteer stints. As needed, Casa Guatemala will accept shorter-term volunteers on a case-by-case basis. Volunteers work twenty-two days out of the month, giving them time to explore Guatemala during their volunteer time.

Cost: Long-term volunteers pay an initial fee of $180, but otherwise their day-to-day expenses are paid for by Casa Guatemala. Short-term volunteers are required to stay at Hotel Backpackers and travel by boat to the orphanage each day, paying $150 per week for food, the hostel, and transportation.

Getting Started: Applications are available on Casa Guatemala's Web site. No interview is required, and Casa Guatemala does not offer formal training or orientation.

Needed Skills and Specific Populations: Casa Guatemala prefers volunteers who have medical training, teaching experience, administrative skills, agricultural background, or general child care abilities. Volunteers should have at least a conversational level of Spanish, and be at least twenty-four years old, but there is no maximum age limit. Casa Guatemala cannot accommodate volunteers with disabilities, though they accept volunteers from around the world, and families with up to four members are welcome.

Catalina Island Conservancy

P.O. Box 2739
Avalon, CA 90704
(310) 510-2595; Fax: (310) 510-2594
E-mail: volunteers@catalinaconservancy.org
Web site: www.catalinaconservancy.org

Project Type: Administrative; Construction; Historic Preservation; Natural Conservation (Land); Scientific Research; Trail
Building/Maintenance

Mission Statement Excerpt: "The mission of the Catalina Island
Conservancy is to be a responsible steward of its lands
through a balance of conservation, education, and
recreation."

Year Founded: 1972

Number of Volunteers Last Year: 1,347

Funding Sources: Private donors, public grants

The Work They Do: The Catalina Island Conservancy protects
and restores the environment on Catalina, promoting and
modeling ecologically sustainable communities to create a
healthier future for the island. Sample programs include
research projects on flora and fauna; a native plant nursery;
educational projects for schools, the community, and visitors; maintenance; and construction projects to support
programs and provide recreational access. Examples of
volunteer projects include building enclosures around rare
and sensitive plant species unique to Catalina Island;
processing and cleaning native seeds; transplanting native
plants; assisting in monitoring of research projects;
removing fences; assisting with maintenance and construction projects; removing weeds; and constructing trails.
Volunteers work alongside staff members who manage each
of the projects. This enables volunteers to gain in-depth
knowledge of each project and how their work plays a vital
part in the conservation and protection of open space on
Catalina Island for future generations to enjoy. Catalina
Island Conservancy offers both "Adventurer" vacations,

which are more physical and include camping at a private camp in the interior of the island, as well as "Explorer" vacations, which are less strenuous and include a stay in a private cottage or condo.

Project Location: All work is done on Catalina Island, California, a seventy-six-square-mile island with valleys, coves, and two-thousand-foot peaks. Most projects are conducted outside in beautiful, remote areas of the island with vistas, and they may require short hikes. Shade is not always available, but temperatures tend to be mild. Work usually entails a mixture of moderate to strenuous activities. Adventurer volunteers stay in canvas tents on raised decks with eight padded bunks, flush toilets, and hot showers that are located on-site. A fully equipped outdoor kitchen with cookware, utensils, barbecue, stove, sink, refrigerator, and coolers are provided. These volunteers also enjoy themed dinners and desserts prepared by local volunteers and restaurants each night.

Time Line: Volunteers are accepted during specific weeks in the months of February, April, May, June, and September for six days. All volunteer vacations require a minimum of six participants per group.

Cost: Adventurer vacations are $180 per person, which includes accommodations for four nights, four evening meals, on-island transportation to and from projects, training, work supplies, and a naturalist activity. Volunteers must pay for transportation to the island and food for breakfast and lunch for four days. Explorer vacations cost $575 per couple, or $288 for an individual, which includes transportation on the project/service days, as well as lunch on the full service day. Explorer volunteers must pay for transportation to the island and food for the week (with the exception of lunch on the full service day) as well as their accommodations in the city of Avalon through Catalina Island Vacation Rentals.

Getting Started: Prospective volunteers should call or e-mail the Catalina Island Conservancy office listed for the Catalina

Adventurer, and for the Catalina Explorer, call Catalina Island Vacation Rentals at (310) 510-2276. No in-person interviews are required. Orientation for both programs are held in Avalon, California, and on-site, and includes an overview of the program, training for specific tasks to be accomplished, and instructions for safely handling tools.

Needed Skills and Specific Populations: Volunteers should be in good physical condition and possess a willingness to work, get dirty, and try new things. Explorer volunteers must be at least twelve years old if accompanied by an adult and eighteen for the Adventurer vacations. Seniors are encouraged to volunteer. While some projects may not be accessible to persons with disabilities, the camp is supplied with a ramp to the tents for wheelchair access.

Catholic Medical Mission Board (CMMB)

10 West 17th Street
New York, NY 10011
(800) 678-5659 or (212) 242-7757; Fax: (212) 242-0930
E-mail: info@cmmb.org or rdecostanzo@cmmb.org
Web site: www.cmmb.org

Project Type: Medical/Health

Mission Statement Excerpt: "Rooted in the healing ministry of Jesus, Catholic Medical Mission Board (CMMB) works collaboratively to provide quality health care programs and services, without discrimination, to people in need around the world."

Year Founded: 1928

Number of Volunteers Last Year: 46 short-term volunteers, 86 long-term volunteers, and 210 mission team members

Funding Sources: Individual donors provide most of CMMB's funding, but it also receives USAID money for specific projects in Haiti, Kenya, and Zambia.

The Work They Do: CMMB primarily places medical volunteers and distributes donated pharmaceuticals in developing countries.

Project Location: CMMB places volunteers in thirty countries in Africa, Asia, Latin America, and the Caribbean. Most volunteers work in mission hospitals or clinics. Many of these facilities are in rural areas with limited resources, though some are in urban areas. Accommodations and food are provided by the host facilities.

Time Line: CMMB places volunteers throughout the year. While a few sites accept volunteers for a few weeks or months, most CMMB volunteers make a six-month to one-year commitment.

Cost: There is a $25 application fee to volunteer with CMMB. The extent of support given depends on the length of the volunteer's stay. All volunteers receive free housing and food. Volunteers who commit to one year or more also receive full health insurance, all travel expenses, and a

A volunteer who is a physical therapist back at home finds her skills in need when volunteering in Tena, Ecuador, as she helps a little girl maneuver with a tiny walker. *Photo courtesy of Catholic Medical Mission Board*

modest monthly stipend. Those volunteering for less than one year receive only insurance coverage.

Getting Started: Prospective volunteers should either download, complete, and send in a preliminary application from the CMMB Web site, or call the volunteer office at the phone number listed. Applications are accepted on a continuous basis, and applicants are expected to interview in person at CMMB's office in New York City. Orientation is done on an individual basis.

Needed Skills and Specific Populations: CMMB only places medical professionals who are licensed in the United States or Canada, including, but not limited to, doctors, surgeons, nurses, physical therapists, occupational therapists, lab technicians, and pharmacists. Some placement sites accept families. Volunteers must be between the ages of twenty-one and seventy-two. Volunteers with disabilities will find that not all sites can accommodate all disabilities. CMMB does not require that volunteers be Catholic, but volunteers must be willing to abide by the morals and ethics established by the Catholic Church.

Centre for Alternative Technology (CAT)

Machynlleth
Powys, SY20 9AZ
United Kingdom
+44 (0) 1654 705950; Fax: +44 (0) 1654 702782
E-mail: barbara.wallace@cat.org.uk
Web site: www.cat.org.uk

Project Type: Agriculture; Community Development; Construction; Education; Natural Conservation (Land); Rural Development

Mission Statement Excerpt: "CAT aims to inspire, inform, and enable people to live more sustainable lifestyles, researching and demonstrating sustainable technologies to a large number of people."

Year Founded: 1973

Number of Volunteers Last Year: 100 short-term and 25 long-term

Funding Sources: Governmental and foundation sources, as well as individual donors

The Work They Do: Consistent with its mission to help people live sustainable lifestyles, CAT operates a number of projects, including a visitor center that receives over sixty-five thousand visitors each year; practical and academic courses ranging from willow weaving to graduate-level coursework; a publishing house; a free information service on alternative technologies; and a consultancy service. Short-term volunteers may undertake one of many different tasks, according to their interests. These may include working on any of the projects listed, or more rudimentary work such as digging holes, weeding and clearing beds, moving compost, or routine maintenance work. Long-term volunteers work within a specific CAT department: Information, Publications, Media, Visitor Centre Marketing, Biology, Engineering, Building, Visitor Centre Maintainance, Displays Maintenance, Productive Gardens, and Display Gardens.

Project Location: The CAT Visitor Centre is in rural Wales, near Snowdonia National Park; it is remote, yet accessible by rail, bus, and road. The site has an independent water supply, and a renewable energy supply from wind, solar, biomass, and hydro power, as well as interactive displays, a restaurant, offices, laboratories, a vegetable field, and woodlands. Short-term volunteers are lodged in a youth hostel–style staff house. Long-term volunteers start in the staff house for a trial week, then are moved to on-site houses or private accommodations in the surrounding area.

Time Line: Short-term volunteers work for one or two weeks, between February and October. Long-term volunteers are accepted for six months at a time, from March through August or September through February. Long-term volunteers undertake a trial week before they commit to a six-month placement to ensure that they fit well with CAT's needs.

Cost: Short-term volunteers pay £10 per night for room and board. Long-term volunteers must be able to cover the cost of their own living expenses, such as accommodation and food, which is estimated to cost £200 per month. However, long-term volunteers receive a free lunch daily and daily travel expenses if they live off-site. Long-term volunteers may also enroll in two CAT courses for free, in topics ranging from solar installation to more theoretical "economics and sustainability" topics.

Getting Started: Short-term volunteer forms are available annually in January for the following spring and summer, and do not require an interview. Prospective long-term volunteers should send a resume and cover letter to CAT; the week-long trial week serves as an in-person interview. All volunteers are given a health and safety training, as well as a tour of the full site. Long-term volunteers will be given additional training as needed.

Needed Skills and Specific Populations: Enthusiasm and interest are the most important qualifications, though long-term volunteers should have specific skills relating to the relevant department. Volunteers must be at least eighteen years old, and senior volunteers are welcome. Volunteers with disabilities are welcome, though not all of CAT's buildings are wheelchair-accessible. Families are welcome on short-term volunteer stints, as long as all members are at least eighteen years old.

Cheyenne River Youth Project (CRYP)

The Main Youth Center and Cokata Wiconi Teen Center
P.O. Box 410
Eagle Butte, SD 57625
(605) 964-8200; Fax: (605) 964-8201
E-mail: info@lakotayouth.org
Web site: www.lakotayouth.org

Project Type: Administrative; Community Development; Youth

Mission Statement Excerpt: "The mission of the Cheyenne River Youth Project is to provide the youth of the Cheyenne River reservation access to a vibrant and secure future through a wide variety of culturally sensitive and enduring programs, projects, and facilities, ensuring strong, self-sufficient families and communities."

Year Founded: 1988

Number of Volunteers Last Year: 33

Funding Sources: The Cheyenne River Youth Project receives financial support through grants, private donations, and local fundraising.

The Work They Do: CRYP is comprised of four major components; the Main Youth Center, the Family Services Program, the two and a half acre Winyan Toka Win ("Leading Lady") Garden, and the Cokata Wiconi Teen Center ("Center of Life"). Volunteers at the Main Youth Center and Cokata Wiconi Teen Center work directly with children aged four to eighteen and provide support in all aspects of the center's work, such as project fundraising, community activities, and building maintenance. Volunteers are responsible for the implementation of planned activities, the development of recreational activities, arts and crafts, sports activities, and meal and snack preparation.

Project Location: CRYP is located on the 2.4-million-acre Cheyenne River Indian Reservation in north-central South Dakota. Dorm-style accommodations are provided at the center for all volunteers.

Time Line: Volunteers are accepted year-round for commitments of six weeks to two years. The average length of a volunteer's stay is around three months.

Cost: Volunteers are provided housing and some meals. Volunteers must travel, at their own expense, to Pierre, South Dakota, by airplane or bus; the Main Youth Center provides transportation from Pierre to the reservation upon the volunteer's arrival.

Getting Started: Prospective volunteers can complete an online application via the organization's Web site. To finalize the application, volunteers must also submit three letters of recommendation, a criminal history background check, and a $250 application fee, for which waivers are available. Once the application is complete, the Main Youth Center will arrange a telephone interview. New volunteers are given an on-site orientation, and must shadow another volunteer for one week before taking on responsibilities.

Needed Skills and Specific Populations: All volunteers must have patience, compassion, energy, dedication, motivation, and commitment. Volunteers who have experience working with children are preferred. Volunteers must be willing to work long hours and view this experience as a full-time job. Volunteers are generally at least eighteen years old, but volunteers as young as sixteen, including those volunteering with their family, will be considered on a case-by-case basis. Senior volunteers and volunteers with disabilities are welcomed, though the position can be physical at times.

Child Family Health International (CFHI)

995 Market, Suite 1104
San Francisco, CA 94103
(415) 957-9000; Fax: (415) 840-0486
E-mail: students@cfhi.org
Web site: www.cfhi.org

Project Type: Medical/Health

Mission Statement Excerpt: "Child Family Health International (CFHI) is a global family of committed professionals and students who work at the grassroots level to promote the health of the world community."

Year Founded: 1992

Number of Volunteers Last Year: 721

Funding Sources: Individual donors

The Work They Do: CFHI provides global health education programs for students of the health sciences, and other students with a strong interest in global health issues. Programs include clinical rotations with local preceptors in a variety of settings each day during the week.

Project Location: CFHI offers global health education programs at seventeen different program sites in Bolivia, Ecuador, India, Mexico, Nicaragua, and South Africa. Housing is with local homestay families, or, in some cases, guest houses where homestay families are not available.

Time Line: All CFHI programs are either four or eight weeks long, and they run year-round. In most cases, programs begin on the first Saturday of each month.

Cost: Program fees are approximately $1,900 for four weeks— exact costs vary from site to site. Program fees include predeparture orientation materials, two to three meals per day, accommodation with a homestay or in a guest house, insurance, airport transfers, an in-country orientation, program fees, and twenty to thirty hours of Spanish classes in Spanish speaking programs.

Getting Started: All applications are processed online via CFHI's Web site. In addition to receiving the predeparture orientation materials mentioned, volunteers are invited to attend two predeparture Web conferences, where they can connect with other program participants and ask CFHI program staff any outstanding questions they may have. In addition, CFHI on-site local coordinators and medical directors hold weekly in-country meetings. Volunteers also receive debriefing materials to assist them in their return home and have access to CFHI alumni opportunities and services.

Needed Skills and Specific Populations: CFHI programs are open to all students of the health sciences and premedical students. Non-health science students with a strong interest in global health issues are also welcome to apply. CFHI programs are not open to already qualified, registered health professionals. Volunteers must be at least twenty-one years old. Senior volunteers are accepted, but the large majority of CFHI volunteers are in their twenties. Prospective volunteers with disabilities are welcome to apply, but they should consult closely with CFHI's program staff to make sure that the selected site is accessible. CFHI does not typically host volunteers with families, but is willing to consider this on a case-by-case basis.

An Introduction to Traditional Medicine

By Christine Henneberg

Child Family Health International

We have arrived in Dehradun by train from Delhi, snaking our way to this bustling small city through the foothills of the Indian Himalaya. As students in the Traditional Medicine program, our days are scheduled and full. In the mornings, we spend several hours in a small homeopathic clinic, where a local doctor treats middle-aged and elderly patients for mostly chronic conditions. In the afternoons, we split our time between a modern "nursing home" (a private obstetrician's hospital) and lectures in the home of a distinguished reiki master, who reads to us from ancient-looking texts and demonstrates healing techniques at his dining room table. We also spend a week in Rishikesh and another week in the rural site of Than Gaon, assisting in rural clinics and hiking to remote villages for health visits.

Even with all the adventures of daily life in India, there is something protective and reassuring about sharing the experience with a small group of other international students. When the sharp edge of cultural alienation slices one of us, we have each other to turn to—for commiseration, shared exultation, or simply the discreet raise of an eyebrow. There is a fellowship amongst our group of five young women: all at different stages of our education, pursuing another angle on the medical field for diverse reasons, we share a common urge to unwind what seems bound up, to dip below the surface and emerge with our heads wet and eyelashes dripping. There is a promise of clarity amidst the muddled confusion of this foreign place.

Fourteen months later, I return to India as an alumni fellow to work with CFHI's Infectious Disease program. New students arrive, and I am their mentor and liaison, providing answers and directions when I can, or turning their questions back to them—which is often more beneficial. I also assist with daily logistics and communication, and help incorporate feedback from students and medical partners into the program. In this role, my time is less structured than when I was a program participant; my days are irregular, and my work is self-directed. While I spend little time in the hospitals and clinics, I spend lots of time talking to students about the million things they see each day—a newborn baby wrapped in a dirty sari and weighed on a produce scale, a college student stricken with leprosy, an entire family infected with tuberculosis.

One thing CFHI emphasizes in its global health electives is that while their programs are meant to be educational—for the benefit of the students—they are not intended to work at the expense of the host communities. This means that every physician preceptor is reimbursed for his or her time spent with CFHI students. Students are asked not to go into clinics or hospitals that don't have formal partnerships with CFHI, where they might inadvertently burden the staff and patients. And to every country where CFHI sends its students, they send with them boxes of donated medical supplies to support under-resourced clinics in that community. A key component of the alumni fellowship is to see that the "Recover" component of CFHI's clinical partnerships is being realized on the ground—that the donated supplies are making it to the clinics where they are most needed.

My work often takes me alone into the streets of Bombay as I rush to meet students at a clinical site, head across town for a briefing with our medical director, or simply take some time to myself after a long day of people-oriented work. One afternoon while stopped at a traffic signal on my way home, a small cohort of young boys flocks to my rickshaw, waving shabby flower bouquets in my face. They wear tattered shorts and dirty T-shirts, and I see the signs of undernourishment on their faces that we've been taught to recognize: dry flaking skin, thinned hair. They call out in broken English: "Ma'am, one flower! One hundred rupees one flower, ma'am!" The rickshaw driver turns a fraction of the way around from his front seat, half-interestedly watching my response. I smile at the boys and shoo them gently away: "Nahi chahiye, Jaao! I don't want any. Go on!" Traffic begins to move again, and the driver revs his engine. "Ma'am, one flower le lo! Go on, take one!" Their cries grow more desperate as we begin to roll forward, "Ma'am, one flower!" . . . Picking up speed now . . . "One flower ma'am! Goodbye ma'am! Happy New Year! Happy Christmas!" In this moment, stretched out and distorted like a piece of gum under my foot, the voices fading behind me make me want to cry.

There's a strange difference, in a foreign place, between being alone and being with others. Things that in the safety of company and likeness would seem almost comical are suddenly wretched and frightening. I think I see a hint of a smile on the driver's face in the rearview mirror; but, like my mood, it is tinged with tragedy.

I have seen through working with CFHI that I will be part of a community of colleagues devoted to the same mission of bringing quality health care to the world's poor. But being a doctor for the underserved will often be lonely work. Of this I have become quite certain. To work in a community where my presence makes a difference, where I am not simply filling a space that would otherwise be filled by another, will mean to go where other doctors do not wish to go. It will mean to face poverty and sickness without the buffer of another body, rich and healthy like mine, beside me. But it will also be social, busy, dynamic work—because to exchange skills and ideas between different cultures is to constantly redefine social contracts, evaluate the meaning behind truths that had always seemed self-evident, and to reel under the force of otherness that is so raw and assaulting when we first encounter it. Eventually, this exchange becomes a force in itself, one we can use to promote the goals of global health equity and increase health choices for poor people.

As students, taking part in this exchange can be one of our greatest opportunities to contribute—until the near future becomes the present, when the health of the all the world's people is in our hands.

Children Walking Tall (CWT)

"The Mango House," House No. 148/3, Karaswada
Mapusa, Bardez, Goa
India
+0091 9822 124 802
E-mail: childrenwalkingtall@hotmail.com
Web site: www.childrenwalkingtall.com

Project Type: Community Development; Education; Human
Rights; Medical/Health; Orphans; Youth
Mission Statement Excerpt: "To give children a childhood
worth remembering."
Year Founded: 2004
Number of Volunteers Last Year: 25
Funding Sources: Foundation, individuals, faith-based organizations, schools, and companies
The Work They Do: CWT assists low-income families by
providing education and health care for children. CWT
operates a drop-in center where children can obtain food
and first aid, as well as formal or informal education.
CWT's objective is to add fun and interest to these kids'
lives. Volunteers assist in this mission by helping with the
kids: providing child care, creating resources, implementing
projects, helping with medical care, playing games, and
distributing clothes and food in local communities.
Project Location: CWT is located near Mapusa, Goa, in India.
The Mango House is a large, old, Portuguese house that has
been painted to create a child-friendly environment. Some of
the volunteers' work is also done in the low-income neighborhoods, which can be hot and dusty. Volunteers are
responsible for finding their own accommodations, which
are available nearby for a range of prices.
Time Line: While volunteers are welcome throughout the year,
most volunteers choose to arrive between October and May.
Volunteers must commit to at least three months of
volunteering.

A volunteer makes good use of a small, portable chalkboard to teach children who live in a local slum in Goa, India. The project title is Basic Education and the goal is to both educate these children one-on-one as well as encourage their families to enroll the children into the proper local schools. *Photo courtesy of Robert Lyon*

Cost: Volunteers make a £50 deposit, which is returned after the initial three months have passed. There are no other program fees, though volunteers are responsible for all of their own travel and living costs; food and accomodations are not provided by CWT.

Getting Started: CWT has a limited number of volunteer slots available, and these are often claimed quickly. Prospective volunteers are encouraged to apply at least three months in advance by contacting CWT through the Web site. An informal orientation, which covers child safety, rules, and regulations, is provided to volunteers upon arrival. Volunteers do not have to complete an interview, but do need to provide the results of a police background check from their country of origin.

Needed Skills and Specific Populations: While CWT does not require that volunteers have any specific skills, a background in teaching or in Hindi language is very helpful.

Volunteers must be at least eighteen years old; there is no maximum age, as long as volunteers can cope with the heat of India. CWT would consider having volunteers with disabilities, though there are not currently any special accommodations available; the building is not wheelchair-accessible.

China Summer Workcamp
Sponsored by Philadelphia Yearly Meeting of the Religious Society of Friends

1515 Cherry Street
Philadelphia, PA 19102
(617) 504-3103
E-mail: chinaworkcamp@pym.org
Web site: www.pym.org/workcamp/China/china.htm

Project Type: Education
Year Founded: 2001
Funding Sources: Faith-based sponsors, mostly from the
Religious Society of Friends (Quakers)
The Work They Do: American volunteers work with others
from China, Japan, and Korea to teach English to children.
Volunteers also teach about environmental issues and other
subjects of their choosing, engage in building community
across cultures, and experience and understand rural living.
Project Location: The work camp is in a rural area of China's
Hunan province. The volunteer group also travels through
Beijing or Shanghai on the way to Hunan and visits a nearby
city. Participants live and work in a school building used
exclusively by the work camp. Sleeping accommodations are
large dormitory rooms and meals are Chinese food prepared
by local residents. The work camp is an international
community, with American, Chinese, Japanese, and Korean
participants living together, sharing chores, and teaching in
teams.
Time Line: The work camp takes place each summer in July and
August and lasts about four weeks.
Cost: The program fee is $1,500. This includes all transporta-
tion within China, housing, and food. International airfare is
not included. All accommodations and travel within China is
arranged by the program.
Getting Started: Prospective volunteers should visit the China
Summer Web site, listed, to read past participants' stories

and more detailed information about the work camp. Applications are available online and are due in March. Pre-program orientation is provided long distance via phone and e-mail. Basic teacher training and on-site orientation takes place during the first few days.

Needed Skills and Specific Populations: Knowledge of Chinese language is not required for participation in the work camp, as most Chinese volunteers will have sufficient English ability. Previous teaching or tutoring experience is useful but not necessary. An open mind and sense of adventure are key. Volunteers must be at least sixteen years old. Family members are welcome to volunteer together.

CHOICE Humanitarian
(The Center for Humanitarian Outreach and Inter-Cultural Exchange)

7879 South 1520 West, Suite 200
West Jordan, UT 84088
(801) 474-1937; Fax: (801) 474-1919
E-mail: expeditions@choicehumanitarian.org
Web site: www.choicehumanitarian.org

Project Type: Agriculture; Community Development; Construction; Economic Development; Education; Medical/Health; Rural Development

Mission Statement Excerpt: "CHOICE Humanitarian's goal is to provide the world with a community development model that ends poverty. We hope to spread this model in a way that is environmentally and socially responsible, always keeping sustainability at the core of everything we do."

Year Founded: 1982

Number of Volunteers Last Year: 300

Funding Sources: Foundation support and individual donors

The Work They Do: CHOICE Humanitarian works with motivated villages to alleviate and, hopefully, to eventually end poverty. They accomplish this by training leadership and providing organizational skills to villagers in the developing world. CHOICE volunteers work side by side with villagers on grassroots projects such as building schools, greenhouses, water systems, and community health posts. Volunteers can choose how physically demanding they want their experience to be, as CHOICE offers both strenuous and nonphysical opportunities. CHOICE measures success not in physical structures but in cultural understanding and global awareness.

Project Location: CHOICE works in Mexico, Guatemala, Bolivia, Kenya, and Nepal. Work sites are generally outside and range from very cold to very hot. Volunteers are usually in housed camp-like settings in schools or community centers and are required to bring a sleeping bag and air mattress. Outside of the village, volunteers usually stay in hotels.

Time Line: CHOICE sends expeditions of volunteers at set times throughout the year, for one to two weeks.

Cost: CHOICE's program fee ranges from $1,494 to $1,895, which covers room and board and orientation costs. Volunteers are responsible for their own international transportation costs.

Getting Started: Applications can be downloaded from CHOICE's Web site or are available by e-mail or fax. There are no application deadlines; applications are accepted until a trip is full. Interviews are not required, but are encouraged as CHOICE likes to get to know their volunteers before the trip begins. CHOICE usually has two two-hour orientation meetings about one month before the trip, and can be completed in-person in Utah or over the phone. These orientations cover general topics such as cultural awareness and norms, as well as more specific topics such as effective packing.

Needed Skills and Specific Populations: No specific skills are needed to volunteer with CHOICE, though volunteers should be open-minded and "willing to challenge their perceptions of where they are in the global community." CHOICE does not have any minimum age and encourages families to volunteer together, but requests that children under the age of thirteen be particularly well-behaved. Senior volunteers are welcome to apply, though they might want to talk with CHOICE to ensure that they meet general health requirements. Volunteers with disabilities are welcome to volunteer with CHOICE, and should contact the office to determine which volunteer trip can best accommodate their needs.

Christian Peacemaker Teams (CPT)

P.O. Box 6508
Chicago, IL 60680
(773) 277-0253; Fax: (773) 277-0291
E-mail: delegations@cpt.org
Web site: www.cpt.org

Project Type: Human Rights; Political Action; Social Justice

Mission Statement Excerpt: "Christian Peacemaker Teams (CPT) offers an organized, nonviolent alternative to war and other forms of lethal intergroup conflict. CPT provides organizational support to persons committed to faith-based nonviolent alternatives in situations where lethal conflict is an immediate reality or is supported by public policy."

Year Founded: 1988

Number of Volunteers Last Year: 140

Funding Sources: Donations from church congregations and individuals, including a small percentage from church denominations. CPT also receives some small grants from private, church, or human rights–oriented foundations. CPT is an initiative of the Historic Peace Churches (Mennonites, Church of the Brethren, and Quakers) with support and membership from a range of Catholic and Protestant denominations.

The Work They Do: CPT focuses on violence deterrence, human rights observation and documentation, accompaniment of vulnerable individuals or groups in conflict areas, and nonviolent public actions. Volunteers meet with local peace-makers and populations affected by violent conflict, engage in human rights documentation, and participate in nonviolent direct action. Volunteers also commit to sharing their experiences with a wider audience upon return to their home communities.

Project Location: As of this writing, volunteers work in Palestine, Iraq, Colombia, in native communities in Canada, and on the Arizona–Mexico border, but this list changes as human rights situations change around the world. Volunteer teams stay in modest accommodations in the city, such as apartments or modest hotels or hostels with shared rooms, and they may travel to the countryside, where accommodations are similar to camping. Volunteers are housed together with at least two people (often more) per room. Depending on the location, volunteers may be required to walk over rough terrain, scramble over muddy riverbanks, or endure extreme heat or cold. Two meals per day are provided.

Time Line: The schedule changes yearly, but there are volunteer opportunities available throughout the year, though not always in every location. In general, locations accept volunteer teams four to six times per year for periods of one to two weeks in length.

Cost: Program fees run from $300 to $3,500, depending on project location. Cost includes international airfare except for U.S. or Canadian projects.

Getting Started: Prospective volunteers should fill out an application for a "Short Term Delegation." These applications can be downloaded from the CPT Web site or are available from the Chicago office. CPT does not require any special training prior to delegation participation, nor an interview.

Needed Skills and Specific Populations: Volunteers should have experience or an interest in working for human rights and cross-cultural understanding, a commitment to nonviolence, and a willingness to participate in nonviolent public witness, team worship, and reflection. The minimum age to volunteer with CPT is eighteen; many participants have been in their seventies and a few have been age eighty and older. However, a degree of physical stamina, such as the ability to walk up to two or three miles over rough terrain, is required. CPT may not be able to accommodate persons with certain kinds of disabilities (for example, limited transportation options in the West Bank might preclude the acceptance of a volunteer who uses a wheelchair for that program).

Citizens Network for Foreign Affairs (CNFA)

1828 L Street NW, Suite 710
Washington, DC 20036
(888) 872-2632 or (202) 296-3920; Fax: (202) 296-3948
E-mail: ewallace@cnfa.org
Web site: www.cnfa.org

Project Type: Agriculture; Economic Development;
Professional/Technical Assistance; Rural Development

Mission Statement Excerpt: "The Citizens Network for Foreign
Affairs (CNFA) is . . . dedicated to stimulating economic
growth around the world by nurturing entrepreneurship,
private enterprise, and market linkage."

Year Founded: 1985

Number of Volunteers Last Year: 78

Funding Sources: USAID

The Work They Do: CNFA specializes in engaging private
companies of all sizes in partnerships to expand economic
activity and increase incomes. Through its volunteer
program, CNFA helps people build a free market–based
food and agricultural system. Since 1993, more than twelve
hundred volunteers have participated in this program. In
order to achieve the greatest impact, CNFA sends multiple
volunteers to long-term projects, with each volunteer assignment building upon previous ones. CNFA's long-term projects seek to develop private farmer associations,
cooperatives, private agribusinesses, women's and young
farmer groups, and other organizations that can help people
increase their incomes. Volunteers provide help to a wide
variety of groups including dairy processors and producers,
beef cattle farmers, mushroom producers, honey producers,
fruit growers, and greenhouse producers. The majority of
volunteer hosts are democratically structured farmers' associations and cooperatives or small-scale agribusinesses.
Typical assignments focus on strengthening associations,
developing marketing skills, business planning, and developing financial management skills. Occasionally, CNFA will

field a volunteer to train in crop production or processing for an individual farmer or agribusiness enterprise.

Project Location: CNFA volunteers work in the former Soviet states of Ukraine, Belarus, and Moldova. Volunteer site locations vary from rural villages to capital cities. In cities, volunteers are provided an apartment, and they have full access to bathing and cooking facilities, as well as to laundry and cleaning services. In villages, each volunteer and a translator will stay with a host family or in a rented apartment. Although lodging conditions are modest, every effort is made to provide comfort for the volunteer during his or her stay. The host family, if there is one, also provides meals.

Time Line: Volunteers are accepted throughout the year, for periods of sixteen to nineteen days. The minimum volunteer stint is sixteen days, and there is no maximum length of time for volunteers.

Cost: There is no program fee; all costs for volunteers are covered by CNFA.

Getting Started: Potential volunteers may submit an application and resume online, which is followed by an interview by phone or e-mail. Other than a short briefing, volunteers receive no training. It is assumed that any appropriate volunteer will already have professional experience in agriculture, so training should not be needed.

Needed Skills and Specific Populations: CNFA seeks experienced volunteers from a variety of specialties: farmers and ranchers, cooperative specialists, food processing professionals, agribusiness executives, extension agents, agricultural organization leaders, and others. Volunteers should have at least five years of experience in their fields, and senior citizens are encouraged to volunteer. Volunteers with disabilities are welcomed, but no special accommodations may be made. CNFA volunteers must be U.S. citizens or green card holders. First-time volunteers with CNFA may not bring family members with them; volunteers with a track record of successful assignments will be allowed to bring their spouses or children along on a case-by-case basis.

Colorado Trail Foundation (CTF)

710 10th Street, #210
Golden, CO 80401
(303) 384-3729; Fax: (303) 384-3743
E-mail: ctf@coloradotrail.org
Web site: www.coloradotrail.org

Project Type: Natural Conservation (Land); Trail
Building/Maintenance

Mission Statement Excerpt: "The mission of the Colorado Trail
Foundation is to provide and to maintain, through voluntary and public involvement, . . . a linear, nonmotorized,
sustainable recreation trail between Denver and Durango,
Colorado."

Year Founded: 1974

Number of Volunteers Last Year: 400

Funding Sources: Primarily private donors

The Work They Do: CTF maintains the 485-mile, high-altitude,
nonmotorized trail between Denver and Durango,
Colorado. Volunteers rehabilitate sections of eroded trail,
build bridges, create waterbars to divert water off the trail,
install culverts, and reroute sections of the trail.

Project Location: Volunteers work in national forests along the
spectacular Colorado Trail and camp in tents, which volunteers must provide. Campsites are reached by conventional
vehicle, a four-wheel-drive vehicle, or backpacking. Elevations range from six thousand to eleven thousand feet. A
description of each camp and work site is given with the
crew registration materials. CTF provides the food for each
volunteer crew.

Time Line: Volunteers are accepted in the months of June, July,
and August. Volunteers work weekends, from Friday
evening through Sunday afternoon, or for a full week,
Saturday through Saturday.

Cost: Weekend crew members pay $25, and weeklong crew
members pay $50. However, although volunteers may sign
up for multiple weekend or weeklong crews, they pay the

program fee only once per year. Transportation costs to Colorado are not included in the program fee.

Getting Started: Prospective volunteers can download a registration form and waiver from CTF's Web site; these are also available by calling or e-mailing the office listed. CTF does not require interviews as a part of the registration process. Trail crew leaders conduct a crew orientation session, a trail building session, and a tool safety session on the first day.

Needed Skills and Specific Populations: Volunteers must be at least sixteen years old; there is no maximum age limit, and previous trail work experience is not required. Due to the remote and rugged nature of their work, CTF cannot accommodate volunteers with disabilities. Families are welcome to volunteer with CTF, but all members must meet the minimum age requirement.

Concordia International Volunteers

19 North Street
Portslade, BN41 1DH
United Kingdom
+44 (0) 1273 422218; Fax +44 (0) 1273 421182
E-mail: info@concordia-iye.org.uk
Web site: www.concordia-iye.org.uk

Project Type: Agriculture; Archeology; Construction; Education; Historic Preservation; Natural Conservation (Land); Youth

Mission Statement Excerpt: "Concordia is a charity committed to international volunteering as a means to promoting intercultural understanding and peace."

Year Founded: 1943

Number of Volunteers Last Year: 200

Funding Sources: Concordia is run in conjunction with an active farm, the proceeds from which support the volunteer program.

The Work They Do: Concordia offers short-term volunteer projects in the areas of conservation, restoration, archaeology, construction, the arts, social work, and education. Concordia's projects cover a wide range of areas, but a few examples of projects include dune restoration in northern France, reforestation in Ecuador, constructing housing for seniors in India, and teaching art to children in Mexico.

Project Location: Concordia operates in over sixty countries in Europe, North America, the Middle East, Latin America, Africa, and Asia. Accommodations vary by site, but are usually basic, such as in tents, town halls, schools, gymnasiums, youth hostels, or occasionally in homestays. Volunteers are expected to bring and use a sleeping bag and to share their living space with other volunteers.

Time Line: Volunteer projects are available throughout the year for two to four weeks.

Cost: Volunteers pay a program fee of £150 to Concordia, and an additional project fee of £80 to £150 to the host organization on-site if the project takes place in Latin America, Asia, or Africa. Volunteers are also responsible for their travel costs, visa, and insurance.

Getting Started: Applications may be completed on Concordia's Web site. Volunteers going to Africa, Asia, and Latin America must attend a compulsory weekend training in Brighton, United Kingdom, for an additional £30.

Needed Skills and Specific Populations: Volunteers must be at least eighteen years old for most projects, though some projects allow volunteers as young as sixteen years old to participate. Concordia does not have a maximum age limit. Volunteers with disabilities should contact Concordia, who will do their best to help identify a suitable project. All volunteers must be resident in the UK in order to apply, regardless of citizenship. Some projects are designated as family friendly.

Conservation Volunteers Australia (CVA)

P.O. Box 423
Ballarat Vic, 3353
Australia
+(61) 3-5330-2600; Fax: +(61) 3-5330-2922
E-mail: info@conservationvolunteers.com.au
Web site: www.conservationvolunteers.com.au

Project Type: Historic Preservation; Natural Conservation
(Land); Trail Building/Maintenance

Mission Statement Excerpt: "To attract and manage a force of
volunteers on practical conservation projects for the better-
ment of the Australian environment."

Year Founded: 1982

Number of Volunteers Last Year: More than 10,000

Funding Sources: Government and private sources

The Work They Do: CVA takes on large-scale, critical environmental problems that can be addressed only through a significant amount of hands-on labor. CVA completes more than
two thousand individual conservation projects each year.
Examples of projects include planting more than one million
trees annually; assisting with manual clearance of invasive
weeds, such as buffel grass in the beautiful surrounds of Uluru
(Ayers Rock); assisting with trail projects on Fraser Island, the
largest sand island in the world; surveying endangered yellow-
footed rock wallabies in the Flinders Ranges of southern
Australia; creating koala habitats; and restoring historic buildings, including the first settlement and gold rush–era proper-
ties. Volunteer activities are hands-on, labor-intensive projects
such as planting trees, removing weeds, clearing trails,
completing carpentry projects, and radio-tracking animals.

Project Location: Any at given time, up to sixty projects may be
occurring simultaneously across Australia. Volunteers
should be prepared to be outside all day, taking into
account the climate conditions and season when they are
participating. CVA teams live together on or near the
project site. Accommodations vary according to project and

location. Typical accommodations can include RVs, hostels, bunkhouses, and camping, for which tents are provided. Volunteers should bring a sleeping mat, sleeping bag, and mosquito netting. Volunteers are expected to help with the preparation of meals and the cleaning up of dishes, plus minor domestic duties, as required.

Time Line: Projects operate year-round. Individual projects can last from one day or a weekend up to several weeks. There is a recommended maximum stay of twelve weeks; most volunteers stay for approximately six weeks.

Cost: The program fee is A$598 for two weeks, A$1,037 for four weeks, and A$1,500 for six weeks; this covers all meals, accommodations, and project-related travel. Volunteers are responsible for their own airfare to the project's point of departure within Australia.

Getting Started: Prospective volunteers should contact CVA through its Web site, via e-mail, or by mail. Volunteers join a team with a maximum of ten volunteers and one CVA team leader. The team leader is responsible for managing the group's health and safety, for explaining the goals and aims of the project, and for providing on-site skills training to enable volunteers to safely and effectively complete the project. All volunteers complete a comprehensive orientation that includes an introduction to CVA, discussions on occupational health and safety, project details, and planned activities. Further orientation at the start of each individual conservation project outlines the reasons for and aims of the activity. Each day also has at least one safety briefing session.

Needed Skills and Specific Populations: All projects involve physical activity, so volunteers should be reasonably fit and healthy. Volunteers must listen carefully and comply with instructions from team leaders. International volunteers must be at least eighteen years old, and volunteers up to age seventy are "very welcome" to volunteer with CVA. CVA recommends that individuals with disabilities review the organization's Web site and judge for themselves whether this would be an appropriate activity. If so, please contact CVA to discuss your particular needs.

Coral Cay Conservation (CCC)

Elizabeth House, 39 York Road
London, SE1 7NJ
United Kingdom
+44 (0) 20 7620 1411; Fax: +44 (0) 20 7921 0469
E-mail: info@coralcay.org
Web site: www.coralcay.org

Project Type: Natural Conservation (Land); Natural Conservation (Sea); Scientific Research

Mission Statement Excerpt: "Providing resources to help sustain livelihoods and alleviate poverty through the protection, restoration, and management of coral reefs and tropical forests."

Year Founded: 1986

Number of Volunteers Last Year: More than 400

Funding Sources: No outside sources

The Work They Do: Coral Cay Conservation (CCC) carries out tropical forest and coral reef conservation projects. Volunteers help collect scientific data, which is then used to form sustainable management recommendations. Volunteers can split their time between a marine expedition and a forest expedition.

Project Location: CCC volunteers work in remote, tropical environments in Tobago, the Philippines, and Papua New Guinea. Volunteers stay in fairly basic dormitories.

Time Line: Projects run year-round and have monthly start dates. The minimum stay is one week on marine projects, and (due to the remote location of Papua New Guinea) four weeks on terrestrial projects. There is no maximum stay.

Cost: Program fees for marine expeditions start at £460 for one week and program fees for forest expeditions start at £1,380 for four weeks. Program fees include accommodations, food, and training. The costs of flights, insurance, and some equipment are not included.

Getting Started: Prospective volunteers can download an enrollment packet from CCC's Web site or contact the office to request that one be sent via mail. If required, science and scuba training can be provided on-site.

Needed Skills and Specific Populations: Volunteers do not need to have scientific or scuba training before volunteering. Volunteers must be at least sixteen years old; there is no maximum age limit. Families are welcome to volunteer, but all members of the family must meet the minimum age requirement. CCC accepts volunteers from around the world. Volunteers with disabilities should contact CCC's office to discuss their particular situation.

A Day in the Life of a Science Officer

By Wing-Yunn Crawley

Coral Cay Conservation

The author is a CCC Science Officer, Philippines Rainforest Conservation Project

----

I wake at five thirty to the sounds of the mountain leaders talking in low voices as they prepare breakfast. After pulling some clothes on, I leave the cocoon-like interior of my hammock and set about waking the volunteers up for breakfast at six. They emerge bleary eyed, but are all awake after a delicious breakfast of scrambled eggs and rice and, of course, the customary hot cup of milo. An Asian house shrew (*Suncus murinus*) pokes its flat, grey head out from under some tree roots and peers at me for a second as I brush my teeth. There are so many animals here in the forest that we don't see, the only clues of their presence being their calls or the rustling of leaves. We pull on our wet trekking boots, grab binoculars and I.D. guides, and set off to do our first survey of the day— a bird point count.

Chattering Mountain white-eyes (*Zosterops montanus*) flitter quickly through the canopy above us as we sit quietly in a forest clearing. One stops to feed on a berry, affording us a glimpse of this small, delicate bird before it disappears in an instant behind the leaves. We check the mammal lines, re-baiting the traps and measuring any rats or shrews that have been caught before releasing them. Surveys for butterflies, herpetiles, and vegetation take up the rest of the afternoon, and before I know it, it's nearly six o'clock and time to open the mist nets.

For me, this is the best part of the day. From the moment a Musky fruit bat (*Pterochirus jagori*) took aim and managed to urinate on me on my very first survey, I was hooked! Although some may say they are not the most pleasant of fruit bats (they aren't called "musky" for nothing) they are strong for their size and boy, do they have attitude. Then there's the magnificent Philippine tube-nosed fruit bat (*Nytimene rabori*), instantly recognisable by the separate, tubular nostrils, yellow spotted wings, and dark stripe running down its back. This critically endangered species is endemic to the Philippines. The female tube-nose caught in the net is actually carrying her young—a tiny creature, tucked underneath her wing. We quickly release her without taking any measurements to minimize possible stress and are ecstatic at seeing evidence of a breeding population with our own eyes.

The volunteers continue to check the nets every half an hour, calling to James (my fellow science officer) and myself when there are any bats. The nets are closed at ten and after hanging their boots up, the volunteers take themselves back to their hammocks for a well-earned sleep. I take a minute to look around, and as the mist rolls in, the hammocks resemble silent spaceships suspended beneath the trees. At this moment, I realize that there is nowhere else where I would rather be.

Cross-Cultural Solutions (CCS)

2 Clinton Place
New Rochelle, NY 10801
(800) 380-4777 or (914) 632-0022; Fax: (914) 632-8494
E-mail: info@crossculturalsolutions.org
Web site: www.crossculturalsolutions.org

Project Type: Community Development; Developmental Disabilities; Education; Medical/Health; Orphans; Women's Issues; Youth

Mission Statement Excerpt: "Our mission is to operate volunteer programs around the world in partnership with sustainable community initiatives, bringing people together to work side-by-side while sharing perspectives and fostering cultural understanding."

Year Founded: 1995

Number of Volunteers Last Year: Over 4,000

Funding Sources: Occasional funding from private donors

The Work They Do: CCS operates international programs that offer a wide range of volunteer opportunities. Volunteer placement is based on the needs of the local community and on each individual's skills and interests. Each volunteer is required to fill out a Skills & Interest Survey that helps CCS place the volunteer with a local organization. Specific examples of volunteer positions available with CCS include: taking care of children in day-care centers and orphanages; teaching conversational English; conducting educational activities for teenagers; working with women's groups; caring for and developing activities for the elderly; observing and assisting with a local health professionals; taking care of people with mental and physical disabilities; and taking care of people living with HIV/AIDS. CCS is a recognized leader in the international volunteer field; it is in Special Consultative Status with the United Nations and in partnership with CARE, one of the world's largest international humanitarian organizations. CCS has been profiled in more than five hundred news outlets.

A volunteer shares a moment, and a tender touch, with an elderly woman at a day care center which receives elderly people, abandoned women, and malnourished children in Salvador, Brazil. The volunteer worked with this organization, founded by Mother Teresa, for six weeks, both in the center and helping to deliver foodstuffs twice weekly to the poorest families in the community. *Photo courtesy of Cross-Cultural Solutions*

Project Location: CCS volunteer programs are located in Brazil, China, Costa Rica, Ghana, Guatemala, India, Morocco, Peru, Russia, South Africa, Tanzania, and Thailand. Volunteers work in partnership with sustainable community initiatives in settings such as schools, orphanages, elderly homes, community homes, clinics, and offices. CCS provides a Home-Base for all volunteers in each given country, which typically consists of a comfortable house in a local, residential neighborhood. Clean, modest accommodations with shared rooms are the standard. Accommodations always have basic amenities such as linens and running water, as well as hot water where available. As part of the CCS program, staff cooks prepare and serve daily meals and snacks based on the regional cuisine. Staff drivers provide daily and airport transportation.

Time Line: Volunteer programs are offered year-round. Volunteers stay for one to twelve weeks, though longer programs may be arranged on an individual basis.

Cost: CCS's program fee is $2,588 for two weeks and $297 for each additional week. Included in the program fee are all accommodations, meals, and in-country transportation; cultural and learning activities including excursions to nearby points of interest and special events; and in-country travel medical insurance. International airfare is not included in the program fee. Only 10 percent of CCS's program fee goes toward administrative expenses.

Getting Started: Prospective volunteers can enroll in a program via CCS's Web site or by contacting CCS. Because CCS participants are from all over the world, there is an in-country orientation that is run by the in-country staff.

Needed Skills and Specific Populations: No specific skills, background, or experience are required to volunteer with CCS, though volunteers must have at least a basic knowledge of the English language. The minimum age for unaccompanied volunteers is usually eighteen, though some sites may accept sixteen- and seventeen-year-olds. The minimum age for a child traveling with a parent or guardian is eight; CCS has worked with hundreds of families at all of their sites. Senior volunteers are warmly welcomed. Volunteers with disabilities are also welcomed and CCS has experience in placing volunteers with disabilities in certain locations. Volunteers from all countries are welcome, provided that they can obtain a visa for their country of service.

All I Had to Offer Was Myself

By Zubin Mathai

Cross-Cultural Solutions

The author volunteered at a computer instructions center in New Delhi, India, for three weeks in July of 2003.

When the first set of students trickled in, smiling and excited at seeing working computers and a clean lab, it started to sink in. It finally hit me full force one day when working with a student. He already knew how to type and the placement of all the keys on the keyboard. He knew how to type from a book I had shown to him numerous times before. Yet after typing each letter, with imploring eyes and a pleading, unsure voice, he would call me over from helping the other students. He would call me over not to show him what the next letter was, but just so that someone would be standing next to him as he typed it. He needed someone's silent presence to give him the confidence to hit a key, and be there to smile in appreciation when he did. No matter how many times I would gently encourage him to type on his own, it would not sink in. I realized then that I was making a difference and a contribution just by being who I was. I never lost patience with that student, or any other. No matter how many times he called me over, I would stand by him. In that or any other moment, when faced with someone's need to feel connected, all I had to offer was myself.

Cultural Destination Nepal (CDN)

G.P.O. Box #11535
Kathmandu
Nepal
+(977) 1 437-7623 or +(977) 1 437-7696;
Fax: +(977) 1 437-7696
E-mail: cdnnepal@wlink.com.np or
info@volunteernepal.org.np
Web site: www.volunteernepal.org.np

Project Type: Community Development; Developmental Disabilities; Education; Medical/Health; Rural Development; Youth

Mission Statement Excerpt: "Cultural Destination Nepal (CDN) aims to introduce the participant to Nepal's diverse geographical and cultural environment and to promote intercultural understanding through experiential learning in Nepal."

Year Founded: 1996

Number of Volunteers Last Year: 15

Funding Sources: None outside of volunteer fees

The Work They Do: Most volunteers teach English, social studies, mathematics, science, or environmental studies in Nepali schools. CDN also provides placement in nonprofit organizations that work in the areas of women's issues, the environment, disabled children, and other areas; however, volunteers in these more specialized fields must be qualified both through work or previous volunteer experiences and through their education. Volunteers also have the opportunity to participate in outdoor activities and excursions, as well as in cultural exchanges. Secondary projects may also be available at the placement site.

Project Location: All volunteers work in Nepal. During the two-week orientation, volunteers stay with a host family near CDN's offices; during the volunteer project, volunteers reside with a host family or in a hostel.

Time Line: Volunteers begin their volunteer experience as part of a group in February, April, June, August, or October. Volunteers commit to two- to four-month stints, with the average volunteer staying three to four months.

Cost: The program fee is €650. The fee includes a two-week orientation program (pre-service training); lodging with a host family; two meals a day (breakfast and dinner); a cultural orientation tour; cross-cultural orientation; a hiking day trip; lectures on Nepali religion, cultures, political system, history, and gender relations; guided meditation; cultural activities; volunteer placement; a village excursion; a jungle safari; white-water rafting; and in-country transportation. Expenses not included in the program fee are the volunteer's airfare to and from Nepal, insurance, personal expenses, visa fees, and entrance fees to tourist sites visited during training.

Getting Started: Contact CDN and request an application form, which must be returned by registered mail along with a resume, four copies of passport-sized photographs, and a nonrefundable application fee of €50. CDN offers what appears to be a very impressive two-week orientation program, which includes a general orientation to Nepali customs, language (taught by professional language teachers), and community interaction skills, all conducted while volunteers stay with host families. The cultural orientation includes discussions about Nepali history and a tour of historic cities within the Kathmandu Valley. Interestingly, it also includes a tour of basic service providers such as the post office, banks, and health clinics. The orientation also includes a one-day hiking trip outside of Kathmandu and lectures on religion, culture, history, politics, geography, necessary health precautions, women in Nepal, and various other topics that explain the diversity of Nepali life. Volunteers can also request lectures if they want to learn more about a particular topic during orientation.

Needed Skills and Specific Populations: Volunteers must be at least eighteen years old and have a high school diploma, though no other specific skills are required. Senior volunteers are welcomed; the eldest CDN volunteer to date was sixty-five years old. Volunteers with disabilities are welcomed, but may not be able to participate in all of the planned activities. Couples are welcomed and encouraged to apply.

Cultural Restoration Tourism Project (CRTP)

410 Paloma Avenue
Pacifica, CA 94044
(415) 563-7221
E-mail: info@crtp.net
Web site: www.crtp.net

Project Type: Agriculture; Archaeology; Community Development; Construction; Economic Development; Historic Preservation; Natural Conservation (Land); Rural Development

Mission Statement Excerpt: "The mission of the Cultural Restoration Tourism Project (CRTP) is to help communities around the world restore artifacts of cultural importance, promote responsible tourism, encourage cultural interaction, and provide a model of alternative funding for other nonprofit organizations or grassroots organizers."

Year Founded: 1998

Number of Volunteers Last Year: More than 100

Funding Sources: No outside funding sources

The Work They Do: CRTP is dedicated to the restoration of culturally significant buildings and to community development around those buildings. Currently, it is restoring a monastery in Nepal and an oasis in Egypt. Community development work, such as agricultural projects, education, and cottage industry development, is carried out along with the building projects. CRTP's volunteer opportunities consist of a wide variety of construction tasks and community work, including working in the garden and helping out in the kitchen or on the construction site. Depending on volunteers' experiences and backgrounds, they may be handling a shovel, a paintbrush, or a chisel.

Project Location: CRTP's current projects are located in rural, remote areas of Egypt and Nepal. Solar or hydroelectric power and emergency communications are available. Accommodations are in traditional housing for the area and are shared with other travelers. The sites are environmentally beautiful, and living quarters are in the local villages. Meals are prepared by the indigenous staff and are shared among the volunteers and locals.

Time Line: CRTP offers programs during many parts of the year. The average volunteer stay is two weeks.

Cost: The program fee to volunteer with CRTP is approximately $1,250 per week, which includes travel within the country, accommodations, and food while at the work site. Volunteers must also pay for their travel to the country of service.

Getting Started: Prospective volunteers should call or e-mail CRTP via the phone number or e-mail address listed. There are no set deadlines for applications, and no interviews are required. Training is completed on-site.

Needed Skills and Specific Populations: No previous skills or experience are required. To date, CRTP's youngest volunteer was fourteen and the oldest was seventy-six. Prospective volunteers with disabilities are encouraged to call the office and make an inquiry. Families are welcome to volunteer with CRTP.

Dakshinayan

F–1169, Chittaranjan Park, First Floor
New Delhi—110019
India
+91 98365-96426
E-mail: info@dakshinayan.org
Web site: www.dakshinayan.org

Project Type: Education; Rural Development; Youth
Mission Statement Excerpt: "Dakshinayan is a volunteer-based
    organization providing education and health care to tribal
    and other rural communities in India."
Year Founded: 1992
Number of Volunteers Last Year: 30
Funding Sources: None; Dakshinayan is self-funded.
The Work They Do: Dakshinayan offers volunteers the oppor-
    tunity to teach primary education classes to children in
    remote villages in India. Volunteers help teach basic English,
    games, and art. Dakshinayan's objective is to provide people
    who are concerned about development issues a unique
    opportunity to observe and experience the culture of rural
    India and to study the problems of communities while
    gaining an in-depth perspective of the myth and reality of
    poverty in an economically developing nation.
    Dakshinayan's emphasis is not on work but rather on
    volunteer participation in ongoing project activities and
    community life. Therefore, work and activities are not
    organized especially for the volunteers.
Project Location: Dakshinayan's project is located in the Sundar
    Pahari Block of Godda District in the new tribal state of
    Jharkhand, India. Volunteers are usually placed on projects
    that are remote and that do not have electricity or running
    water. Living conditions are basic, and food consists of
    simple vegetarian meals made from whatever vegetables are
    available locally.
Time Line: Volunteers are accepted year-round, but they must
    apply at least one month before they wish to depart, and

they must arrive in New Delhi before the fifth of the month in which they wish to begin work. Volunteers must commit to at least one month of work, and have a maximum stay of four months.

Cost: Dakshinayan's program fee is $300 per month, which includes food and accommodation while at the project. Transportation costs to and from the project are not included.

Getting Started: Prospective volunteers should request, complete, and return a questionnaire by e-mail, which will then be screened. No orientation is given nor interview required, though Dakshinayan provides some instructions and informal conversations before departure.

Needed Skills and Specific Populations: No special skills or certification are required, as most volunteers teach basic English or mathematics to small children. A volunteer who cannot teach either subject may teach the children about the volunteer's own culture. Volunteers must be eighteen to thirty. Dakshinayan cannot accommodate volunteers with disabilities or families, though couples may volunteer together. Volunteers must be very culturally sensitive, as they are placed in rural villages that have had little exposure to other cultures.

Earthwatch Institute

3 Clock Tower Place
Maynard, MA 01754
(800) 776-0188; Fax: (978) 4
E-mail: info@earthwatch
Web site: www.earthwat

Project Type: Archaeology; Community Development; Historic
Preservation; Natural Conservation (Land); Natural Conservation (Sea); Scientific Research

Mission Statement Excerpt: "Earthwatch Institute engages
people worldwide in scientific field research and education
to promote the understanding and action necessary for a
sustainable environment."

Year Founded: 1971

Number of Volunteers Last Year: 4,000

Funding Sources: Some money from private sources

The Work They Do: Earthwatch Institute expeditions are short-
term volunteer opportunities to directly assist qualified and
respected scientists in their field research and to work on
critical and current issues. Research topics span a wide
range of scientific study and include climate change,
ecology, zoology, archaeology, and cultural impacts. The
range of tasks on Earthwatch Institute expeditions is enormous, from using dental picks to coax free a dinosaur bone
to freeing a bird from a mist net. Other examples of
possible volunteer activities include counting fish on a coral
reef, recording the mating rituals of monkeys, interviewing
poor farmers or homeless women, and utilizing scientific
instruments (from a gravity meter to a satellite tracking
system to a pair of tweezers and a magnifying glass). Other
volunteers might whisk the dust off of a bowl that was last
seen by a Roman soldier in the first century A.D. or dig up
bones of dinosaurs from the late Triassic Period. In addition
to individual opportunities, teams are often available for
teens, families, and groups.

Location: Volunteer projects are carried out in forty
countries around the world, from the United States to
Tanzania to Brazil. Much of Earthwatch Institute's work
takes place in wildlife reserves, at important historical sites,
and in national parks. In some cases, volunteers work in
areas that are inaccessible to tourists, in pristine regions that
only researchers are allowed to enter. Accommodations and
food arrangements vary widely and might take the form of
hammocks, dorm rooms, country inns, formal hotels, or
condos. Food ranges from spaghetti cooked over a fire to
four-course meals in a safari camp. Earthwatch Institute's
online project descriptions provide specific details for each
trip.

Time Line: Projects are offered year-round, though each project
takes place in a specific time frame. Most projects are ten to
fourteen days long, but one-week and three-week options
are available. The shortest projects take place over a
weekend, and the longest projects run twenty-two days.

Cost: Program fees range from $199 to $4,000, with the
average being about $2,500. The program fee includes
accommodations and food, travel during the expedition,
and any permits that are needed. Only 12 percent of the
program fees go to administrative overhead costs; the
remainder goes toward paying for the volunteer's expenses
and for the scientific research project. Volunteers must
provide their own airfare to the work site, and pay for other
personal expenses. Earthwatch Institute estimates that the
average volunteer spends about $750 on airfare and $250
on other expenses.

Getting Started: Prospective volunteers can sign up for an expedition online, over the phone, or through the mail. Volunteers then receive an expedition briefing that includes all of
the necessary program details. In the field, volunteers are
given one or more training sessions that cover all needed
skills with the exception of scuba certification, which is
required by one or more projects. Some projects require

Volunteers on Earthwatch's Amazon Riverboat exploration record data for a fish population survey near Iquitos, Peru. *Photo courtesy of Earthwatch Institute*

volunteers to have extensive backpacking and camping experience before their arrival.

Needed Skills and Specific Populations: Other than family teams, which provide options for children and their guardians, all projects have a minimum age requirement of either sixteen or eighteen. Senior volunteers are encouraged to work with Earthwatch Institute. Volunteers with disabilities are welcomed provided that the type and level of disability can be accommodated by the specific project. Expeditions that require a high level of fitness or scuba certification are clearly identified in their online descriptions.

Eco-Center Caput Insulae—Beli (ECCIB)

Beli 4, 51559 Beli
Island of Cres
Croatia
+385 51840525
E-mail: caput.insulae@ri.t-com.hr
Web site: www.supovi.hr

Project Type: Archeology; Natural Conservation (Land); Rural
Development; Scientific Research

Mission Statement Excerpt: "Protect and preserve natural diversity and work toward the protection of original values and
cultural-historical heritages."

Year Founded: 1993

Number of Volunteers Last Year: 350

Funding Sources: Government and private funding

The Work They Do: Eco-Center Caput Insulae—Beli (ECCIB)
works to protect Eurasian griffon vultures and the natural
and historical heritage of the island of Cres in Croatia.
Volunteers help conduct observations of griffon vultures,
learn about and maintain historic stone walls, assist with
trail maintenance, build labyrinths, and staff and maintain a
historical interpretation center.

Project Location: Volunteers live and work in the village of Beli,
to the north of the Adriatic island of Cres, in Croatia. The
village dates back to 4,000 B.C.E., and two thousand years
ago it was a Roman settlement. Volunteers stay in dormitories that have shower and kitchen facilities, and cooking
tends to be communal.

Time Line: Volunteers are accepted from March through
October. Volunteers must stay at least one week, and the
maximum volunteer stint is six months. The average volunteer stays for two or three weeks.

Cost: One-week projects cost between €108 and €164, while
two-week projects cost between €135 and €298. Three-
week projects are €162 to €364, and four-week projects cost
€190 to €430. Food is an additional €8.50 per day. The

program fee includes travel from the town of Cres to the village of Beli, accommodation, training, and insurance; it does not include travel to Cres or visas.

Getting Started: Prospective volunteers may access an application form on ECCIB's Web site, or can contact the organization by e-mail or phone. Applications should be sent in at least one month before travel, preferably more for the summer months. Prospective volunteers should closely read ECCIB's Web site and volunteer contract, as this must be signed on the first day. Also on the first day volunteers are given an introductory lecture that includes information on the Eurasian griffon vulture and the surrounding area. For the first few days, volunteers accompany a coordinator or an ecocenter staff member to learn more about the work done at the center. Later during their stay, volunteers take a daylong hike along the ecotrails in the area and have the opportunity to explore the island of Cres.

Needed Skills and Specific Populations: Volunteers must be at least eighteen years old, speak English or Croatian, and be in good physical condition, which includes the ability to swim. Senior citizens are welcome to volunteer with ECCIB, as are volunteers with disabilities who meet the physical requirements. Families may volunteer with ECCIB between mid-March and mid-April.

Ecologia Youth Trust

The Park, Forres
Moray, IV36 3TD
Scotland
+44 (0) 1309 690995
E-mail: info@ecologia.org.uk
Web site: www.ecologia.org.uk

Project Type: Education; Orphans; Youth

Mission Statement Excerpt: "Ecologia Youth Trust promotes and fosters the process of positive and creative change in the world through youth, ecology, and education."

Year Founded: 1995

Number of Volunteers Last Year: 25

Funding Sources: Foundations, individuals

The Work They Do: Ecologia supports the Kitezh Children's Community in western Russia by sending volunteers there to assist in the community's work. Kitezh is an entirely child-centered, therapeutic education community where families raise orphaned children who have had traumatic early childhood experiences, and educate them along with their own children. Volunteers live with a family, teach English to children, and take part in the daily working and social life of the community through gardening, cooking, and building. Russian-language speakers have the opportunity to use their linguistic skills and often provide translation services.

Project Location: The Kitezh Children's Community is three hundred kilometers south of Moscow. Located on one hundred hectares of land, it has a number of wooden houses, a school, a church, and a farm, with natural woodlands and a lake nearby. Winters can be quite cold and snowy, and summers can be hot and buggy. The rural nature of the village means that contact with city life is minimal. Volunteers live with a family in shared accommodation and are expected to take part fully in family and community life, helping with the children and in the kitchen and vegetable gardens.

Time Line: Volunteers are accepted throughout the year for a minimum of two months and a maximum of twelve months. Though the community prefers that volunteers stay for at least six months, the average volunteer commits to two to three months.

Cost: Program fees are prorated per month, beginning at £900 for two months and going up to £1,410 for six months. The program fee includes the volunteer's visa, room and board, and a transfer from Moscow. The volunteer's travel to Moscow from their country of origin is not included in the program fee.

Getting Started: Applications are accepted throughout the year. Prospective volunteers should first complete an Introductory Questionnaire, available on Ecologia's Web site. Applications include two references, a police background check, and a phone interview. Ecologia provides written materials before departure and support via e-mail during the volunteer experience.

Needed Skills and Specific Populations: While no specific skills are required to volunteer with Ecologia, volunteers will find it helpful to have some of the following skills: a working knowledge of Russian; English-teaching experience; experience working with children; construction; woodworking; cooking; and gardening. Volunteers must have a strong interest in children, a willingness to adapt to a new culture, and a desire to participate fully in the life of the community. Volunteers must be at least eighteen years old, and senior volunteers in good health are welcome. Volunteers with physical disabilities will find that the Kitezh village, since it is so rural, will probably not be suitable for them. Some families have volunteered successfully with Ecologia in the past, though others have found that their children have a hard time integrating with the other children because of the language barrier. Prospective volunteers should be aware that they may encounter behavioral difficulties with some children, and that self-reliance and self-motivation are the keys to a successful volunteer experience.

Ecovolunteer Program
Meijersweg 29, 7553 AX
Hengelo
The Netherlands
+(31) 74-2508250; Fax: +(31) 74-2506572
E-mail: info@ecovolunteer.org
Web site: www.ecovolunteer.org

Project Type: Natural Conservation (Land); Natural Conservation (Sea); Scientific Research

Year Founded: 1992 as a part of a larger organization; became an independent organization in 1998

Number of Volunteers Last Year: Approximately 500

Funding Sources: None; self-supported

The Work They Do: The Ecovolunteer Program offers a large number of diverse volunteer opportunities in wildlife conservation, animal rescue, and fieldwork. Sample projects include: researching elephants in Cameroon, surveying giant otters in Bolivia, caring for rescued animals at a sanctuary in Brazil, identifying sustainable products in the Colombian rainforest, assisting at a big cat rescue facility in Florida, taking care of gibbons in Thailand, tracking wolves in Russia, and collecting data on dolphins off the Italian coast. In all of these projects, volunteers participate as hands-on assistants. All projects are conducted by local nongovernmental organizations according to local standards. A high level of adaptability and flexibility is sometimes required of volunteers to cope with different organizations around the world.

Project Location: The Ecovolunteer Program runs approximately thirty projects per year in North America, South America, Asia, Africa, Oceania, and Europe. Accommodations are usually quite basic, such as a field station, a home, a cabin on a research vessel, or a tent; rooms are generally shared, as are kitchen and bathroom facilities.

Time Line: There are always projects available throughout the year, though not all projects are available at all times. While some specific projects run year-round, others are seasonal, depending on, for example, the migratory patterns of birds. Lengths of projects vary, but volunteers can set their own dates of arrival and departure. In general, the Ecovolunteer Program expects a minimum of a week-long commitment and a maximum commitment of six months.

Cost: Program fees range from approximately $300 for some one-week projects to $1,500 for some two-week projects, but they vary based on the project and the length of the volunteer experience. Included in the program fees are lodging and, usually, food; when food is not included, it is almost always available nearby and is quite inexpensive. Not included in the program fee are transportation costs, travel insurance, and any visa expenses. Volunteers are required to make a nonrefundable deposit of at least $100 when the booking is confirmed, with the balance due at least six weeks before departure.

Getting Started: Prospective volunteers should apply via the Web site listed. Projects usually include on-the-job training, and some also offer an introductory day or lectures.

Needed Skills and Specific Populations: Most projects require participants to be at least eighteen years old, though a few mandate that volunteers be at least twenty or twenty-one years old. Similarly, most projects do not have a maximum age, though there are a few exceptions to this; others may require specific skills, such as the ability to swim. Most of Ecovolunteer Program's projects are not suitable for volunteers with disabilities, but final decisions will be made on a case-by-case basis by the project manager, who will review the applicant's file.

El Porvenir

48 Clifford Terrace
San Francisco, CA 94117
(713) 568-9179; Fax: (413) 618-4048
E-mail: info@elporvenir.org
Web site: www.elporvenir.org

Project Type: Community Development; Construction; Rural Development

Mission Statement Excerpt: "El Porvenir partners with poor communities in Nicaragua to improve their quality of life through sustainable development of drinking water, sanitation, and reforestation projects, and health education."

Year Founded: 1990

Number of Volunteers Last Year: 112

Funding Sources: Faith-based and private sources

The Work They Do: El Porvenir works with villagers to build wells, latrines, communal wash facilities for bathing and washing clothes, fuel-saving stoves, and community tree nurseries. Water and sanitation projects may include building a communal washing facility near the village well, which will relieve women of the burden of carrying water long distances to wash clothes; rehabilitating a well to ensure that the community has access to safe drinking water; or building latrines to prevent the spread of disease and to protect the water source. Reforestation projects include clearing brush areas, planting seedlings, fencing areas, and building smoke-free, fuel-saving family cookstoves. Villagers who are assisted by this project live in adobe or brick homes with dirt floors, and they rarely have electricity. The conditions are poor, but the villagers are committed to improving their lives and they welcome the volunteers to their communities. Volunteers work alongside villagers mixing cement, laying bricks, cutting and tying wire, sifting sand, and filling bags for planting trees. The tasks range from easy to difficult, and the volunteers decide which tasks they will perform. All of El Porvenir's projects are initiated, built, and maintained by the villagers, and El Porvenir purchases its materials in Nicaragua, supporting locally owned businesses whenever possible.

Project Location: Projects are carried out in central Nicaragua in the small villages near the towns of El Sauce, Camoapa, San Lorenzo, Terrabona, and Ciudad Dario. Volunteers stay in modest hotels in nearby towns and travel daily via four-wheel-drive trucks to the work sites in small villages. Most meals are eaten in restaurants, though some are eaten in the host communities.

Time Line: Trips are offered throughout the year, usually in January, February, March, June, July, August, September, and November, and they are one to two weeks in length.

Cost: A two-week trip with El Porvenir costs $1,050, plus airfare. The program fee includes food, lodging, all in-country transportation, two bilingual guides, travel and health insurance, and activity fees. Volunteers are responsible for their own transportation to and from Nicaragua. Two hundred dollars of the program fee goes directly to the project being constructed.

Getting Started: Prospective volunteers should contact El Porvenir via e-mail or phone to request an information form. Orientation and a brief history of Nicaragua are provided to volunteers upon arrival.

Needed Skills and Specific Populations: A parent must accompany volunteers who are younger than eighteen. El Porvenir offers two Elderhostel trips per year for volunteers over fifty-five years old. Volunteers with disabilities are welcomed as long as they can climb in and out of a four-wheel drive truck, climb steps, and live comfortably in a tropical climate. Refrigeration is available for medications. Volunteers from outside the United States should check Nicaragua's visa regulations before applying.

Engineering Ministries International (EMI)

130 East Kiowa, Suite 200
Colorado Springs, CO 80903
(719) 633-2078; Fax: (719) 633-2970
E-mail: info@emiusa.org
Web site: www.emiworld.org

Project Type: Community Development; Construction; Professional Technical Assistance; Rural Development

Mission Statement Excerpt: "EMI's vision is to mobilize design professionals to minister to the less fortunate in developing nations—we proclaim the Gospel of Jesus as we help others change their world—through the development of hospitals, schools, orphanages, bridges, water supplies, electricity, and more."

Year Founded: 1982

Number of Volunteers Last Year: 200

Funding Sources: Individual donors and faith-based organizations

The Work They Do: EMI primarily works in two ways: designing relief projects that mitigate physical and spiritual poverty, such as hospitals, schools, orphanages, bridges, and water supplies; and by serving Christian missionaries by providing free design services for infrastructure that enables them to serve the poor and preach the Gospel with greater effectiveness and impact. EMI volunteers use their specific technical skills in pursuit of these goals.

Project Location: EMI has completed over seven hundred projects in over eighty economically developing countries around the world. Projects have been located in Africa, Asia, Central America, South America, Europe, the Middle East, and the South Pacific. EMI volunteers serve in both urban and rural placements, and usually work in conjunction with local missionary teams who provide guidance and support, including accommodations.

Time Line: EMI carries out projects throughout the year, usually for two weeks at a time, though occasionally there are longer trips, up to a year in length.

Cost: EMI's program fee is $600, which covers accommodations, in-country travel, and meals. Volunteers must pay for their own airfare. EMI estimates that most volunteers pay between $1,200 and $3,000 total for their volunteer vacation.

Getting Started: Prospective volunteers can read about planned trips on EMI's Web site, split into winter, spring, and fall opportunities. Applications are also available on the Web site, and project leaders interview all applicants in advance of the trip. Training is included as a part of the volunteer experience.

Needed Skills and Specific Populations: Volunteers must have a technical skill that matches the need of the planned trip; examples of these skills include, but are not limited to, architecture, civil engineering, structural engineering, surveying, and electrical engineering. Because of this, almost all of EMI's volunteers have at least a college degree. Senior volunteers are encouraged to participate in EMI's trips, and volunteers with disabilities may also be able to participate on a case-by-case basis. EMI is a Christian organization, but accepts both Christian and non-Christian volunteers.

Explorations in Travel (ET)

2458 River Road
Guilford, VT 05301
(802) 257-0152; Fax: (802) 257-2784
E-mail: explore@volunteertravel.com
Web site: www.volunteertravel.com

Project Type: Education; Natural Conservation (Land); Trail
Building/Maintenance

Mission Statement Excerpt: "To provide qualified volunteers for
grassroots organizations working to protect environments,
develop sustainable industries, and animal welfare and rehabilitation."

Year Founded: 1991

Number of Volunteers Last Year: 15

Funding Sources: None; self-funded

The Work They Do: ET assists independent organizations in
locating volunteers in the areas of education, animal
welfare, wildlife rehabilitation, and conservation. Volunteers
typically teach, help with conservation work, and care for
animals.

Project Location: ET operates programs in Costa Rica, Puerto
Rico, Ecuador, Belize, and Guatemala. Most work sites are
in rural, less developed locations. Some work may be physical; it can be hot and humid, and there will be insects.
Actual physical conditions vary from site to site. In some
cases volunteers live with local host families in a rural
setting; in other cases they share housing with other volunteers. ET arranges for housing.

Time Line: Projects go on throughout the year. Most sites prefer
that volunteers stay for a minimum of one month.

Cost: There is a $35 application fee and a $700 program fee.
Additionally, volunteers make a $100 donation to their host
organization. Volunteers are responsible for all travel,
lodging, and meal costs.

Getting Started: Prospective volunteers should e-mail ET for an
application; all volunteers are required to complete an inter-

view by phone. The volunteer's supervisor provides orientation on-site.

Needed Skills and Specific Populations: Volunteers must be at least eighteen years old. Senior citizens are welcomed. Some sites may be accessible to volunteers with disabilities. ET places volunteers from all over the world, but it does not assist with obtaining visas. ET requests volunteers that are "mature and self-motivated." Most of ET's sites are not appropriate for families.

Farm Sanctuary

P.O. Box 150
Watkins Glen, NY 14891
(607) 583-2225; Fax: (607) 583-2041
E-mail: intern@farmsanctuary.org
Web site: www.farmsanctuary.org

Project Type: Administrative; Agriculture; Political Action;
Social Justice
Mission Statement Excerpt: "Farm Sanctuary works to end
cruelty to farm animals and promotes compassionate living
through rescue, education, and advocacy."
Year Founded: 1986
Number of Volunteers Last Year: 100
Funding Sources: Individual donors and corporate grants
The Work They Do: Farm Sanctuary volunteer interns help take
care of and feed hundreds of rescued animals and run the
organization's two shelters. Their Volunteer Internship
Program provides a way for volunteers to get closely
involved in the work of a national animal advocacy organization. Interns live at the shelters and get daily hands-on
experience with animals. Interns also get the unique experience of living and working with other like-minded people.
The program is designed to be educational and offers many
educational opportunities on a variety of topics of the
interns' choosing. Interns visit a working stockyard to see
what it is like. They also have the option of working
directly with the animals at the shelters or working in other
departments (campaigns, development, communications,
education, or administration).
Project Location: Farm Sanctuary owns two farms: a 175-acre
shelter in upstate New York, near Ithaca, and a 300-acre
shelter in northern California, thirty miles west of Chico.
These farms house more than one thousand rescued cows,
pigs, chickens, turkeys, sheep, goats, rabbits, donkeys,
ducks, and geese. On-site housing is offered to all Farm

Gloria, one of many resident pigs at Farm Sanctuary, surrounded by a group of admiring fans (volunteers!). Many volunteers choose to work directly with the animals, doing everything from assisting the caregivers and caring for special needs animals, to feeding the animals and cleaning animal housing areas. Volunteers can also serve in many other ways, from publicity to visitor programs and giving tours. *Photo courtesy of Farm Sanctuary*

Sanctuary volunteers, and it includes shared bedrooms, bathrooms, and kitchen facilities.

Time Line: Farm Sanctuary internships are available year-round. Positions are filled on an ongoing basis as applications are received; summer months are the most popular for volunteers, so prospective summer volunteers should apply by the end of February. Volunteer positions begin on the first day of every month. Volunteers must commit to at least one month of service. All volunteers work a full-time, forty-hour-per-week schedule. The shelters are open seven days a week, so volunteer schedules generally include weekends and holidays.

Cost: There is no program fee to volunteer with Farm Sanctuary, and housing is provided at no charge, however there is a $150 deposit that is refundable upon completion of the internship. Volunteers must provide their own transportation to the work site and are responsible for buying and preparing their own food. Weekly trips to the grocery store are provided for volunteers without vehicles.

Getting Started: Prospective volunteers can complete an online application, available at Farm Sanctuary's Web site, or can call the phone number listed and request an internship application. Applicants are asked to submit two letters of recommendation on their behalf, and need to complete a phone interview. Volunteers receive an orientation on their first day, which covers expectations, an overview of the program, farm and house rules, and protocols. Further specific training is given to each volunteer in their individual department.

Needed Skills and Specific Populations: Volunteers must be at least eighteen years old. They must have a strong commitment to Farm Sanctuary's goals and a personal commitment to veganism. Interns live a vegan lifestyle for the duration of the internship, which includes diet (no meat, dairy products, eggs, honey, or other animal byproducts), personal care items (cruelty-free and no animal by-products), and clothing (no leather, fur, silk, wool, etc.). Volunteers with disabilities are welcome, but may not be able to work in all departments, depending on the disability.

Foundation for Sustainable Development (FSD)

517 Potrero Avenue, Suite B
San Francisco, CA 94110
(415) 283-4873
E-mail: info@fsdinternational.org
Web site: www.fsdinternational.org

Project Type: Agriculture; Community Development; Economic
  Development; Education; Human Rights; Women's Issues;
  Youth
Mission Statement Excerpt: "Our mission is to overcome the
  effects of poverty by empowering underserved communities
  and their citizens to be agents of their own sustainable
  change and growth."
Year Founded: 1995
Number of Volunteers Last Year: More than 100
Funding Sources: Private donors and grants
The Work They Do: FSD offers four main types of volunteer
  experiences: internships ranging from nine to fifty-two
  weeks, short-term volunteer placements that last from one
  to eight weeks, Service Learning Trips (SLTs) for students
  and professionals, and the ProCorps program for
  experienced professionals and retirees. The work done by
  volunteers depends on the program and place selected, but
  all projects offer cultural immersion, development training,
  project management experience, and exposure to relationships and professional opportunities, and all are collaborative efforts with the grassroots organizations they are there
  to support.
Project Location: Projects take place in Argentina, Bolivia,
  India, Kenya, Nicaragua, and Uganda. Both rural and urban
  placements are available. Living conditions can be pretty
  basic, but almost all sites have running water and electricity.
  Program participants usually stay with host families, and
  intern opportunities are available year-round.

Time Line: Volunteer and intern opportunities are available
year-round. FSD's Web site has complete, up-to-date information on program start dates.

Cost: Program fees vary by country, but they range from about
$1,000 to $3,000. The program fees cover all in-country
expenses including room, board, transportation, training
materials, language lessons (except in Latin America),
communications, a host organization grant or a service
project grant, a group leader, translation, logistical support,
health insurance and emergency evacuation coverage, orientation and debriefing sessions, and program support. It does
not include airfare to and from the country of service.

Getting Started: Prospective volunteers can download an application from FSD's Web site; applications are accepted on a
rolling basis. FSD requires that all volunteers complete an
extensive phone interview to determine which program best
fits the individual volunteer. FSD provides an information
packet prior to departure, as well as a one-week in-country
orientation and training.

Needed Skills and Specific Populations: Volunteers should have
a demonstrated interest in international development.
Spanish is required for volunteering with the Latin
American internship program. Volunteers must be at least
eighteen years old; senior citizens are welcomed. FSD is able
to accommodate some volunteers with disabilities, but not
families.

Friends of the Cumbres
Toltec Scenic Railroad

6005 Osuna Road NE
Albuquerque, NM 8710?
(505) 880-1311; Fax: (505) 85
E-mail: cinerail@aol.cou
Web site: www.cumbrestoltec.org

Project Type: Archaeology; Construction; Historic Preservation;
Museum; Natural Conservation (Land)

Mission Statement Excerpt: "The Friends is organized to serve a
public purpose—the historic preservation of the Cumbres
and Toltec Scenic Railroad."

Year Founded: 1988

Number of Volunteers Last Year: 497

Funding Sources: Some funding from private sources; membership dues

The Work They Do: The Friends is in charge of interpretation,
preservation, and restoration of this historic railroad,
including rolling stock and structures. This work includes
repairs, reconstruction, painting, car lettering, rail line
clearing, interior repairs to locomotive cabs, landscaping,
archaeological study of previously existing structures, and a
docent program. Most volunteers help with woodworking,
painting, electrical work, carpentry and construction, and
landscaping and gardening. Other volunteers help to document historic restoration work, serve as docents, or work on
archaeological studies.

Project Location: Volunteers work in northern New Mexico and
southern Colorado along the sixty-four-mile railroad line,
which is at high elevations that range from seventy-eight
hundred to ten thousand feet above sea level. Volunteers are
responsible for their own accommodations; a large
percentage stay in one of three local campgrounds, and the
remainder stay in bed-and-breakfasts or motels.

Time Line: Volunteers are accepted for two weeks in each of the
months of May, June, and August. Volunteers must commit

151

least one five-day work week, Monday to Friday, though many volunteers stay for two consecutive weeks. The exception to this is docents, who are utilized from Memorial Day through mid-October.

Cost: The program fee is $40 per week, plus a one-time insurance charge of $15 per year. The $40 fee covers a daily sack lunch and daily snacks and drinks. Volunteers must provide for their own transportation, lodging, breakfasts, and dinners.

Getting Started: Prospective volunteers should download registration materials from the Friends' Web site or request them from the main office. People must join the organization before participating as volunteers, but no interview is necessary. Volunteers select up to three preferred assignments from the list of scheduled work session projects; these choices are submitted along with the registration materials. Every effort is made to assign volunteers to a requested project, and volunteers are notified ahead of time of their assignment. On the Monday of each work week, a safety meeting is held and provides basic information for the entire week. After the safety meeting, volunteers meet with their team leaders and the rest of their volunteer groups for a project-specific orientation, then begin their work.

Needed Skills and Specific Populations: Volunteers should come into this experience with skills already in place; they should not expect technical training. Volunteers for the regular programs must be at least thirteen years old; though there is a junior volunteer program for youth aged ten to twelve, who may take on limited, supervised responsibilities. Senior volunteers are welcomed and may request "light duty" if there are health issues or limitations. However, volunteers should remember that the work is all at high elevation and in a remote area with limited medical facilities. Volunteers with disabilities may find access around the railroad yard difficult because of the railroad tracks. In addition, support cars for volunteers are actually boxcars, and volunteers are required to enter them via freestanding stairs. The Friends welcome any volunteers with disabilities who can work within those limitations. Families are welcome to volunteer together, as long as children are in the junior volunteer program, are supervised, and recognize that they may not be able to volunteer in all of the Friends' projects.

Friends of the Great Baikal Trail (FGBT)

300 Broadway, Suite 28
San Francisco, CA 94133
(510) 717-1805; Fax: (415) 788-7324
E-mail: baikalwatch@earthsland.org
Web site: greatbaikaltrail.org

Project Type: Community Development; Economic
Development; Historic Preservation; Natural Conservation
(Land); Natural Conservation (Sea); Trail
Building/Maintenance

Mission Statement Excerpt: "Our organization is designed to
promote sustainable economies in eastern Russia, first and
foremost by encouraging the development of ecotourism in
the region."

Year Founded: 1991

Number of Volunteers Last Year: 839

Funding Sources: Government and private sources

The Work They Do: FGBT helps to recruit and organize teams
of international volunteers to work on any of dozens of
trail-building projects that occur each summer in the parks
and nature reserves around Lake Baikal, the largest and
deepest lake in the world. International volunteers work
alongside local people to build the Great Baikal Trail as a
way to promote low-impact tourism to the region. In some
instances, volunteers help with design, interpretation (both
language and natural interpretation), and other, less manual
aspects of the FGBT's work. However, most of the work
involves digging, leveling, and the construction of campsites
and other wooden structures along the trail. Half of the
members of volunteer groups are Russians from local towns
and cities, and half are non-Russian citizens.

Project Location: Volunteers work at one of twenty-five work
sites along the shores of Lake Baikal in Russia. Most work
sites are within one or more of the national parks around
the lake. Several of the project areas run into the mountain

ranges that surround the lake. Most work sites are located in wilderness areas and are often not easy to access by roads or other public transport, although most are accessible by boat. Accommodation is almost always in tents, which are provided by FGBT. Food, which is also provided by FGBT, is prepared at campsites. Most trail-building sites are located within walking distance of the lake, where volunteers can swim and hang out on the shore. The national parks approve each work site, along with the trails themselves, to make sure that environmental impact is minimal.

Time Line: Projects run from June to September, and each lasts two weeks. Volunteers can work on two consecutive projects, and volunteers with extensive trail-building experience may sign up for more than that.

Cost: Volunteers pay a program fee of $380 for two weeks, which covers all of the on-site program costs, including food and lodging in tents, language interpretation, and training. Volunteers are responsible for their travel to Irkutsk via Moscow (which involves traveling by either air or train), as well as to the project site. Volunteers may elect to pay an additional $100 for help in getting to the project site from Irkutsk. Volunteers are also responsible for covering all Russian travel visa fees.

Getting Started: Prospective volunteers should send an e-mail to the address listed, or they may visit the GBT Web site to find an application and a list of project dates and locations. Interviews are not required before volunteering. Orientation and training take place on the first full day of each project, and include cultural pointers. Training in the proper and safe use of tools is also given on the first day, with "reminder training" given daily. Prospective volunteers should be aware that passport holders from some nations, particularly African ones, may have problems obtaining visas to enter Russia.

Needed Skills and Specific Populations: No trail-building or Russian language skills are required, though the FGBT encourages people who possess these skills to apply. Volunteers must be in good health and have both a sense of adventure and a willingness to work hard. Volunteers must be at least eighteen years old (though exceptions to this rule can be made for volunteers traveling as part of a school group led by teachers or parents). Senior volunteers who are physically capable of the hard work and wilderness living are also heartily welcomed. Volunteers with disabilities may be able to volunteer with FGBT in the future, once a fully accessible portion of the Great Baikal Trail is completed.

Frontier

50–52 Rivington Street
London, EC2A 3QP
United Kingdom
+44 (0) 20 7613 2422; Fax: +44 (0) 20 7613 2992
E-mail: info@frontier.ac.uk
Web site: www.frontier.ac.uk

Project Type: Education; Natural Conservation (Land); Natural
Conservation (Sea); Scientific Research
Mission Statement Excerpt: "Frontier's mission is to conserve
the world's most endangered wildlife and threatened habitats and to build sustainable livelihoods for marginalized
communities in the world's poorest countries. To create
solutions that are apolitical, forward-thinking, community-
driven, and innovative and which take into consideration
the long-term needs of impoverished communities."
Year Founded: 1989
Number of Volunteers Last Year: 270
Funding Sources: Government and private donors
The Work They Do: Frontier works in conjunction with coun-
terpart organizations and government departments to carry
out biodiversity, habitat, and socioeconomic surveys in areas
of great value to conservation, but where there are communities which suffer through a range of problems such as
environmental conflict, acute poverty, and deprivation.
Volunteers are responsible for the collection and processing
of field data, reconnaissance trips to assess possible new
survey sites, participating in remote satellite camps, equipment maintenance, and ensuring a well-run base-camp.
Frontier also has a smaller number of teaching opportunities
abroad. In general, Frontier's programs fall into the general
categories of convservation, education, diving, animal
welfare, ethical adventures (which combine volunteering
and traveling), and language (combining language acquisition with volunteering).

Project Location: Frontier currently operates almost one hundred projects in more than twenty-nine countries, on all seven continents. Lodging is provided in communal tents or huts; food is cooked by the group and mostly consists of the local staple, such as rice or noodles, supplemented with fresh fruit, vegetables, bread, meat, fish, herbs, and spices.

Time Line: Frontier's projects run throughout the year. Volunteers can join projects for four, eight, ten, or twenty weeks.

Cost: Program fees begin at £695 for four weeks; £1,195 for eight weeks; £1,295 for ten weeks; and £2,495 for twenty weeks. The program fees include an orientation session in the United Kingdom, accommodation, transfers, food, group expedition equipment, and—for U.K. residents only—insurance and visa. Volunteers are responsible for their flights and personal equipment.

Getting Started: Prospective volunteers can apply online; all volunteers must complete a short telephone interview. Within a week of their interviews, applicants will be notified in writing whether their application has been successful. An optional weekend orientation program takes place in the United Kingdom six weeks before departure. Health and safety, scientific, and (as needed) scuba training are provided upon arrival.

Needed Skills and Specific Populations: Frontier volunteers do not need a science or teaching background; above all, Frontier values resilience, resourcefulness, flexibility, and imagination. Volunteers also need to be in good physical shape, be team players, speak fluent English, and be able to use their initiative. Volunteers must be at least seventeen years old, and most volunteers are in the seventeen to thirty range; senior volunteers are not encouraged to volunteer with Frontier. Given the physical demands of Frontier's remote projects and locations, many volunteers with disabilities may not be able to work with this organization.

Galapagos ICE: Immerse Connect Evolve

Rodriguez, Lara, y Genovesa
Puerto Ayora, Galapagos
Ecuador
+593 52526-088
E-mail: epozo@galapagosice.org
Web site: www.galapagosice.org

Project Type: Community Development; Education; Medical/Health; Natural Conservation (Land); Rural Development; Youth

Mission Statement Excerpt: "By fostering community-building interactions between residents of the Galapagos, citizens of Ecuador, and volunteers beyond Ecuador's borders, and by securing donations of necessary equipment, time, and money at home and abroad, Galapagos ICE seeks to empower local residents to improve their educational, medical, and economic opportunities."

Year Founded: 2005

Number of Volunteers Last Year: 74

Funding Sources: Individual donors and faith-based organizations

The Work They Do: Galapagos ICE volunteers have taken on a broad range of projects, including photo documentaries of Galapagenian children; kinesiology workshops with senior citizens; art workshops with schoolchildren; ESL teaching; HIV/AIDS prevention workshops, and health screenings for adults. Volunteers with specialized skills may find opportunities to utilize these skills in teaching or helping others, including in the areas of health, education, ESL, science teaching, or marketing.

Project Location: Galapagos ICE primarily works on Santa Cruz Island, though they have also had volunteers on Isabela Island. Most volunteers stay with host families, though some choose to stay in apartments or hotels.

Time Line: Volunteers are accepted year-round for one week to six months.

Cost: Volunteers pay a $50 application fee, as well as all of their own living costs. Galapagos ICE recommends that volunteers budget $150 to $200 per month for housing and $10 per day for food; volunteers staying with host families pay $350 per month, which includes all meals. Flights to the Galapagos are relatively expensive, and there are several park entrance fees and airport arrival/departure taxes that must be paid.

Getting Started: Prospective volunteers should contact Galapagos ICE via e-mail. Completed applications require a resume, two references, and the $50 application fee. All volunteers receive a short orientation upon arrival, and further training as needed.

Needed Skills and Specific Populations: The minimum age for volunteers is eighteen, unless a group of high school students volunteer together; there is no maximum age for volunteers. Galapagos ICE welcomes volunteers with disabilities and families, though both of these populations should organize their trip well ahead of their arrival.

Gibbon Conservation Center (GCC)

P.O. Box 800249
Santa Clarita, CA 91380
(661) 296-2737; Fax: (661) 296-1237
E-mail: gibboncenter@earthlink.net
Web site: www.gibboncenter.org

Project Type: Education; Natural Conservation (Land); Scientific Research

Mission Statement Excerpt: "The mission of the Gibbon Conservation Center is to prevent the extinction of this small Southeast Asian ape and to advance its study, propagation, and conservation by establishing secure captive gene pools. . . . We educate the public, assist zoos and rescue centers in better captive management, encourage noninvasive behavioral studies, and support ongoing field conservation projects."

Year Founded: 1976

Number of Volunteers Last Year: Approximately 180, including 17 live-in volunteers

Funding Sources: Private donors and grants from foundations

The Work They Do: GCC is the only facility in the world devoted exclusively to gibbons, an increasingly rare ape. GCC houses nearly forty gibbons, among them six of the thirteen living species, including the only Javan gibbons in captivity in the United States. GCC specializes in nonintrusive behavioral studies on gibbons that are conducted by students, scientists, and volunteers working at the center, and it also has the largest gibbon library in the world. Volunteers have three work options. Primate keepers work directly with the care of gibbons, including feeding, cleaning, and changing water. This role may also include administering medication, doing behavioral observations, and assisting with administrative duties. Most resident volunteers are primate keepers, and they work from approximately 7 A.M. to 5 P.M. seven days per week. Center assistants may do maintenance work, take behavioral observations, clean, and help with administrative tasks; they also keep a minimum distance of six feet from all enclosures. Clerical assistants help with administrative tasks and may do behavioral observations.

Project Location: All volunteers work at the GCC site, which is located about one hour north of Los Angeles. GCC is on five acres in a rural canyon area on the outskirts of a medium-sized city and is in a desert area. Weather conditions can be extreme, reaching from a high of 105 degrees in summer months to a low of 35 degrees at night in the winter. GCC provides free lodging to resident volunteers in an older, basic travel trailer with free access to bathroom, kitchen, and laundry facilities. Volunteers are responsible for providing their own food and personal items.

Time Line: Volunteers are welcome seven days a week year-round. Resident volunteers must commit to a minimum of one month; there is no stated maximum stay. Many volunteers stay for several months, with the average being two months. Resident volunteers who have completed at least one month in the past may volunteer again for less than one month.

Cost: There is no program fee to volunteer at GCC, but in order to ensure that GCC remains fully staffed at all times individuals wanting to secure a volunteer position will be required to put down a $200 deposit at least three months prior to their expected start date at the GCC. The deposit is fully refundable on the last day they are scheduled to volunteer at the center, as long as they serve the full number of scheduled days in good standing. If the volunteer leaves the position early, for whatever reason, their deposit will not be refunded. Volunteers are responsible for their own transportation to and from the work site, as well as for personal expenses incurred during the volunteer experience. GCC also requires a number of medical exams and inoculations before volunteers may enter the facility. Volunteers must have valid health insurance coverage.

Getting Started: Prospective volunteers may download an application from the GCC Web site or contact the office to receive an application. Applications must include a resume, a cover letter, and two letters of recommendation; GCC does not require interviews of prospective volunteers. A one-week training session is required, and it covers mandated procedures and GCC's own goals of cleanliness, welfare, breeding, and safety. The training is conducted by an experienced primate keeper.

Needed Skills and Specific Populations: GCC wants volunteers who are self-motivated and have a love for animals. No smoking is allowed at the center. All volunteers must be at least eighteen years old, and resident volunteers must be at least twenty years old. There is no maximum age for volunteers, as long as they are capable of undertaking strenuous work. Volunteers who serve as primate keepers must be physically fit. Volunteers with disabilities will be considered on an individual basis. Families may be able to volunteer with the GCC under specific circumstances, but children must be supervised at all times.

Global Citizens Network (GCN)

130 North Howell Street
St. Paul, MN 55104
(651) 644-0960 or (800) 644-9292; Fax: (651) 646-6176
E-mail: info@globalcitizens.org
Web site: www.globalcitizens.org

Project Type: Community Development; Education; Rural
Development; Social Justice

Mission Statement Excerpt: "Global Citizens Network sends
short-term teams of volunteers to communities in other
cultures, where participants immerse themselves in the
culture and daily life of the community. Each volunteer team
is partnered with a local grassroots organization active in
meeting local needs."

Year Founded: 1992

Number of Volunteers Last Year: More than 150

Funding Sources: Individual private donors

The Work They Do: GCN carries out community development
and cultural immersion programs. Participants stay with
local families or at other facilities within the community
while working on site-directed development projects. Examples of volunteer projects include building health clinics,
renovating a youth center, and teaching in a primary school.

Project Location: Projects take place in the United States
(Arizona, Kentucky, and Washington) as well as internationally in Canada, Kenya, Tanzania, Nepal, Thailand, Mexico,
Guatemala, Ecuador, Peru, and Brazil. GCN arranges
lodging and other accommodations while in the project
location.

Time Line: Projects take place throughout the year and last
from one to three weeks. Participants may arrange for back-
to-back volunteer stints for a total of six weeks.

Cost: Costs vary according to the length and location of the
project, but they range from $975 for sites in the United
States to $2,425 for international programs. Program fees
include food and lodging, a donation to the project, training

materials, emergency medical and evacuation insurance (for non-U.S. sites), and a T-shirt. A portion of the fees go to cover GCN program costs. Volunteers are responsible for their own transportation costs. Discounts are available for returning volunteers, children, groups, and those who register early.

Getting Started: Prospective volunteers can download an application from GCN's Web site or call or e-mail to request an application. Interviews are encouraged but not required. Predeparture orientation is provided to volunteers by the team leader via e-mail or telephone. During the first evening of the volunteer experience, all teams hold an orientation meeting; daily team meetings are held for the duration of the project.

Needed Skills and Specific Populations: Trip participants must have a willingness to experience and accept a new culture. No specific physical or occupational skills are required. Volunteers must be at least eight years old, and participants under the age of eighteen must be accompanied by an adult. Senior citizens are "absolutely!" encouraged to volunteer with GCN. Prospective volunteers with disabilities should confer with GCN before applying to ensure that accommodations will be available. Because of their unusually low minimum age requirement, GCN is particularly family friendly.

Global Crossroad

415 East Airport Freeway, Suite 365
Irving, TX 75062
(800) 413-2008; Fax: (972) 636-1368
E-mail: info@globalcrossroad.com
Web site: www.globalcrossroad.com

Project Type: Construction; Education; Medical/Health; Natural
Conservation (Land); Natural Conservation (Sea); Orphans;
Women's Issues

Mission Statement Excerpt: "Global Crossroad's focus on grassroots projects, cultural immersion, and travel learning
opportunities reflects the unique, alternative approach that
we have adopted to garner memorable experiences for our
volunteers."

Year Founded: 2002

Number of Volunteers Last Year: More than 1,400

Funding Sources: None; Global Crossroad is self-funded.

The Work They Do: Global Crossroad offers volunteer placements in a variety of projects. In each host country, Global
Crossroad has developed a project working with disadvantaged children and teaching English; additional projects vary
depending on the country. Conservation projects range from
maintaining trails in national parks to supporting reforestation, from sea turtle conservation on the Pacific Coast to
bird conservation and various other wildlife conservation
projects in Africa. Community development projects include
working with local women's groups on microcredit development in India, assisting the elderly in a nursing home in
Costa Rica, working on a community organic fertilizer
farm, and even assisting with a variety of projects in a single
community pertaining to self-sustainability. Volunteers may
help care for children in an orphanage, teaching them
English, leading them in games and activities, helping to
cook and distribute food at mealtime, and mentoring the
children. Volunteers in health care projects assist a local
doctor or nurse in a health clinic or hospital to the extent

that their skills and experiences allow. Conservation projects offer the widest variety of activities for volunteers, from the physical labor of maintaining trails through national parks to tracking native birds through the Kereita Forest in Kenya as part of a research project. There are also a number of wildlife projects throughout Africa—even lion conservation/breeding/reintroduction in some countries.

Project Location: Global Crossroad currently operates in over thirty-four countries, including: Argentina, Australia, Bolivia, Brazil, Cambodia, Chile, China, Costa Rica, Ecuador, El Salvador, Ghana, Greece, Guatemala, Honduras, India, Kenya, Lesotho, Mexico, Namibia, Nepal, Nicaragua, Peru, the Philippines, South Africa, Spain, Sri Lanka, Tanzania, Thailand, Tibet, Togo, Vietnam, and Zimbabwe. Because of the enormous variety of projects and host countries, the work settings vary tremendously. Projects involving children are usually indoor projects and are usually set in an orphanage, children's home, or school. Conservation projects are usually outdoors, and they often involve considerable physical labor. Depending on the exact placement, lodging may be with a host family, at a hostel, or at a lodge. Most lodging is with host families, especially in Africa and Latin America. Food is included as part of the placements and is usually provided by the host family; volunteers staying at hostels or hotels may eat there or at local restaurants.

Time Line: Projects begin on the first and third Mondays of each month. The minimum volunteer stint is two weeks, and the maximum is usually twelve weeks (this can some-times be extended to twenty-four weeks, depending on the country's visa regulations). The average volunteer works for Global Crossroad for about six weeks.

Cost: Global Crossroad's program fees run from $800 to about $2,500, averaging about $1,500. Most program fees include all housing, meals, comprehensive travel insurance, and airport transfers. The program fee does not include airfare to the host country, visa and airport fees, or immunizations.

Getting Started: Prospective volunteers can either apply online through Global Crossroad's Web site, or by completing and

167

A volunteer standing with her class in the Christian Nursery Prep & Junior Secondary School, located in the town of Teshi, Ghana. She was particularly touched by the children's obvious need for and appreciation of the one-on-one attention she was able to lavish on them during her two-week stay. *Photo courtesy of Suzanne Gerber*

submitting an application form (which can be downloaded from the Web site or requested from the head office) and submitting it via post. Prior to arrival in their chosen countries, volunteers receive a predeparture booklet and placement details. On the first day of their projects, volunteers receive a one-day orientation session that covers safety, health, culture and customs, general information on the country, and an introduction to the project, host family, and living conditions. A one-week language and cultural orientation course is offered as an optional beginning for the volunteer trip.

Needed Skills and Specific Populations: Health care placements require that the volunteer have a health care background, such as being a medical student, nurse, therapist, or having extensive volunteer experience in a hospital. Teaching positions in China and Thailand require that the applicant be a native English speaker; positions in Thailand also require a Bachelor's degree. Volunteers aged fifteen and under must be accompanied by a parent or close adult relative, and Global Crossroad has hosted a number of families; volunteers aged sixteen and seventeen may volunteer unaccompanied, but must have a permission letter from their parents. Senior volunteers in good health are welcome to volunteer. Volunteers with disabilities should contact Global Crossroad's office to discuss their specific needs.

Global Deaf Connection (GDC)

2901 38th Avenue South
Minneapolis, MN 55406
(612) 724-8565; Fax: (612) 729-3839
E-mail: travel@deafconnection.org
Web site: www.deafconnection.org

Project Type: Education; Human Rights; Social Justice; Youth

Mission Statement Excerpt: "Our mission is to develop self-sustaining cycles of Deaf education and leadership skills through advocacy, multicultural exchange, college scholarships, and mentor support. These cycles will empower Deaf people in developing countries to achieve greater access to universal human rights which will increase their social and economic self sufficiency."

Year Founded: 1997

Number of Volunteers Last Year: 11

Funding Sources: Government sources, foundations, individual donors, and faith-based organizations

The Work They Do: GDC helps teach Deaf adults in a Jamaican college-preparatory program. Thirty Deaf adults have been participating in this intensive, two-year tutoring program to prepare to take the college entrance exams. Those who pass the exams will enroll in a four-year teacher training college in Jamaica. GDC will provide scholarships and Jamaican Sign Language interpreters. The goal is to have at least one Deaf teacher in each of Jamaica's thirteen Deaf schools so that Deaf children in Jamaica will have teachers and role models who can sign in their native language. As a result, nearly two thousand Deaf students taught by Deaf teachers will result in improved academic performance. Volunteers usually work directly with the Deaf students and assist teachers in classroom instruction. Volunteers may also work with teachers of the Deaf in schools.

Project Location: Volunteers work in Jamaica. Accommodations are generally arranged for volunteers, and may include dorm-style housing with communal eating areas, or perhaps more rugged conditions.

Time Line: GDC generally operates in set dates during the summer months, especially in July and August. Volunteers commit to a minimum of one week and a maximum of two months; the average stay is about four weeks.

Cost: GDC's program fee is between $2,000 and $4,000. This fee covers airport transfers as well as room and board, though it does not cover the cost of international airfare.

Getting Started: Volunteers apply through GDC's sister organization, World Endeavors, with application deadlines generally falling a few weeks before travel. Volunteers must complete an interview in person, or through videophone or Web cam, before being accepted into the program; phone interviews are not conducted and the applicant is responsible for arranging their own technology for the interview. An orientation is given to volunteers when they arrive in Jamaica, including Jamaican culture, proper attire, cultural norms, safety, and transportation.

Needed Skills and Specific Populations: Deaf, hard of hearing, and hearing people are all welcome to volunteer with GDC, though they must all be fluent signers of a world sign language, and willing to learn a new sign language at the volunteer site. Volunteers must be at least eighteen years old, and there is no maximum age limit. Volunteers with disabilities, especially those who are Deaf, are encouraged to volunteer with GDC. Families are welcome, and those with children under age eighteen can request a waiver to the age limit, which will be determined on a case-by-case basis.

Global Eco-Spiritual Tours (GEST)

250 South Ocean Boulevard, Suite 266
Delray Beach, FL 33483
(561) 266-0096; Fax: (561) 266-0092
E-mail: global@paradista.net
Web site: www.globalecospiritualtours.org

Project Type: Agriculture; Community Development; Natural
Conservation (Land); Social Justice

Mission Statement Excerpt: "Our primary goals are to make
contributions to the educational and health care needs of
impoverished children through our member donations; to
improve the environment in our tour region with simple
sustainable development projects through our member
work; and to introduce and educate our members to expand
their perspective of other cultures and religions in our tour
region."

Year Founded: 2001

Number of Volunteers Last Year: 8

Funding Sources: Self-funded through program fees

The Work They Do: GEST offers trips that combine ecotourism
and spiritual awareness. As a part of the ecotourism aspect
of the trip, volunteers undertake ecological volunteer projects such as planting sapling trees, installing solar panels on
remote homes, cleaning up littered campsites along mountain trails, participating in summer harvest festivals at water
mills, locating and identifying endangered species for scientists, bottling pure mountain spring water for local charities,
and marking glacial retreats during the summer melt. Volunteers also participate in local cultural life by visiting and
exploring monasteries, attending meditation and prayer
sessions, constructing sand mandalas, and visiting with local
families.

Project Location: GEST operates its tours in the Himalayan
Mountains of northern India, an ancient Buddhist setting
for people who wish to investigate questions of ecology and

spirituality. Volunteers stay in hotels, guest houses, and tents during their tours.

Time Line: GEST's tours usually run in early August. They offer a twelve-day, set itinerary that the group follows together.

Cost: The program fee of $2,500 includes accommodations and all meals. Twenty percent of the program fee is donated to schools and health clinics in the tour area; 60 percent goes toward the cost of running the program; and the remaining 20 percent is used for administrative costs. The program fee does not include international airfare, but it does include in-country transportation costs.

Getting Started: Prospective volunteers can register online via GEST's Web site or by calling the office listed. A $750 deposit, which may be partially refundable, is required at the time of registration, and no interview is required. A full application, physician-signed health statement, and the balance of the program fee are due at least thirty days before departure. GEST limits its tours to ten volunteers per group, and volunteers are selected, for the most part, on a first-come, first-served basis. Generally, GEST plans to send just one group per year, but it can plan a second group if there is sufficient demand.

Needed Skills and Specific Populations: Given the project's location in the Himalayan Mountains, volunteers should expect to work at high elevations. Volunteers must be in good physical condition and be capable of walking or hiking one to five miles per day; volunteers must provide a signed medical statement from a doctor indicating that they are fit for the program. "Responsible teenagers" and older people may volunteer, with no maximum age limit. Volunteers with non-ambulatory disabilities may volunteer. Though GEST mostly attracts independent volunteers, families are also welcome.

Global Humanitarian Expeditions (GHE)

602 South Ogden Street
Denver, CO 80209
(303) 858-8857; Fax: (303) 649-9017
E-mail: kim@humanitariantours.com
Web site: www.humanitariantours.com

Project Type: Community Development; Economic
Development; Education; Medical/Health; Orphans
Mission Statement Excerpt: "The mission of Global
Humanitarian Expeditions is to recruit and connect volun-
teers to meaningful experiences with charitable
organizations in the United States and around the world."
Year Founded: 2002
Number of Volunteers Last Year: 170
Funding Sources: Individual donors
The Work They Do: GHE provides education, community
development, and health care services to children in need.
Projects include setting up and running mobile dental clinics
that provide dental care and education to children; building
schools; working with local communities to develop income-
generating programs that help the communities maintain
autonomy and become self sufficient; and working with
teachers to develop teaching curriculum. Volunteers assist in
these projects through providing dental care as a dentist or
hygienist; managing patient flow in and out of clinics;
teaching oral hygiene instruction; keeping records; and
training teachers in reading, writing, and math education
skills; or participating as part of the community
development team by working with local communities to
develop income generating programs.
Project Location: GHE works in Nepal, India, Vietnam,
Guatemala, and Nicaragua. The work sites vary greatly
from project to project, but most take place in rural village
locations that are within driving distance of larger cities.
Dental clinics are set up in school classrooms, as are education and community development projects. GHE's school-

building projects are more physically demanding than other projects. All lunches are brought in from nearby restaurants that are safe for volunteers to eat. GHE also provides bottled water for volunteers at the project site and in their hotels at night. Accommodations vary depending on location and type of project, but, in general, volunteers stay in two or three star hotels. In some cases, especially in Nepal and Nicaragua, volunteers may camp during part or all of their volunteer experience, in which case GHE provides tents, food, showers, bathrooms, and other necessities for volunteers.

Time Line: GHE operates ten to twelve volunteer projects each year between January and May, and between July and November. Projects run for a minimum of seven days and a maximum of one month.

Cost: GHE's program fee for one week of volunteering is $890, which includes most meals, accommodations, and all in-country transportation; volunteers are responsible for their own airfare to the country of service. However, GHE also offers volunteers the opportunity to follow their week of volunteering with a week of sightseeing, in which case the program fee is approximately $3,600, but this fee includes international airfare from Los Angeles or San Francisco. The exception to this is Guatemala, which is just $2,080 for the volunteering-plus-sightseeing option.

Getting Started: Prospective volunteers complete an application packet, available upon request from GHE. The application packet includes information on the volunteer's experiences, skills, and expectations. Volunteers should apply at least six to eight months before their desired departure date. Interviews are not required, but GHE does talk with prospective volunteers by phone before departure. Training and orientation is completed in-country, and volunteers receive a predeparture packet of information.

Needed Skills and Specific Populations: Medical volunteers must have appropriate licensure, but nonmedical volunteers are not required to have any specialized credentials, just flexibility and a willingness to serve the host community. The minimum age is twelve years old, but only one or two children will be accepted on each project; there is no maximum age for volunteers. GHE welcomes volunteers with disabilities, and encourages these volunteers to talk with a staff member to determine which placement might be most appropriate to accommodate their specific needs. Families are welcome to volunteer with GHE, but all family members are expected to volunteer and assist with the project.

Global Routes

1 Short Street
Northampton, MA 01060
(413) 585-8895; Fax: (413) 585-8810
E-mail: mail@globalroutes.org
Web site: www.globalroutes.org

Project Type: Community Development; Construction; Education; Natural Conservation (Land); Orphans; Rural Development; Youth

Mission Statement Excerpt: "Global Routes . . . [sends] students all over the world to participate in community service projects."

Year Founded: 1985

Number of Volunteers Last Year: 300

Funding Sources: None; Global Routes is self-funded.

The Work They Do: Global Routes volunteers participate in projects focused on construction, working with children, and environmental conservation. Working in groups, volunteers build community centers, schoolhouses, playgrounds, and health clinics in rural communities. Volunteers can also teach English and work with youth to create summer camps, soccer camps, and other youth-focused activities.

Project Location: Projects take place in Argentina, Belize, China, Costa Rica, the Dominican Republic, Ecuador, Ghana, India, Kenya, Mexico, Nepal, Peru, Tanzania, Thailand, and Vietnam. Accommodations are with host families or in group living quarters in rural villages, and food is provided at these.

Time Line: High school programs run three to five weeks in the summer; college and gap-year programs run seven weeks in the summer and twelve weeks in the fall, winter, and spring.

Cost: Program fees range from $4,000 to $6,500. All fees include accommodation, food, and all in-country costs other than personal expenses. Volunteers must provide their own airfare.

Getting Started: Applications are available on Global Routes'
  Web site, and a phone interview is required. The in-country
  orientation lasts from four to ten days.

Needed Skills and Specific Populations: Volunteers must be at
  least fourteen years old to participate in high school
  programs, and seventeen years old for college programs; all
  programs are designed for high school and college students.
  Volunteers with disabilities cannot be accommodated,
  though Global Routes has organized some individualized
  family trips in Africa, Asia, and Latin America.

Global Service Corps (GSC)

300 Broadway, Suite 28
San Francisco, CA 94133
(415) 788-3666 x128; Fax: (415) 788-7324
E-mail: gsc@globalservicecorps.org
Web site: www.globalservicecorps.org

Project Type: Agriculture; Community Development; Education;
   Medical/Health; Orphans; Professional/Technical Assistance;
   Rural Development; Youth
Mission Statement Excerpt: "Global Service Corps's mission is
   to design and implement volunteer vacation and service-
   learning community development programs that benefit the
   volunteers and positively impact the communities they
   serve."
Year Founded: 1992
Number of Volunteers Last Year: 155
Funding Sources: No outside funding; GSC is self-supporting.
The Work They Do: GSC is a nonprofit international volunteer
   organization that provides volunteer opportunities for people
   to live and work in Thailand or Tanzania. In Thailand, volunteers work on HIV/AIDS education and prevention, public
   health, English education, and cultural immersion projects.
   Specifically, volunteers teach HIV/AIDS education and
   prevention in Thai secondary schools; teach English in
   primary or secondary schools, monasteries, or orphanages; or
   observe doctors, nurses, and other health professionals in
   hospitals. Programs available in Tanzania involve public
   health, sustainable agriculture and hunger relief, and
   HIV/AIDS prevention. GSC volunteers assist with agricultural
   demonstration plots, help teach sustainable agriculture
   methods of farming, and provide HIV/AIDS awareness talks
   and seminars. GSC also runs an HIV/AIDS education and
   prevention summer day camp in Tanzania as well.
Project Location: GSC's projects in Thailand are located in the
   Singburi Province; in Tanzania, projects are located in
   Arusha. Volunteers are immersed in the cultures in which

they work. Volunteers stay with local host families in homes that are "comfortable by Western standards." All meals and project-related transportation are provided by host families, and host families often include their volunteer guests in outings and activities and teach them about culture, lifestyles, and family customs. Each volunteer has his or her own furnished room, and GSC can arrange for friends or couples to stay together.

Time Line: Projects are carried out year-round with monthly start dates in each country. Applications are accepted on a rolling basis. Participants must volunteer for at least two weeks, with a maximum of six months; the average volunteer stays for one month.

Cost: Program fees begin at $2,705. The program fees include airport pickup and project transportation, hotel, hostel, or homestay accommodation, all meals, a weekend excursion, project administration, and support. International airfare is not included in the program fee.

Getting Started: Prospective volunteers can download a copy of the application form from the GSC Web site. The completed application form should be sent in with a resume, one-page personal statement, and a $300 refundable deposit. Upon signing up for a project, volunteers receive an orientation manual with information on the country and the program, a reading list, a packing list, and other health and travel tips. Volunteers also receive an on-site orientation, which is conducted by the in-country coordinators.

Global Volunteer Network (GVN)

P.O. Box 30-968
Lower Hutt, 6001
New Zealand
+(800) 963-1198
E-mail: info@volunteer.org.nz
Web site: www.volunteer.org.nz

Project Type: Agriculture; Community Development; Construction; Education; Medical/Health; Natural Conservation (Land); Orphans; Trail Building/Maintenance

Mission Statement Excerpt: "Our vision is to connect people with communities in need. We do this by supporting the work of local community organizations through the placement of international volunteers."

Year Founded: 2001

Number of Volunteers Last Year: 2000

Funding Sources: No outside sources

The Work They Do: GVN offers volunteer opportunities in areas of teaching, environmental work, wildlife care, orphanages, disabled children, medicine, HIV/AIDS education, and economic sustainability. Working with partner organizations, volunteers may teach in a school in Ghana, help in an orphanage with disabled children in Romania, work with mistreated wildlife in Thailand, or participate in reforestation projects on the Galapagos Islands.

Project Location: GVN runs projects in Cambodia, China, Costa Rica, Ecuador, El Salvador, Ghana, Honduras, India, Kenya, Nepal, New Zealand, the Philippines, Romania, Russia, South Africa, Tanzania, Thailand, Uganda, the United States, and Vietnam. Volunteers generally live and work in the same conditions as members of the host community.

Time Line: Projects are available throughout the year and range from two weeks to six months in length. The average volunteer project is about six weeks long.

Cost: All volunteers pay an application fee of $350, which

180

allows them to participate in as many projects as the volunteer wishes for five years. Program fees vary by project, but they average about $900 for six weeks. Each program fee covers accommodation, meals, and most in-country costs; volunteers are responsible for airfare, insurance, and visas.

Getting Started: Volunteer application forms are available on GVN's Web site. Applications are accepted on a rolling basis. Partner organizations provide training and orientation programs; the length and content of this training and orientation varies from program to program. Applicants are not required to complete an interview as a part of the application process.

Needed Skills and Specific Populations: With the exception of medical projects, most programs do not require specialized skills. Families, except those with very young children, are welcome on a number of GVN's programs. Most projects require volunteers to be at least eighteen years old; the minimum age for the Russia and Romania project is twenty-one. Senior volunteers are welcomed, but are advised that some project sites are more physically strenuous than others. Prospective volunteers with disabilities will be considered on a case-by-case basis.

Paper Into Pearls

By Erina Khanakwa

Global Volunteer Network

In January of 2007, I traveled to Uganda where Global Volunteer Network arranged for me to volunteer with an amazing project called Paper into Pearls, which is spearheaded by the founder of GrassrootsUganda.com, Malcolm Trevena. I joined Malcolm and his craft teacher, Rose Ochwo, and we traveled together to Buvunya, a small village far off the main road. The reason for visiting Buvunya was to teach a group of interested women how to make beads from sheets of old calendar paper.

In the late morning, ladies started trickling into our host's house. The women were shy and quiet, whispering between themselves and repositioning the babies tied to their backs in colorful Chentenges (sarong-like wraparounds). When the project is explained to the women, suddenly they open up, energized and hopeful by the prospect of earning an income. Zaina Nalubanga is a petite twenty-two-year-old mother of three beautiful girls. Since finishing primary school, she has been a housewife, mother, nurse, and farmer. Her husband works as a bodaboda rider (Moped taxi driver) and earns around US$1.50 a day for his work. This low wage can barely cover all of the family's basic needs, much less expensive medical costs such as malaria prophylaxis and treatment for Zaina's hernia. She looks past us or at the ground as she tells us, "I would use the money to pay the school fees for my children to go to school . . . with this I could buy clothes and milk." When asked what making these beads means to her she smiles shyly, holding her youngest on her hip and says, "It makes me happy and gives me hope that I will improve myself." Another participant states, "It would make me proud if someone bought the necklaces, it cures the boredom and we get paid."

It's varnishing time the next morning, and the ladies' delight is genuine and contagious as the beads hang on the washing line out back to dry in the sun. But more than the excitement that they've made necklaces is the new sense of hope among them. Hope for the family to have a little more money, for school fees to be paid, or maybe even open a business one day. The women sit down, smile, and begin another delicately wrapped rainbow bead. And as they collect their beads into small piles of achievement, it's easy to see that even here, in a village that most people have never heard of, something special and promising is happening. For more information and to buy some Paper into Pearls jewelry, please go to www.grassrootsuganda.com.

Global Volunteers

375 East Little Canada Road
St. Paul, MN 55117
(800) 487-1047
E-mail: email@globalvolunteers.org
Web site: www.globalvolunteers.org

Project Type: Community Development; Economic
   Development; Education; Orphans; Rural Development;
   Social Justice; Youth
Mission Statement Excerpt: "Global Volunteers' goal is to help
   establish a foundation for peace through mutual
   international, cross-cultural understanding."
Year Founded: 1984
Number of Volunteers Last Year: 2,500
Funding Sources: Global Volunteers receives a small number of
   private donations, mostly from individuals.
The Work They Do: Global Volunteers supports development
   partnerships in more than one hundred host communities
   through on-going volunteer assistance, direct project
   funding, and child sponsorships. Volunteers work on locally
   initiated projects that include teaching conversational
   English, caring for at-risk children, constructing and
   repairing community buildings and facilities, working to
   develop and promote natural resource conservation, and
   assisting with medical care. Working in cooperation with
   local people, past Global Volunteers have built schools in
   Tanzania and China; constructed community buildings in
   Australian, Costa Rican, and Jamaican villages; built new
   homes in Appalachia; assisted with physical therapy for
   Ecuadorian and Peruvian children with disabilities; taught
   English to future leaders of China, eastern Poland, southern
   Italy, Hungary, Tanzania, Ghana, and Greece; and provided
   care to vulnerable babies in Romania and Brazil, and
   orphans in Peru and southern India. Volunteers serve on
   teams of between ten to twenty individuals, and are led by

staff country managers, most of whom are are citizens of the host community.

Project Location: Global Volunteers maintains development partnerships in Australia, Brazil, China, the Cook Islands, the United States, Peru, India, Tanzania, Ghana, Hungary, Romania, Poland, Portugal, Greece, Ireland, Italy, Costa Rica, Mexico, Jamaica, Vietnam, South Africa, and Ecuador. Accommodations vary by site, but most teams are lodged in tourist hotels. Other lodging includes guest houses or "indoor camping" in community centers. Global Volunteers arranges for all lodging and meals.

Time Line: More than 170 programs are scheduled annually, and are available year-round. The standard service program is two or three weeks, but one-week options are available for most programs, and extended stays up to twenty-four weeks are available in a few host communities.

Cost: Program fees range from $895 for one week in the continental United States to $2,650 for three weeks in Italy. Each fee includes a direct contribution to long-term development projects and covers the volunteer's meals and accommodations, as well as ground transportation in the host country. Volunteers must also pay for their airfare to the work site. Only 16 percent of Global Volunteers' program fee goes toward administrative overhead. Discounts are available for groups, families, students, and people who apply online.

Getting Started: An online application is available at Global Volunteers' Web site; prospective volunteers can also call the office to speak with a volunteer coordinator, who can give advice on which programs might be the most suitable. Applicants must provide personal references and complete a health and skills questionnaire. Volunteers receive predeparture orientation materials that outline Global Volunteers' procedures and philosophy as well as project and country information. The first few days of each program are devoted to extensive orientation sessions, team-building exercises, and community introductions, as well as to basic language instruction.

Global Volunteers team members participate in lively "field trips" with disabled children in Quito, Ecuador, including wheelchair races. *Photo courtesy of Elizabeth Rooney, Global Volunteer team member*

Needed Skills and Specific Populations: Global Volunteers welcomes families, and has one of the lowest minimum age requirements; it accepts volunteers as young as six for some programs, and as young as eleven for others. Senior volunteers are encouraged to volunteer with Global Volunteers. Volunteers with minor disabilities may be able to serve with Global Volunteers, depending on project size and logistics; specifics should be discussed with a volunteer coordinator. Volunteers who wish to teach English must be native speakers.

My Love Affair

By Elizabeth Rooney

Global Volunteers

It was love at first sight. I looked into his soulful brown eyes and was smitten. For three intense weeks he was with me, in my arms. My heart spilled over with love for this dear, dear fellow. Then it was over. I left him. Yes, I left him behind in Romania.

He is four-month-old Adrian, at the time the youngest and smallest of the more than thirty children—almost all under age four—at the Failure to Thrive Clinic at Tutova Hospital. Adrian has a cleft lip and palate, which make it difficult for him to eat. During my stay we struggled to discover the best way for me to hold him—propped upright on my right knee with the bottle tilted toward the left side of his mouth—so that he could drink his whole bottle without losing any.

Adrian is only the latest to steal my heart. Last year, on my first visit, it was Abel, a charming, one-year-old bundle of energy and one of my motivations for returning this year. Not long before my second visit, Abel had surgery to correct his crossed eyes. I witnessed Abel's improved vision at work one day when he spotted everyone's favorite rattle on the far side of the playroom and charged across to claim it.

It is unusual for a village in Romania to have its own hospital; a local landowner donated his property for this purpose in 1912. Tutova is a small agricultural village in Vaslui County, the poorest region in Romania and, indeed, in the European Union. The Failure to Thrive Clinic was established in 1970. I was at the hospital as a participant in one of the many international volunteer programs run by Global Volunteers. This

NGO has been sending volunteers to serve in 160 communities in thirty countries for more than twenty years. Global Volunteers has been involved in Tutova since 1998. Teams of up to twenty volunteers come for two or three weeks to spend time with the children. This trip was my third with Global Volunteers and my second to Romania. I didn't think anything could be better than my first time at the clinic. But coming back a second time and seeing how happy and healthy my kids were was an even more rewarding experience.

On my last day there, I find myself holding the kids longer and hugging them more intensely. I hold Adrian close and whisper my dreams for him. Then it's Abel's turn. For once he sits still on my lap instead of trying to climb me. He may not understand a word as I express my hopes for his life but he must feel my vibe, for he sits quietly with his head on my chest. It is agonizing to leave them. But they will never leave me; they are forever in my heart.

Global Works

2342 Broadway
Boulder, CO 80304
(303) 545-2202; Fax: (303) 545-2425
E-mail: info@globalworkstravel.com
Web site: www.globalworkstravel.com

Project Type: Community Development; Construction; Education; Natural Conservation (Land); Natural Conservation (Sea); Rural Development; Trail Building/Maintenance

Mission Statement Excerpt: "Global Works strives to provide young adults with rewarding service, language learning, and adventure travel programs, which foster personal growth and promote social and cultural awareness for the participant and the communities involved."

Year Founded: 1990

Number of Volunteers Last Year: 440

Funding Sources: No outside funding sources; Global Works is self-funded.

The Work They Do: Global Works is an environmental and community-service travel program for high school students that offers options for language learning and homestays. Examples of past work done by volunteers include an archaeological dig in France, working with Seeds of Hope in Ireland, environmental work in the Gredos Mountains of Spain, home construction in Puerto Rico, community construction projects in Costa Rica and in Fiji, protecting sea turtles in Martinique and Mexico, work with a kiwi habitat in New Zealand, and work with day-care centers in Ecuador and Argentina.

Project Location: Projects are available in Spain, France, Ireland, Fiji, New Zealand, Australia, Costa Rica, Puerto Rico, Ecuador, Mexico, Panama, Peru, Argentina, and Martinique. Groups of volunteers usually stay together in inns, bed and breakfasts, hostels, or eco-lodges. Individual volunteers on language immersion trips are housed with local families in a homestay.

Time Line: Global Works' programs range from two to five weeks during the summer.

Cost: Program fees run from $3,295 to $5,695, and include room and board. Airfare costs are not included.

Getting Started: Prospective volunteers should visit the Web site listed to complete an online application; most trips fill up by March prior to departure. Short, friendly telephone interviews are required in order to clarify Global Works' expectations and guidelines with prospective volunteers. Training is provided in-country as a part of the program by the adult leaders and by local organizations.

Needed Skills and Specific Populations: Volunteers must be willing to challenge their typical comfort zones and have a desire to live, work, and travel with others. Volunteers with disabilities may be able to volunteer with Global Works, which will be determined on a case-by-case basis. Global Works' programs are restricted to teenagers, but can also organize custom service trips for schools, universities, families, clubs, or organizations.

Global Xperience

Thamesbourne Lodge, Station Road, Bourne End
Bucks, SL8 5QH
United Kingdom
+44 (0) 1628 648680; Fax: +44 (0) 1628 819382
E-mail: info@globalxperience.com
Web site: www.globalxperience.com

Project Type: Community Development; Construction; Education; Medical/Health; Natural Conservation (Sea); Orphans; Youth

Mission Statement Excerpt: "To assist sports and community development in disadvantaged communities in Africa and Latin America and to raise awareness of development issues by enabling volunteers to actually work directly in the field."

Year Founded: 2002

Number of Volunteers Last Year: 450

Funding Sources: None outside of program fees

The Work They Do: Global Xperience offers two types of volunteer placements: the first are sports coaching placements, wherein volunteers provide a structured environment for youth to participate in sports, utilizing good equipment provided by Global Xperience. Sports range from soccer and tennis to basketball and rugby. The second kind of volunteer placement is non-sports projects, which include education, construction, providing care in orphanages, and conservation placements.

Project Location: Global Xperience operates in Latin America and Africa, mostly in cities. Accommodations are basic but comfortable, usually in dormitory settings or with homestays. Because volunteers work in urban settings, local transportation and other amenities are usually easily found.

Time Line: Global Xperience has projects that depart every month. Volunteers work for four to twelve weeks, with most opting for longer stays.

A volunteer works directly with Ghanian school children in an after school art and design club. Art is often neglected in the curriculum to make room for core subjects like English, math, or science. The other great side of this project is that the volunteers get to spend time with local African artists, learning their techniques and the history surrounding their artwork. *Photo courtesy of Global Xperience*

Cost: Global Xperience's program fee is £1,295 for five weeks and £100 for each additional week. The program fee includes all accommodations and meals, airport transfers, activities, orientation, and local support. Volunteers are responsible for their own travel to the country of service, visas, spending money, in-country travel, and other personal expenses.

Getting Started: In general, prospective volunteers should apply at least six weeks before they wish to depart; Global Xperience aims to confirm the volunteer's placement within seven days of receiving the application, which can be submitted online. Volunteers must provide the name of one referee, and complete a phone interview. Once in country, volunteers are given an orientation that includes safety, cultural norms, an introduction to the city, and training with local coaches. Global Xperience also provides predeparture advice on logistics and travel bookings.

Needed Skills and Specific Populations: Volunteers must be hard working, proactive, and flexible enough to cope with the challenges of living and working in an economically developing nation. A few projects require specialized skills, such as physiotherapy. Most volunteers are between ages eighteen and thirty-six, though there is no maximum age limit. Prospective volunteers with disabilities should contact Global Xperience before registering in order to ensure that their specific needs can be met at the site. Families generally do not volunteer with Global Xperience because of the eighteen-year-old minimum age requirement.

Coaching Field Hockey in a South African Township

By Emily Crow

Global Xperience

Why did you decide to go overseas to coach sports?
When I was planning my gap year (a year European students typically take "off" before starting at college or university), I knew that I really wanted to travel and see some more of the world, but at the same time I really wanted to widen my experiences by not just visiting places but by doing some kind of volunteer work and by immersing myself in the local culture. In addition, playing hockey has been a big part of my life for quite a few years, so it seemed natural that when I was researching different volunteer experiences abroad, the one I was instinctively drawn towards was the one that offered the opportunity to coach hockey!

What was a typical day like?
A typical coaching day began for us at approximately 8:30, when we'd get up and head to breakfast, where we also made our sandwiches to take to coaching with us. The coaches were split evenly into two groups, one of which left for coaching at 9:00 and the other at 10:00. Coaching sessions usually lasted between one and a half and two hours—for example, on Wednesdays we left at 10 A.M. and coached at one school from 10:30 until 12, and then at a different school from 1 P.M. until 3. On return to the accommodation, I'd then usually drop my bags and head straight down to visit the Maranatha children, who lived in an area attached to our accommodation and were

staying at Maranatha having usually come from abusive homes or similar. I usually spent about an hour and a half with the kids most evenings—we would help them with their homework and just generally play with them. Dinner was at 6 and afterwards we'd either have a quiet night in or head down to the bars on the Beachfront.

What were the local people and culture like?
The people in Port Elizabeth were definitely amongst the most friendly we met in the whole of my time in South Africa— nowhere was this more evident than when we were driving along in the combi, and people would hoot and wave at us all! The culture took some getting used to—whilst apartheid ended thirteen years ago it was clear that there were still obvious black, white, and coloured areas of town, which was a real eye-opener for me.

What did you achieve during your placement?
The placement definitely allowed me to achieve a much more in-depth understanding of township culture in South Africa, and illustrated to me the segregation that persists despite the end of apartheid. Volunteering also allowed me to pass on my hockey skills to the kids—which was immensely rewarding because they improved visibly during my time there. My time spent in South Africa has turned me into someone with a lot more confidence; after all, I arrived in the country knowing no one but twelve weeks later these strangers are now some of my close friends! Learning to live with forty new personalities is certainly a challenge but one that I think has prepared me well for university.

What did you achieve in sport from the experience?
Whilst in South Africa I joined a local hockey club called Gelvan, based in the Northern areas of PE, and played regularly for their ladies side. Working with this team gave me the opportunity to work on my own hockey skills, while also

allowing me to indulge myself by playing on their (very nice!) Astroturf—a far cry from the pitted grass pitches we coached the kids on. Through Gelvan I was also invited to attend trials for the Eastern Province U21 team, which was a very nerve-wracking but incredible experience!

Would you do it again or recommend it to others and if so why?

I'd do this whole experience again without a shadow of a doubt—I had the time of my life! I think the coaching and building a great rapport with the children was one of the most rewarding things I've done in a long time, and definitely helped me mature. The entire trip was made up of incredible moments, which I know will stay with me for the rest of my life!

Globe Aware

6500 East Mockingbird Lane, Suite 104
Dallas, TX 75214
(214) 823-0083; Fax: (214) 823-0084
E-mail: info@globeaware.org
Web site: www.globeaware.org

Project Type: Community Development; Construction; Economic Development; Education; Orphans; Rural Development; Youth

Mission Statement Excerpt: "Globe Aware seeks to promote cultural awareness and sustainability by engaging in locally chosen development projects that are safe, culturally interesting, and genuinely beneficial to a needy community."

Year Founded: 2002

Number of Volunteers Last Year: 550

Funding Sources: Fully funded by donations from individuals

The Work They Do: Globe Aware's main focus is to carry out work that leads to greater independence and health for local communities. For example, volunteers fix playgrounds, paint murals, and give one-on-one attention and care to orphans. In other programs, volunteers build modified adobe stoves that reduce fuel consumption and dramatically decrease the contraction of upper respiratory disease from smoke inhalation. Globe Aware takes on a broad spectrum of work projects at most sites.

Project Location: Globe Aware currently works in Latin America (Mexico, Costa Rica, Peru, Brazil, and Cuba), Asia (Thailand, Nepal, Laos, China, Cambodia, and Vietnam), Africa (Ghana), and Eastern Europe (Romania). Work sites vary tremendously. For example, the Cusco, Peru, work site is a cobblestoned, double courtyarded facility with flushing toilets and hot water. In Thailand, volunteers may teach in clean rural classrooms or build homes in hot and humid (but beautiful) outdoor environments. Food, water, and accommodations are always provided. At project sites in Thailand and Costa Rica there is no hot water, but it is rarely missed due to the warm outside temperatures.

Time Line: Each program is offered for at least one week every
month, with the exception of the Thailand program, which
is available November through May. Most programs last
one week, Saturday to Saturday, but some of Globe Aware's
volunteers choose to extend their programs by up to three
weeks at the additional charge of $750 per additional week.

Cost: Program fees range from approximately $900 up to
$1,500. Each fee covers the cost of meals, accommodation,
on-site travel, emergency medical evacuation, medical insurance, donations to the various community projects, and an
orientation package. Airfare is not included in the program
fee.

Getting Started: An application is available on the
organization's Web site, or Globe Aware can fax, mail, or e-
mail the application to prospective volunteers; interviews
are not required. Orientation materials are sent to
volunteers upon registration, and the first day upon arrival
is devoted to orientation activities.

Needed Skills and Specific Populations: No specialized skills are
necessary to volunteer with Globe Aware. Volunteers under
sixteen must fill out a special waiver. Senior volunteers are
welcomed. Volunteers with disabilities are welcomed,
though there are limitations within each program. For
example, the program in Cusco may not suit those who use
wheelchairs because the living accommodations and work
place are on cobblestone. Globe Aware encourages families
volunteering together as a way to expose children to
cultural learning and promote cross-cultural awareness.

Go Differently

19 West Road, Saffron Walden
Essex, CB11 3DS
United Kingdom
+44 (0) 1799 521950; Fax: +44 (0) 870 486 1577
E-mail: info@godifferently.com
Web site: www.godifferently.com

Project Type: Agriculture; Community Development; Economic
Development; Education; Historic Preservation; Natural
Conservation (Land); Youth

Mission Statement Excerpt: "Go Differently offers small group
and tailormade ethical vacations, volunteering, and voluntourism tours based on the appreciation and respect of the
local people and the environment."

Year Founded: 2002

Number of Volunteers Last Year: 350

Funding Sources: Private individuals

The Work They Do: Go Differently offers opportunities both
for voluntourism—two-week country tours that include
both vacationing and volunteering—as well as single location volunteer projects that do not include travel and
tourism. Their projects include living and working with
elephants in Thailand, teaching English in village schools,
and community development projects.

Project Location: Go Differently offers volunteer vacations in
Thailand, Vietnam, Cambodia, and Laos. Volunteers typically stay with families, sometimes in quite basic conditions,
or in small, locally owned hotels. Voluntourists, on the
other hand, stay in a combination of both locally owned
hotels and more luxurious facilities. Potential volunteers
who have concerns about their level of comfort should
discuss this in advance with Go Differently to ensure that
they are choosing a suitable trip.

Time Line: Voluntourism trips can be operated at any time with
a minimum of two participants; see Go Differently's Web
site for details. Volunteer projects that are not a part of a

tour can be joined at any time. The minimum stay is one week, with most volunteers staying for two weeks. Longer volunteer stints can be arranged, and may be eligible for a discount.

Cost: Volunteer projects start at $640 per week, and voluntourism trips begin at $1,700 for two weeks. The program fee includes accommodation, food, and logistical and linguistic support throughout the trip. Volunteers are responsible for the cost of their travel to the project's start point.

Getting Started: Prospective volunteers should contact Go Differently to discuss their specific interests and to check availability of volunteer projects. Interviews are not required, but applicants do complete a Volunteer Questionnaire to ensure a proper match between volunteer and project. Go Differently does not provide formal training, but does give each volunteer documentation that details the daily routine, a packing list, local contact information, and cultural considerations.

Needed Skills and Specific Populations: The only required skill is good spoken English for the English teaching positions, though even there sometimes other major European languages may be an acceptable substitute. While Go Differently encourages children to volunteer, all volunteers under age eighteen must be accompanied by a parent or other responsible adult. Families may enjoy discounts based on sharing rooms, as available. Go Differently welcomes volunteers of all nationalities, senior volunteers, and volunteers with disabilities, and will work to accommodate special needs as possible.

Greenforce

1218 Delaware Avenue
Wyomissing, PA 19610
(740) 416-4016
E-mail: usainfo@greenforce.org
Web site: www.greenforce.org

Project Type: Community Development; Natural Conservation (Land); Natural Conservation (Sea); Rural Development; Scientific Research; Trail Building/Maintenance; Youth

Mission Statement Excerpt: "Implement the requirements of Section 3c of the Rio Earth Summit 1994, to provide environmentally and economically balanced biodiverse regions. Incorporating local requirements utilizing international aid plans."

Year Founded: 1996

Number of Volunteers Last Year: 250–300

Funding Sources: Some funding from private agencies such as the Red Cross or World Wildlife Federation

The Work They Do: Greenforce takes on a number of different projects, all of which are centered around improving the environment and human interactions with the environment. This mission includes work as diverse as creating a national park or a marine park, undertaking environmentally aware community programs to provide local employability, and implementing sustainable fuel programs to reduce deforestation. A specific example of one of Greenforce's projects is the establishment of a marine park island in Fiji as a World Heritage site to protect the environment. Once this was completed, volunteers then trained the local villagers to dive, both to monitor the reef and also to earn an income as dive guides, and to work as boat handlers for visiting scientists. Diving equipment and boats were also donated. The island is now a freestanding, self-monitoring, self-financing reserve.

Project Location: Projects are carried out in Australia, the Bahamas, China, Ecuador, Fiji, India, Nepal, South Africa,

Spain, and Tanzania. The first week of each project is spent in the host country's capital for training, during which time volunteers reside either in a hostel or a home. While carrying out a project, volunteers are housed in simple, but clean and safe, local housing, such as a Malay stilt house, a Fijian *bure,* or Maasai *kraal.*

Time Line: Greenforce volunteers depart to work on projects every January, April, July, and October. The minimum time commitment is one week, and the maximum is one year. The average volunteer stays for about three months.

Cost: Greenforce's program fees change by country, but in general begin at £1,300 for three weeks, and goes up to £2,400 for ten weeks. This covers all meals, accommodations, medical insurance, and language lessons. Volunteers must provide their own international flight to the expedition location.

Getting Started: Prospective volunteers can download an application from Greenforce's Web site or contact the office to request a brochure. Greenforce offers predeparture orientation packets and an online forum; more extensive training is given once the volunteer arrives on the site.

Needed Skills and Specific Populations: Volunteers must be at least eighteen years old. Senior volunteers are welcomed, and Greenforce requests that someone break its record for the oldest volunteer, which is currently held by a seventy-six-year-old.

Habitat for Humanity Internatic
Village Work Teams

P.O. Box 369
Americus, GA 31709
(229) 924-6935 ext. 7530; Fax: (267) 2
E-mail: gv@habitat.org
Web site: www.habitat.org/gv

Project Type: Administrative; Community Development; Construction; Economic Development; Human Rights; Political Action

Mission Statement Excerpt: "Habitat for Humanity works in partnership with God and people everywhere, from all walks of life, to develop communities with people in need by building and renovating houses, so that there are decent houses in decent communities in which every person can experience God's love and can live and grow into all that God intends."

Year Founded: 1976

Number of Volunteers Last Year: 12,000 in the Global Village Work Teams Program

Funding Sources: Government funds for land and infrastructure

The Work They Do: One of the most well-known and beloved volunteer organizations in the United States, Habitat for Humanity International's Global Village Work Teams consist of short-term house-building trips designed to give concerned people a firsthand opportunity to observe and contribute to Habitat's work. Working alongside homeowners and local volunteers, team members assist low-income people in home-building projects. Volunteers are needed for all stages and tasks in these construction projects. Global Village Work Team participants learn about poverty housing, development challenges, and Habitat's ecumenical Christian ministry.

Project Location: Global Village Work Team volunteers work in one hundred nations around the world. Most work sites are in rural areas of economically underdeveloped countries, ey tend to be very basic. Team leaders and in-country abitat hosts make arrangements for volunteers' food, accommodations, and local transportation.

Accommodations tend to be in hotels in more urban areas, and on church or school floors in the more rural areas.

Time Line: Global Village Work Team projects run year-round for ten to twenty days each.

Cost: Program fees range from $1,000 to $2,500. The program fee includes room and board, in-country transportation, travel insurance, and a donation toward the host community's building program. Airfare to the host country is not included in the cost.

Getting Started: Prospective volunteers can apply online via the Habitat for Humanity International's Global Village Work Teams Web site. Volunteers are given orientation guides, and are guided by in-country team leaders. Prospective volunteers must be interviewed by phone before being accepted into the program.

Needed Skills and Specific Populations: Volunteers do not need any prior experience or specific skills. Participants between the ages of fourteen and eighteen must either be accompanied by a parent or guardian or be part of a chaperoned school, church, or institution group. Senior volunteers are welcomed. Accommodations for volunteers with disabilities vary by work site and by disability. Individuals and groups of people with diverse backgrounds are encouraged to participate in the Global Village Work Teams Program. Participants must be in good health, as the work assignments often require strenuous manual labor.

Hands Up Holida

5 Kendal Place
London, SW15 2QZ
England
(201) 984-5372
E-mail: info@handsupholidays.c
Web site: www.handsupholidays.c

Project Type: Administrative; Community Development; Education; Medical/Health; Natural Conservation (Land); Orphans; Trail Building/Maintenance

Mission Statement Excerpt: "Hands Up Holidays' mission is to provide inspiring ecotours and exceptional service for its guests that enable them to experience incredible sights in a destination and blending that with meaningful, fulfilling volunteering opportunities."

Year Founded: 2006

Number of Volunteers Last Year: 80

Funding Sources: Individuals

The Work They Do: Hands Up Holidays provides opportunities to combine sightseeing with "a taste of volunteering." They cater to people who are "time-poor," but who want to make a difference while on vacation. Hands Up Holidays consults with local communities to identify what projects a small group of enthusiastic volunteers could take on for an average of four or five days at a time or for a longer period of time. Most volunteers work in the areas of repair and renovation, building, teaching, or environmental conservation, such as tree planting, turtle rescues, or bird monitoring and tagging.

Project Location: Hands Up Holidays offers opportunities in thirty countries, mostly in Africa, Asia, and Latin America, as well as in Eastern Europe and the Pacific. Volunteers typically stay in four-star hotels, with some five-star accommodations available. Volunteers can also be placed in homestays upon request.

Hands Up Holidays offers scheduled departures throughout the year, though most are in peak tourism seasons; they can also craft tailor-made trips. Most guests volunteer for four days, with a maximum dependent on visa availability; most volunteers travel for fourteen days, four of which are spent volunteering and the balance of time is spent sightseeing.

Cost: Program fees include guides, a donation to the project, accommodations, entrance fees, and meals as indicated in the itinerary. These fees, which do not include international airfare, range from £600 for fifteen days in Nepal to £12,850 for eighteen days in New Zealand; the average program fee is £2,000 for fifteen days. Accommodations range, roughly corresponding with price, from simple hotels, homestays, and guesthouses, up to luxury hotels and lodges.

Getting Started: Hands Up Holidays recommends that volunteers book their trip at least sixty days in advance to ensure availability. Police background checks are required for volunteers who wish to work with children. Interviews may be required for volunteers who wish to utilize special skills or who wish to travel for longer periods of time. A predeparture information packet is sent to volunteers, and a local guide provides an in-country orientation after arrival.

Needed Skills and Specific Populations: While Hands Up Holidays does not require any specific skills, they can help to find projects for people who have specializations that they wish to utilize for the benefit of others. Unaccompanied volunteers must be at least eighteen years old; volunteers under this age may be allowed if accompanied by an adult, though this is determined in consultation with the parents. Senior volunteers are encouraged, but may need to provide a doctor's certificate if over age sixty. If at all possible, Hands Up Holidays will accommodate the needs of volunteers with disabilities, but this may not be possible in all cases. Families are welcomed to volunteer with Hands Up Holidays, though they should consult with the organization prior to booking a trip to ensure that the volunteer project (and sightseeing activities) are appropriate.

Health Volunteers Overseas (HVO)

1900 L Street NW, Suite 310
Washington, DC 20036
(202) 296-0928; Fax: (202) 296-8018
E-mail: info@hvousa.org
Web site: www.hvousa.org

Project Type: Education; Medical/Health; Professional Technical Assistance

Mission Statement Excerpt: "Health Volunteers Overseas is dedicated to improving the availability and accessibility of health care in developing countries through training and education."

Year Founded: 1986

Funding Sources: Donations from individuals and foundations, as well as government funding

The Work They Do: HVO provides clinical education and training in various disciplines including anesthesia, burn management, dentistry, dermatology, hand surgery, hematology, internal medicine, oral and maxillofacial surgery, orthopedics, pediatrics, and physical therapy. HVO also provides needed education-related materials and equipment to program sites to reinforce educational programs. Volunteers are involved in a variety of activities including clinical training, teacher training, curriculum development, and student and faculty mentoring. They lecture, serve as clinical instructors, conduct ward rounds, and demonstrate various techniques in classrooms, clinics, and operating rooms.

Project Location: Volunteer assignments with HVO are available in more than twenty-five economically developing countries in Africa, Asia, the Caribbean, Latin America, and Eastern Europe. Amenities and the comfortableness of the work sites and accommodations vary by location.

Time Line: HVO's programs are ongoing, and the organization accepts volunteers year-round. Volunteers typically serve for one month, though there are some stints where volunteers can serve for two weeks. Longer placements are also available.

Cost: HVO does not charge program fees, but it requires participants to become members to help provide support for the organization's administrative costs. Volunteers are responsible for their international travel, and many sites provide room, board, and daily transportation.

Getting Started: Prospective volunteers should visit HVO's Web site or call the number listed. HVO has a predeparture orientation process that includes communication by phone, e-mail, and fax. All volunteers receive HVO's *Guide to Volunteering Overseas,* a booklet that contains information on international travel, safety and health precautions, and cross-cultural communication skills, as well as teaching and training tips. In addition, volunteers receive an orientation packet that includes a packing list, training and program details, and site-specific information on housing, travel, food, personal needs, and weather.

Needed Skills and Specific Populations: HVO volunteers must be fully trained and licensed health care professionals. In addition, HVO prefers volunteers with three to five years' professional experience, since activities include teaching and training. There is no language requirement for volunteers. The most successful HVO volunteers are well-trained, flexible, adaptable, and open to new experiences. There is no minimum age required to volunteer with HVO, and senior volunteers are welcomed. Qualified volunteers with disabilities are welcomed, though they should work with HVO staff to assess the feasibility of assignments. Family members often accompany HVO volunteers, and in some sites may be able to volunteer as teachers, administrators, or in some other capacity.

Independent Living Alternatives (ILA)

Trafalgar House, Grenville Place
London, NW7 3SA
United Kingdom
+44 (0) 20 8906 9265; Fax: +44 (0) 20 8959 1910
E-mail: PAServices@ILAnet.co.uk
Web site: www.ILAnet.co.uk

Project Type: Community Development; Human Rights;
Medical/Health; Social Justice
Mission Statement Excerpt: "To promote the right of disabled
people to live independently."
Year Founded: 1989
Number of Volunteers Last Year: 35
Funding Sources: Service fees from clients
The Work They Do: ILA provides a comprehensive range of
personal assistance services to disabled people. Volunteers
provide personal assistance to disabled people to enable
them to live independently; this might include personal
assistance such as helping someone to get dressed, have a
bath, and utilize a toilet, or more practical assistance such
as shopping and housework.
Project Location: London and Cumbria, England. Volunteers
live in the disabled person's home; during their time off,
they reside in shared volunteer accommodations. ILA pays
for the volunteer's room and board, travel expenses, and a
living allowance.
Time Line: ILA does not have specific starting and end dates for
volunteer projects. Volunteers commit to a minimum of four
months and maximum of one year.
Cost: There is no cost to volunteer with ILA, but volunteers
must pay for their own travel to London, insurance, and
any visa costs.
Getting Started: ILA has an open application process, with no
deadlines. Phone interviews are required of all prospective
volunteers. ILA provides training as needed for volunteers in
areas such as food safety, fire safety, first aid, and hygiene.

Needed Skills and Specific Populations: While not essential, volunteers will find a driver's license to be helpful. Volunteers must be at least eighteen years old, and there is no maximum age for volunteers. Volunteers with disabilities may be able to volunteer with ILA, depending on their disability. Families may be able to volunteer together in some circumstances.

Institute for International Cooperation and Development (IICD)

P.O. Box 520
Williamstown, MA 01267
(413) 458-9466; Fax: (413) 458-3323
E-mail: info@iicd-volunteer.org
Web site: www.iicd-volunteer.org

Project Type: Agriculture; Community Development; Education; Human Rights; Medical/Health; Orphans; Rural Development

Mission Statement Excerpt: "Move humanitarian development forward by working towards achieving the objectives outlined in the Declaration of Human Rights."

Year Founded: 1987

Number of Volunteers Last Year: 100

Funding Sources: Individuals and a private organization

The Work They Do: IICD takes on a number of projects but are primarily concerned with fighting AIDS and with improving education around the world. Most volunteers work in the areas of HIV/AIDS prevention work, the environment, agriculture, and education.

Project Location: IICD works in Angola, Brazil, Malawi, Namibia, Zambia, Mozambique, and South Africa. Volunteers live at the work site, usually in rural areas without electricity or running water. Volunteers can request an urban placement with more amenities, though.

Time Line: Volunteer projects start in February, May, August, October, and November, and run for nine to thirteen months, or for twenty months.

Cost: IICD charges an enrollment fee of $400. The program fee for nine to fourteen months is $3,800, and $4,400 for twenty-month programs.

Getting Started: Prospective volunteers should call or e-mail the office; IICD does not have application deadlines. Interviews are required, and can be completed in-person or on the phone. Every volunteer receives an extensive orientation and training, lasting two months for volunteers in Brazil and six months for all others.

Needed Skills and Specific Populations: IICD does not require any specific skills, just a lot of stamina. Volunteers must be at least seventeen years old; couples are welcome, but children are not. There is no maximum age limit. IICD is very willing to try to accommodate volunteers with disabilities, and has successfully worked with volunteers with sight disabilities. Volunteers from around the world are welcome, as long as they can obtain a visa for their country of service.

Intercultural Youth Exchange (ICYE)

Latin American House, Kingsgate Place
London, NW6 4TA
United Kingdom
+44 (0) 20 7681 0983; Fax: +44 (0) 20 7916 1246
E-mail: info@icye.org.uk
Web site: www.icye.org.uk

Project Type: Community Development; Education; Human
Rights; Natural Conservation (Land); Orphans; Women's
Issues; Youth

Mission Statement Excerpt: "Operating within an international
network of locally managed ICYE organizations, ICYE UK
encourages intercultural understanding and cooperation
through the exchange of people and ideas."

Year Founded: 1949

Number of Volunteers Last Year: 60

Funding Sources: Foundations

The Work They Do: ICYE offers a wide range of volunteer
placements, including opportunities such as working with
street children in Brazil; promoting HIV awareness in
Mozambique; assisting women's education and development
in India; and protecting sea turtle habitats in Costa Rica.
Volunteer assignments depend on the skills and interests of
the volunteer and the requirements of the project.

Project Location: ICYE works in Latin America, Africa, and
Asia. Volunteers usually live with local host families in
settings ranging from rural villages to large cities. ICYE
locates accommodations for volunteers.

Time Line: ICYE offers both short-term volunteer opportunities
of three to sixteen weeks, which depart throughout the year,
as well as long-term six or twelve month opportunities,
which depart in January and August.

Cost: Short-term volunteer opportunities' program fee begins at
£750, which covers international flights, accommodations,
food, health insurance, and airport transfers. Long-term
volunteer programs are £3,300 for six months and £3,900

for twelve months, which includes international travel costs, room and board, health insurance, training and orientation before departure and on arrival, thirty hours of language instruction, and pocket money. Part of the program fee helps to defray the costs of volunteers from Latin America, Africa, and Asia to operate in disadvantaged communities in the UK.

Getting Started: Interested volunteers should contact ICYE by e-mail; there are no application deadlines, and ICYE can conduct the required interview by phone. ICYE offers predeparture training, training in-country, and ongoing training during and after the volunteer experience.

Needed Skills and Specific Populations: Specific needed skills vary from project to project, but all volunteers must be enthusiastic, dedicated, and passionate. Volunteers must be at least eighteen years old, and long-term volunteers may not be older than thirty. ICYE welcomes volunteers with disabilities and will make appropriate living and project arrangements. Families may volunteer together as long as all members meet the minimum age requirement.

International Cultural Adventures (ICA)

160 #2 Quail Nest Road
Naples, FL 34112
(888) 339-0460
E-mail: info@icadventures.com
Web site: www.icadventures.com

Project Type: Agriculture; Community Development; Education; Medical/Health; Orphans; Rural Development; Youth

Mission Statement Excerpt: "The mission of ICA is to enlighten the mind and enrich the spirit of each program participant by providing unique opportunities to acquire new perspectives on their life and gain a greater understanding of our global community through extraordinary cultural, educational, and volunteer service experiences abroad."

Year Founded: 1996

Number of Volunteers Last Year: 52

Funding Sources: None; self-funded

The Work They Do: ICA offers both custom-designed volunteer opportunities and a regularly scheduled volunteer program. Project areas include education, environmental conservation, agriculture, health care and nutrition, child development, care of seniors, small business development, orphanages, and construction. Some specific examples of volunteer work available through ICA include weeding and ox-driven field plowing with local farmers in order to plant potatoes; teaching English to young monks in a rural monastery; constructing beds for an orphanage in order to accommodate street children; repairing windows and painting an inspirational mural for a local secondary school; raising funds and constructing a new computer laboratory at an orphanage; working alongside a local doctor in the oncology department of a modern hospital; teaching art and theater to primary school students; serving meals to street children in a shelter; and collecting toys, books, and games and establishing a game room for the children of an orphanage.

Project Location: Most of the established projects take place in Peru, India, and Nepal, though customized programs can be created in other countries. In the established programs, volunteer opportunities exist in urban, semi-urban, and rural locations. Accommodations and work sites are clean, comfortable, and basic. Volunteers in customized programs may choose to stay with a host family, in a guesthouse, or in a hotel. Established programs generally house volunteers with host families.

Time Line: Established programs are available either during the summer for six weeks or as a three-month extended program beginning in February, March, and September. Customized programs can be arranged at almost any time during the year for any length of time.

Cost: The program fee for a customized volunteer experience is negotiated with the participant. Established summer program fees start at $3,990, and established semester-length program fees start at $4,950. Each program fee includes accommodations, transportation to scheduled activities, and most meals. Volunteers must also pay for their domestic and international airfare, visa and passport fees, airport departure taxes, and travel insurance.

Getting Started: Prospective volunteers may contact ICA via the contact information listed and request program information and an application packet. Prospective volunteers must complete a phone interview before beginning. All volunteers receive extensive in-country orientation. The established six-week programs include two weeks of orientation followed by four weeks of volunteering; the established three-month programs start with a month of orientation followed by two months of volunteering. Volunteers in customized programs specify the length of their in-country training.

Needed Skills and Specific Populations: Foreign language skills are not necessary to participate on any of ICA's programs, but volunteers in Peru will have more opportunities to serve if they speak Spanish. Although most projects do not require any special skills, some projects that involve medicine and health care require specific skills of varying levels. The suggested minimum age of participants on any of ICA's programs is eighteen, though younger volunteers may participate with parental consent. In customized group programs, particularly school group programs, participants can be of any age provided that those under age eighteen have parental consent. There is no maximum age limit. ICA also welcomes volunteers with disabilities; specific arrangements for accommodations are dependent on each volunteer's disabilities and the program he or she is considering. Families are welcome to apply with ICA, though they do not have much experience working with families.

International Executive Service Corps (IESC)
1900 M Street NW, Suite 500
Washington, DC 20036
(202) 589-2600; Fax: (202) 326-0289
E-mail: iesc@iesc.org
Web site: www.iesc.org

Project Type: Agriculture; Community Development; Economic
Development; Legal; Professional/Technical Assistance;
Rural Development; Women's Issues
Mission Statement: "Promoting stability and prosperity through
private enterprise development."
Year Founded: 1964
Number of Volunteers Last Year: More than 350
Funding Sources: A majority of the funding for IESC comes
from the U.S. government, primarily USAID, though a
modest amount comes from private donors.
The Work They Do: IESC provides technical and managerial
assistance services to small and medium-sized private businesses and to business support organizations in the developing world and in emerging democracies. IESC pursues its
mission by implementing major development programs
around the world and through the delivery of technical
consultancies by volunteers and professional experts. Volunteer consultants provide technical assistance in IESC's four
major sectors: trade and competitiveness, information and
communications technology, financial services, and tourism
development. Volunteers share their expertise in training
programs, trade development, trade show participation,
trade missions, and quality assurance certification with both
private and governmental organizations. IESC volunteers
work very hard—often six days a week—while on a project,
and they are usually required to produce a professional
"consultant/advisor" report upon completion of an
assignment.
Project Location: IESC's programs operate worldwide, and have
taken place in more than 130 countries. Volunteers usually

stay in hotels or a client's guest quarters in or near a major city, though some clients provide an apartment or other housing.

Time Line: Projects are undertaken as requests come in from overseas. Volunteer assignments last from one week to several months.

Cost: Executives pay nothing to volunteer with IESC, as their work is carried out under cooperative agreements or contracts with organizations that provide funding. Generally, volunteers receive per diem and housing allowances based on U.S. State Department rates.

Getting Started: Prospective volunteers should register online at the IESC Web site. All volunteers receive briefings before and after their arrival at the host country project site.

Needed Skills and Specific Populations: There is no minimum age to volunteer. Senior volunteers are welcomed, but must have been active in their sector within the last three years. Volunteers with disabilities are welcomed, but it is up to the volunteer to determine the appropriateness of the assignment, as IESC cannot guarantee that accommodations overseas will meet the volunteer's requirements. For volunteer projects that last more than four weeks, IESC may pay expenses to have a spouse accompany the volunteer, though spouses are then expected to volunteer locally.

Iracambi Atlantic Rainforest Research Center

Fazenda Iracambi, Caixa Postal No. 1
Rosário da Limeira, CEP 36878-000
Minas Gerais
Brazil
+55 32 3721 1436; Fax: +55 32 3722 3611
E-mail: iracambi@iracambi.com
Web site: www.iracambi.com

Project Type: Administrative; Agriculture; Community Development; Economic Development; Legal; Natural Conservation (Land); Professional/Technical Assistance; Rural Development; Scientific Research; Social Justice; Trail Building/ Maintenance; Youth

Mission Statement Excerpt: "To make conservation of the rainforest more attractive than its destruction."

Year Founded: Iracambi was started as a working farm in 1989 and became established as a nonprofit organization in 1999.

Number of Volunteers Last Year: 144

Funding Sources: Private sources

The Work They Do: Iracambi carries out four specific projects: land use management, forest restoration, income-generating alternatives, and community understanding and engagement. Volunteers help with these projects by working on information technology; marketing; fundraising; Web site maintenance; trail maintenance; plant nursery management; environmental education and farmer outreach; GIS mapping; plant, animal, and bird identification and surveys; medicinal plant work; house maintenance; promotional material design; legal research and advice; and socioeconomic research.

Project Location: Volunteers work at Fazenda Iracambi and in the surrounding towns and villages. Iracambi has four volunteer houses and is in the process of building five new cabins. The houses are very simple and are built in the same style as local houses. Each volunteer shares a room with someone of the same sex, unless they come as a couple.

Volunteers are expected to share cooking and cleaning responsibilities with members of their house.

Time Line: Volunteers are accepted year-round for a minimum of one month and a maximum (because of visa restrictions) of six months.

Cost: The volunteer program fee is $675 for the first month, $645 for the second month, and $615 for each month thereafter. The program fee covers all room and board; volunteers are responsible for all other costs, including airfare to Brazil.

Getting Started: Prospective volunteers should send a cover letter and a CV or resume to the e-mail address listed. The cover letter should detail the areas of work that are of most interest to the applicant. All volunteers are given an orientation to the project, the farm, and their roles.

Needed Skills and Specific Populations: Given the range of roles that need to be filled at Iracambi, the program can find a use for almost any skill a volunteer may possess. Volunteers must be at least eighteen years old, and senior volunteers are welcomed as long as they accept the somewhat basic living conditions. Individuals with disabilities may be able to volunteer with Iracambi, depending on the type of disabilities involved and the type of work they wish to undertake.

i-to-i Meaningful Travel

190 East 9th Avenue, #350
Denver, CO 80203
(800) 985-4864; Fax: (303) 765-5327
E-mail: usca@i-to-i.com
Web site: www.meaningfultravel.com

Project Type: Community Development; Construction; Education; Natural Conservation (Land); Orphans; Rural Development; Youth

Mission Statement Excerpt: "To allow travelers from around the world to give something back to the communities they visit by contributing to worthwhile projects during their stay, sharing skills and experiences, and promoting cultural understanding, and to provide local projects in communities worldwide with a consistent supply of trained and committed volunteer workers who will work toward the project's own goals."

Year Founded: 1994

Number of Volunteers Last Year: 5,000

Funding Sources: No outside sources

The Work They Do: I-to-i offers more than five hundred projects in thirty-four countries designed to help disadvantaged communities and ecosystems around the world. Project offerings are quite diverse, and include protecting endangered Panda in China; rainforest conservation in Ecuador; working with endangered animals in Costa Rica; teaching English in Uganda; working in a community health center for early childhood development in Tanzania; protecting endangered lions in South Africa; building homes for families in Costa Rica and Honduras; and care work, such as helping orphaned children or street youth in Brazil or India.

Project Location: I-to-i offers projects in Argentina, Australia, Brazil, China, Costa Rica, Dominica, the Dominican Republic, Ecuador, Ghana, Honduras, India, Kenya, Laos, Madagascar, Mozambique, Nepal, New Zealand, Peru,

Two volunteers race down the beach in Mombasa, Kenya, carrying local children along for a joyful and wet ride. Mombasa is home to more than thirty thousand street children from all over Kenya, with many more orphaned by HIV/AIDS. Volunteers work with the children in many ways, including recreational. *Photo courtesy of i-to-i*

South Africa, Sri Lanka, Swaziland, Tanzania, Thailand, Tibet, Vietnam, and Zambia. Accommodations depend on the project and range from volunteer houses to home stays.

Time Line: Projects last from one to twelve weeks; the average volunteer serves for two to three weeks.

Cost: Program fees vary by location and length of the project, but a typical two-week placement with i-to-i costs $1,595, which includes accommodations and food, a welcome orientation, and a TEFL (Teaching English as a Foreign Language) course. Volunteers are responsible for providing their own airfare.

Getting Started: Prospective volunteers can call the toll-free number listed to talk with a travel advisor or visit i-to-i's Web site for details and booking arrangements. Every trip includes a standard orientation session upon arrival in the country. The orientation session lasts two or three days and covers administrative issues, health and safety, code of conduct, expectations during the project, how to succeed as a volunteer, and cultural tips. All of i-to-i's teaching and community development projects require volunteers to take a forty-hour online TEFL course before they leave for their

223

projects. I-to-i also offers additional Spanish language lessons as needed.

Needed Skills and Specific Populations: Most of i-to-i's projects do not require specific knowledge or skills, but some media, marketing, and health projects require volunteers to submit their resumes in advance. Volunteers must be at least fifteen years old, and senior volunteers are welcomed. Families with children who meet this minimum age requirement are welcome. Placement for volunteers with disabilities will be done on an individual basis in order to be 100 percent sure that the programs in which they are interested will be able to support them fully.

Jatun Sacha

Volunteer Program, Jatun Sacha Foundation
Casilla 17-12-867, Quito
Ecuador
+(593) 2-243-22240 or +(593) 2-331-8156;
Fax: +(593) 2-331-7163
E-mail: volunteer@jatunsacha.org
Web site: www.jatunsacha.org

Project Type: Agriculture; Community Development; Education;
  Natural Conservation (Land); Natural Conservation (Sea);
  Rural Development; Scientific Research
Mission Statement Excerpt: "Jatun Sacha is dedicated to
  promoting the conservation of forest, aquatic, and *páramo*
  ecosystems of Ecuador through technical training, scientific
  research, environmental education, community
  development, sustainable management of natural resources,
  and the development of leaders with a high participation of
  ethnic groups and women to improve the quality of life of
  the community."
Year Founded: 1989
Number of Volunteers Last Year: 1,185
Funding Sources: Private sources, nonprofit organizations, and
  USAID
The Work They Do: Jatun Sacha focuses on biological conservation and cultural diversity through private reserves, environmental education, and the development of products and
  research that improve the lives of the people in its zones of
  influence and activities. The volunteer program offers
  opportunities in a variety of activities including reforestation
  projects; habitat restoration; organic agriculture;
  agroforestry; orchids, bromeliad, and medicinal gardens;
  construction; alternative animal production; forestry
  programs; community visits; community and health
  programs; environmental education; teaching experiences;
  productive projects; production of organic fertilizers;

sustainable wood production; alternative energy program; sustainable aquaculture; beach clean ups; phenology studies; natural regeneration studies; flora and fauna inventories; and hummingbird and mammal feeding.

Project Location: The volunteer program works with seven biological stations managed by the Jatun Sacha Foundation in national and internationally recognized reserves located in the four major regions of Ecuador. The reserves extend from sea level up to four thousand meters in altitude. This range includes marine, intertidal, and mangrove ecosystems, as well as dry forest, rain forest, cloud forest, pre-mountain and high-mountain forest, as well as the *páramo* and the Galapagos Islands. Each of the reserves also works with local communities. Volunteers are housed at each station's facilities.

Time Line: Volunteers are accepted throughout the year for a minimum of two weeks and a maximum of one year. Jatun Sacha estimates that the average volunteer stays for two months.

Cost: Volunteers pay a $47 application fee ($67 for the Galapagos) and a program fee of $475 per month ($840 for the Galapagos). The program fee covers lodging and all meals. Volunteers are responsible for transportation and all other costs.

Getting Started: Prospective volunteers should send an application letter that indicates their experience in conservation activities, future interests, reasons for applying, and preferred station and participation dates, along with a CV or resume, a recent health certificate, a police record card, two passport-sized photos, and the application fee. Jatun Sacha provides an orientation meeting before volunteers travel to sites that consists of an overview of the foundation, its reserves, and its respective projects; volunteer activities; and directions to the volunteer's reserve. Once at the reserves, volunteers receive a more in-depth orientation on the activities in which they will participate, and they receive on-the-job training throughout their service.

Needed Skills and Specific Populations: Volunteers must have at least a basic knowledge of Spanish and be at least eighteen years old. Senior volunteers who are physically fit are welcomed. Volunteers with disabilities are welcomed, provided that the necessary accommodations can be made. Families can volunteer with Jatun Sacha, but children may not be able to participate in all activities, and there are no day care centers available.

Joint Assistance Centre (JAC)

P.O. Box 6082
San Pablo, CA 94806
E-mail: jacusa@juno.org
Web site: www.jacusa.org

Project Type: Construction; Economic Development; Education;
Medical/Health; Orphans; Women's Issues; Youth
Mission Statement Excerpt: "The international volunteer
programs of the Joint Assistance Centre (JAC) are intended
to provide opportunities for visiting friends from abroad to
see India and learn about its people and their concerns
while traveling."
Year Founded: 1990
Number of Volunteers Last Year: 10
Funding Sources: None; self-funded
The Work They Do: JAC offers a variety of volunteer opportunities, all of which focus on human services work; each
program is individually created and tailored to the
applicant's skills and desired volunteer experience. Examples
of work done by volunteers include cooperating with
villagers on projects in the areas of sanitation, construction,
agriculture, environmental improvement, literacy, women's
welfare, and health, including local herbal medicine. Volunteers can also assist in JAC's New Delhi office; prepare for
and attend conferences on development, disasters, and environmental issues; and teach English.
Project Location: All of JAC's programs take place in various
parts of India, including Delhi, the region of Uttar Pradesh,
and the region of Orissa. Projects may take place in rural
villages or in cities. Volunteers are provided modest accommodations, sometimes with a family or school compound,
and vegetarian food.
Time Line: Volunteers are accepted year-round for a minimum
of three weeks and a maximum of six months.
Cost: JAC's program fee is $150 per month. Accommodations
and food are included in this program fee, as are airport

transfers. Volunteers must provide their own airfare to India.

Getting Started: Prospective volunteers should e-mail JAC at the address listed and request an application. JAC requires an interview and offers an orientation, both by phone.

Needed Skills and Specific Populations: Volunteers must be at least eighteen years old, and senior volunteers are welcomed. JAC has not had any experience hosting volunteers with disabilities but believes that it will be able to accommodate people with a wide range of disabilities. JAC has previously hosted two families and requires that parents be responsible for minors.

Junior Art Club

P.O. Box GP 1301
Accra
Ghana
+233 244-237388
E-mail: jacghana@gmail.com
Web site: www.juniorartclub.org

Project Type: Community Development; Economic Development; Education; Human Rights; Museum; Rural Development; Youth

Mission Statement Excerpt: "Our mission is to use the Junior Art Club as a proven incubator capable of identifying and developing the creative potentials of children and the youth in varied artistic forms and models through possible endless expressions of universal art so as to provide progressive opportunities for the youth in order to raise their standard of living in a sustainable development and eradicate poverty."

Year Founded: 2000

Number of Volunteers Last Year: 25

Funding Sources: Foundations and individual donors

The Work They Do: Junior Art Club utilizes many forms of artistic expression and dissemination of artwork to help children in Ghana express themselves and find ways of earning much-needed funding. Their methods include work-shops, computer lessons, work in museums and galleries (including Ghana's only children's art gallery), guidance and counseling for youth, publications, exhibitions, competitions, festivals, cultural exchanges, and media productions. Volunteers partner with local coordinators to lead workshops and teaching sessions in their area of specialty.

Project Location: Junior Art Club works in the Ghanaian cities of Accra, Ada, Ashaiman, Adeiso, Daboase, and Assin Fosu. The workshops are carried out within existing school struc-tures, usually as after-school programs, though some photography workshops may travel into the field. Junior Art Club provides accommodations for volunteers in hostels with shared kitchens, bathrooms, and living rooms; volunteers share a room with at most two other volunteers. Volunteers may also stay with local host families.

Time Line: Junior Art Club accepts volunteers year-round, and is flexible in terms of start and end dates. Volunteers are accepted for a minimum of one week and a maximum of two years.

Cost: Junior Art Club's program fees start at £400 for one week and go up to £2,000 for three months, then £300 for each additional week after three months. The program fees include materials for workshops, airport transfers, daily transportation to the volunteer site, room and board, and social events with local artists. Volunteers are responsible for their own international transportation to Ghana.

Getting Started: Junior Art Club's application is available on its Web site; there are no deadlines for submitting the application and interviews are not required. Volunteers are given a basic orientation to cultural differences, the Ghanaian monetary system, and the city of service.

Needed Skills and Specific Populations: Volunteers must be knowledgeable about one or more areas of the arts, and be motivated, creative, and committed. Volunteers must speak English and have at least a high school diploma. Volunteers must be between eighteen and seventy years old, and volunteers with disabilities are welcome. Junior Art Club has hosted families in the past and welcomes applications from families.

JustWorks

Unitarian Universalist Service Committee
689 Massachusetts Avenue
Cambridge, MA 02139
(800) 388-3920 or (617) 868-6600; Fax: (617) 868-7102
E-mail: justworks@uusc.org
Web site: www.uusc.org/info/workcamps.html

Project Type: Community Development; Human Rights; Political Action; Social Justice

Mission Statement Excerpt: "The Unitarian Universalist Service Committee advances human rights and social justice around the world, partnering with those who confront unjust power structures and mobilizing to challenge oppressive policies."

Year Founded: 1996

Number of Volunteers Last Year: Approximately 250

Funding Sources: Individual donors

The Work They Do: JustWorks offers short-term work camps that help volunteers examine and understand the causes and damaging effects of injustice. Participants work directly with people in the communities they serve, experiencing social-justice struggles firsthand. Volunteers are taught advocacy skills to address issues of poverty, discrimination, and racism, while learning about human-rights issues and promoting intercultural understanding and reconciliation. Participants may then make use of these skills and newfound knowledge in their congregations, campuses, and communities when they return home. Specific examples of JustWorks programs include electoral-related skills training sessions in Atlanta, Selma, Montgomery, and Birmingham (which was timed to honor the fortieth anniversary of Freedom Summer); a Defending Democracy program held in conjunction with presidential-nominating conventions, which trained volunteers to organize, educate, and register voters; and a program for teenagers that focused on human-rights issues such as race, sovereignty, and culture among Native Americans in the Pacific Northwest.

Project Location: JustWorks program locations change every year. They may be held anywhere in the United States. Accommodations depend on the project; they have included RVs and dormitories in the past.

Time Line: Most JustWorks projects last one week. They are usually held between March and October.

Cost: The program fee varies depending on the camp but generally ranges from $300 to $400. The program fee includes all accommodations, food, and local transportation during the project, but it does not include transportation to and from the project site. In general, JustWorks volunteers eat locally grown food prepared by local people.

Getting Started: To apply for a JustWorks project, prospective volunteers can download an application from the organization's Web site or contact the office via e-mail or phone. Applicants are encouraged to submit their materials at least six to eight weeks before the project's start date; interviews are not required as a part of the application process. Orientation and training is provided on-site at the beginning of each camp.

Needed Skills and Specific Populations: Some camps may require that volunteers have specific skills sets. In general, volunteers must be at least sixteen years old, though some projects are designed specifically for youth and young adults, and some projects have a minimum age of eighteen. Many JustWorks camps are intergenerational, and senior volunteers are encouraged to apply. JustWorks is unable to accommodate individuals with disabilities. Families are encouraged to apply for the JustWorks camps; in particular, families who have previously attended the Civil Rights Journey camp.

Kokee Resource Conservation Program (KRCP)

Hui O Laka/Kokee Natural History Museum
P.O. Box 100
Kekaha, HI 96752
(808) 335-0045; Fax: (808) 335-0414
E-mail: rcp@aloha.net
Web site: www.krcp.org

Project Type: Natural Conservation (Land); Trail
Building/Maintenance

Mission Statement Excerpt: "Kokee Resource Conservation
Program (KRCP) seeks to involve the public in protecting
native ecosystem resources by coordinating volunteers to
conduct essential removal of invasive noxious weeds in
selected areas."

Year Founded: 1998

Number of Volunteers Last Year: 2,100

Funding Sources: Government and private grants

The Work They Do: KRCP focuses on alien species control
projects in the forests of Kokee State Park on Kauai Island,
Hawaii. About one thousand acres are actively managed,
and KRCP removes ginger, guava, privet, and several types
of plants. Other work, such as trail maintenance and
nursery planting, occasionally takes place. Volunteers join
staff members daily to hike and work off-trail, treating
specific weeds in a section of the park. The park has a
variety of forest ecosystems and weed problems, so work
does not become monotonous.

Project Location: All volunteers work in Kokee State Park,
which is three to four thousand feet above sea level and is
made up of swamp, wet forest, and dry forest. Conditions
can be muddy and involve steep terrain; hiking and off-trail
bushwhacking are common. Volunteers should be prepared
for rain, but they may be comforted to know that there are
no snakes. Lodging is in a 1930s bunkhouse, constructed by
the Civilian Conservation Corps as a part of the New Deal,

that has bunk beds, hot running water, and a communal kitchen.

Time Line: Volunteers are accepted year-round for one day to four weeks. The average stay is two weeks. Volunteers work four days each week and have three days off, but are allowed to stay in the bunkhouse for all seven days.

Cost: There is no cost to volunteer with KRCP, and housing is provided free of charge in the bunkhouse. Volunteers are responsible for purchasing their own food, which is obtained in a town that is forty-five minutes away from the site. Transportation to Kokee State Park is difficult, and volunteers should plan on providing their own travel to the work site, such as by renting a car. Volunteers must also have health insurance.

Getting Started: Prospective volunteers should contact KRCP at the address listed and request an application form. Much of the first day of volunteering is spent in training and orientation, and more training is given daily as needed.

Needed Skills and Specific Populations: Anyone who can handle the strenuous, off-trail work is welcomed, including senior volunteers and volunteers with disabilities. Volunteers are expected to work with mild herbicides and machetes. Volunteers under age eighteen should be accompanied by their parents or volunteer as a part of a group, and they are not allowed to use herbicides or machetes.

La Sabranenque

Rue de la Tour de l'Oume
30290 Saint Victor la Coste
France
+0033 466 500 505; Fax: +0033 466 500 077
or
La Sabranenque
c/o Jacqueline Simon
124 Bondcroft Drive
Buffalo, NY 14226
(716) 836-8698
E-mail: info@sabranenque.com
Web site: www.sabranenque.com

Project Type: Historic Preservation; Rural Development

Mission Statement Excerpt: "La Sabranenque works toward the preservation of traditional Mediterranean architecture through work projects aimed at consolidating and rehabilitating sites and through teaching volunteers the construction techniques."

Year Founded: 1969

Number of Volunteers Last Year: 250

Funding Sources: No outside funding; La Sabranenque is self-funded.

The Work They Do: La Sabranenque works on consolidating and rebuilding traditional regional architecture in southern France. Projects range from the paving of a village path to the consolidation of a Romanesque chapel to the complete reconstruction of a complex of houses. Volunteers take an active part in the restoration work, including clearing rubble, cutting stone, walling drystone, paving paths, tiling floors or roofs, and plastering walls. The main construction technique used is stone masonry.

Project Location: Volunteers work in Provence, France. Work sites may be houses, chapels, or medieval castle sites, either within a village or on a hilltop. Volunteers are housed, two to a room, in the restored village of Saint Victor la Coste. Food is prepared by a chef and is described as one of the highlights of the experience.

Time Line: Volunteers are accepted in May through October, and they can stay from one week to several months. The average volunteer stay is one to two weeks.

Cost: La Sabranenque's two-week program fee is $820, which includes housing and full board, all activities, and pickup and drop-off at the Avignon train station. The program fee does not include international airfare or train costs to Avignon. La Sabranenque is run by volunteers, so approximately 90 percent of the program fee goes directly toward program costs.

Getting Started: Prospective volunteers should contact La Sabranenque and request a brochure and an enrollment form. Interviews are not required before starting to volunteer. All volunteers are trained in the traditional construction techniques used while on the job.

Needed Skills and Specific Populations: No construction skills are needed; La Sabranenque's volunteers rarely have experience in this kind of work. Volunteers must be at least eighteen years old; there is no maximum age limit, and La Sabranenque regularly hosts volunteers who are in their sixties. Due to the layout of the village and the access to projects, La Sabranenque may not be able to accommodate people who have difficulty walking. Families frequently volunteer with La Sabranenque.

Landmark Volunteers

P.O. Box 455
800 North Main Street
Sheffield, MA 01257
(413) 229-0255; Fax: (413) 229-2050
E-mail: landmark@volunteers.com
Web site: www.volunteers.com

Project Type: Community Development; Construction; Historic
Preservation; Natural Conservation (Land); Trail
Building/Maintenance; Youth

Mission Statement Excerpt: "The mission of Landmark Volunteers is to encourage public service among high school
students and to foster a sense of social conscience at an age
when the satisfaction of 'giving something back' can influence these teenagers' lives; and to contribute value to
leading nonprofit historical, environmental, social service,
and cultural institutions across the United States."

Year Founded: 1991

Number of Volunteers Last Year: 625

Funding Sources: Individual donors and foundations

The Work They Do: Landmark Volunteers participants primarily do manual work for host organizations, including
clearing and building trails, painting, construction, and
grounds maintenance. Volunteers may also work directly
with the one of the host organization's target populations,
such as disadvantaged or physically disabled youth. Volunteers, who are all high school students, serve in teams of up
to thirteen people under the full-time leadership and supervision of an adult Landmark Volunteers team leader.

Project Location: Landmark works in sixty locations across the
United States. Lodging is arranged in cooperation with the
host organizations and varies by site. Possibilities range
from cabins to dorms to tents to local churches or schools.
At many of the sites the volunteers will have an opportunity
to prepare their meals as a group.

Time Line: Spring projects are available in April and run for one week. Two-week summer programs run from mid-June to mid-August.

Cost: Program fees range from $750 for the spring programs to $1,300 for the summer programs. Each fee covers food, lodging, and adult supervision. Travel arrangements and expenses are the responsibility of each volunteer. Day-off activities are not included in the program fee. There is some scholarship aid available for those who cannot afford the requested payment for participation.

Getting Started: Prospective volunteers can apply via Landmark's Web site. Participants are admitted after a rigorous application process; admission is merit based, and applicants must prove that they are diligent, supportive, and responsible. Applications consist of an essay, a letter of recommendation, and an application form. Landmark has a rolling admissions policy, but volunteers are encouraged to apply early in order to be placed in one of their top choices. Orientation includes team building and a review of expected conduct, as well as site-specific orientation from host organizations. Some Landmark volunteers also receive safety and emergency training.

Needed Skills and Specific Populations: Landmark volunteers must be fourteen and a half and a rising sophomore, junior, or senior in high school. Landmark's nondiscrimination policy states that "we do not discriminate in admissions . . . against any individual on account of that individual's . . . disability."

Lawyers Without Borders (LWOB)

750 Main Street, Suite 1500
Hartford, CT 06103
(860) 541-2288; Fax: (860) 525-0287
E-mail: info@lwob.org
Web site: www.lawyerswithoutborders.org or www.lwob.org

Project Type: Education; Human Rights; Legal; Orphans;
Professional Technical Assistance; Social Justice; Women's
Issues

Mission Statement Excerpt: "Lawyers Without Borders' mission is
to protect the integrity of the legal process, serve the underserved, build capacity in developing regions and regions
emerging from conflict, and promote the culture of pro bono
service in the legal profession, all with a neutral orientation."

Year Founded: 2000

Number of Volunteers Last Year: 60

Funding Sources: Governmental and foundation sources, as well
as individual donors

The Work They Do: LWOB volunteers, who must be lawyers,
engage in the training of other lawyers and judges in trial
advocacy, anticorruption, trial observation, gender issues as
they pertain to the law, fact gathering, data collection, and
observations. LWOB volunteers attend trials, make in-
country arrangements for seminars and training sessions,
interview trainees, observe trainees and trials, collect data
for indicator projects and reports, conduct legally oriented
community outreach, and develop, circulate, and distribute
community focused legal informational materials.

Project Location: LWOB primarily operates in regions in Africa,
including Ethiopia, Liberia, Kenya, Sierra Leone, Namibia,
Nigeria, Rwanda, and Mozambique. Given this broad range
of locations in Africa, work sites and accommodations are
diverse. LWOB volunteers mostly make their own arrangements for accommodations, but, when possible, LWOB
helps volunteers make contact with past volunteers who
worked in that region.

Time Line: LWOB offers flexible volunteer dates throughout the year, but volunteers should be prepared to commit a minimum of two to three weeks, preferably one month or longer. In the past, LWOB has offered opportunities as short as one week and as long as one year.

Cost: LWOB volunteers pay a $75 processing fee after they have been screened and accepted as volunteers. All other expenses, including travel, room and board, and visas are the responsibility of the individual volunteer.

Getting Started: Prospective volunteers may either apply in response to a specific opportunity posted on the LWOB Web site or may indicate their general interest in future volunteer opportunities; in either case, volunteers should send their resume or CV and a cover letter to LWOB. A telephone interview is required before being accepted as an LWOB volunteer. There are not formal orientations or trainings provided to volunteers, but lawyers participating in advocacy training are themselves able to attend trial advocacy training. Volunteers who will be observing trials do have a detailed phone orientation before departure, and all volunteers are provided with an instructional guide.

Needed Skills and Specific Populations: All LWOB volunteers must be lawyers; some projects may have additional requirements in terms of expertise or experience. There is no maximum age for volunteers, and senior volunteers are "treasured and welcomed." Volunteers with disabilities may be able to volunteer with LWOB, depending on the region, the level of conflict, and the facilities in-country. LWOB, in general, cannot host families, unless all members are lawyers. All LWOB volunteers must abide by a neutrality mandate, leaving their politics, agendas, and leanings at home. All are required to sign confidentiality agreements, are generally not allowed to interact with the press, and, due to the sometimes volatile regions involved, there are several hold harmless commitments and releases that prospective volunteers must sign.

Madre

121 West 27th Street, #301
New York, NY 10001
(212) 627-0444; Fax: (212) 675-3704
E-mail: volunteers@madre.org
Web site: www.madre.org

Project Type: Agriculture; Community Development; Economic Development; Education; Human Rights; Medical/Health; Professional/Technical Assistance; Social Justice; Women's Issues

Mission Statement Excerpt: "Madre provides essential support to our partner organizations through our volunteer program, Sisters Without Borders. When requested by our partners, Madre arranges for culturally competent, skilled professionals to work with women and children and to provide assistance to staff and community leaders."

Year Founded: 1983

Number of Volunteers Last Year: 7

Funding Sources: Madre receives support from individual donors, foundations, community organizations, and religious communities.

The Work They Do: Madre addresses many issues of global importance and provides resources and training to sister organizations around the world to help them meet immediate needs in their communities and develop long-term solutions to the crises they face. Examples of Madre volunteer projects include sending volunteer health care professionals to work with the communities of their sister organizations to deliver urgently needed medicines and medical supplies to combat AIDS, breast cancer, pediatric diseases, and other threats to people's health in Latin America and the Caribbean; facilitating trainings and popular education workshops on women's human rights, labor rights, the rights of indigenous people, and sexual and reproductive rights; trauma counseling; agriculture, including organic farming; and budget management and planning.

Project Location: Madre volunteers work in Guatemala, Mexico, Nicaragua, Peru, Kenya, and Palestine. Volunteers sometimes work in rural, underserved communities that lack critical resources such as potable water and electricity. Volunteers usually stay in nearby hotels or hostels or with local families, depending on each volunteer's preference.

Time Line: Volunteers must be able to commit to a minimum of two months; there is no maximum length of time for volunteer projects. Under certain circumstances, volunteer opportunities with a time commitment of one month or less may be arranged for advanced professionals such as physicians and nurses who have necessary language skills and experience working abroad.

Cost: Madre does not charge a program fee, but volunteers are responsible for all of their own costs. Madre will help arrange room and board for volunteers. Depending on the country and placement, volunteer expenses range from approximately $400 to $900 per month, with an average being around $500 to $600 per month; this monthly cost does not include the cost of international airfare.

Getting Started: Prospective volunteers should send a cover letter and resume that states their country or program of interest, relevant skills, background, and level of fluency in appropriate languages for the country of service. Madre's orientations are personalized for each volunteer and generally consist of at least two in-person meetings and background materials on the project and the community in which the volunteer will be working.

Needed Skills and Specific Populations: Volunteers must have experience and professional skills or credentials to work with Madre. Volunteers must be at least eighteen years old, and senior volunteers are welcomed. Volunteers with disabilities are welcome to join a Madre project, depending on the project location and each volunteer's specific disability. Madre does not have specific policies regarding families who wish to volunteer together, but notes that young children's needs may be difficult to accommodate.

Medex International (MEI)

1235 North Decatur Road
Atlanta, GA 30306
(404) 815-7044; Fax: (404) 892-6672
E-mail: info@medexinternational.org
Web site: www.medexinternational.org

Project Type: Medical/Health

Mission Statement Excerpt: "Medex International . . . provides
  health care to some of the world's most underserved people
  and animals. We travel to remote regions of the world and
  bring medical care to people in developing countries as well
  as rural areas of more advanced nations."

Year Founded: 2004

Number of Volunteers Last Year: 63

Funding Sources: Donations from private sources

The Work They Do: MEI provides medical and dental care to
  individuals and families. The organization also trains local
  health care providers, vaccinates and neuters dogs and farm
  animals, and treats acute illnesses in all animals. This care is
  provided by physicians, physician assistants, nurse practi-
  tioners, nurses, physical therapists, dentists, veterinarians,
  and other medical professionals. Nonmedical support volunteers may work in triage or in the pharmacy, do very basic
  lab work, or help with crowd control.

Project Location: MEI works in India and Ecuador. Work sites
  range from thatched roof huts in Ecuador to a newly built
  medical clinic at a Tibetan settlement in India. Volunteers
  often, but not always, work in facilities with no electricity
  or climate control. Living conditions vary, and accommodations might be in an ecolodge, a church, a monastery, or a
  very basic hotel. During any tourism parts of a trip, volunteers stay in first-class hotels.

Time Line: MEI offers one-week trips to Latin America and
  two-week trips to Asia throughout the year.

Cost: The program fee runs from $1,500 to $1,945, which
  includes lodging, most meals, all in-country transportation,

medical supplies, guides, interpreters, and a few days of sightseeing. The program fee does not include international airfare.

Getting Started: Prospective volunteers should fill out the application form found on MEI's Web site. Interviews are not required. Informational materials are sent to volunteers before their departure, and orientation is held the night before medical work begins.

Needed Skills and Specific Populations: Although several nonmedical support volunteers are taken on each trip, volunteers with any medical or veterinarian skills are most needed. Licensed medical professionals are requested to submit copies of their valid medical licenses. Volunteers must be at least ten years old. Senior volunteers are welcomed, but they must be in good shape, as the trips tend to be somewhat physically challenging. Most of MEI's medical sites are in rural areas of developing countries that do not meet U.S. standards for accommodating physical disabilities; availability of work for volunteers with disabilities depends upon the disability of the potential volunteer. Citizens from other countries are welcome to volunteer with MEI. Families are welcome, provided that MEI has space for nonmedical family members, and that all children are over the age of ten.

Medical Ministry International (MMI)

P.O. Box 1339
Allen, TX 75013
United States: (972) 727-5864; Fax: (972) 727-7810
Canada: (905) 524-3544; Fax: (905) 664-8386
E-mail: mmitx@mmint.org
Web site: www.mmint.org

Project Type: Medical/Health
Mission Statement Excerpt: "Medical Ministry International is an opportunity to serve Jesus Christ by providing spiritual and physical health care in this world of need."
Year Founded: 1968 as Medical Group Missions; became Medical Ministry International (MMI) in 1995
Number of Volunteers Last Year: 1,600
Funding Sources: Private sources and some faith-based organizations
The Work They Do: MMI sends volunteer teams of health care professionals to serve the world's poor who have little or no access to medical care. The health care MMI offers is usually all that is available to the recipients. Both medical and nonmedical volunteers are accepted, including dentists, primary care and specialty physicians, surgeons, optometrists, nurses, health educators, other health professionals, translators, technicians, handy people, and general helpers. To provide the very best possible care for patients, only qualified professionals participate directly in surgical or dental procedures. Medical and project directors assign each participant a role, matching his or her skills and training to the needs of the project. Days are full, and volunteers work hard as a team to see as many patients as possible during the week.
Project Location: The organization works regularly in over thirty countries around the world. Work sites vary; some involve a short-term clinic set up in a school or community center for the duration of a project. Others involve a clinic that is moved by volunteers to different areas every few

days. Teams may also work at an existing hospital. Accommodations are usually in a hostel, dorm, or small hotel, all of which have bathroom facilities. MMI usually uses its own cooks to ensure that volunteers and staff members receive healthful food and water.

Time Line: One- and two-week projects are scheduled year-round, though most are for two weeks. It may be possible to stay longer than two weeks, but volunteers will need to work this out with the hosts on location. Some MMI volunteers add tourist travel to the end of their stay.

Cost: The program fee is $775 for a one-week project and $1,075 for a two-week project. All room and board costs are included in the program fee; volunteers must provide their own airfare to the country of service. Each project has a project director and a medical director who will work with volunteers to coordinate all needed medicines and supplies. More than 90 percent of the program fee goes directly into program services.

Getting Started: Prospective volunteers can apply online, download an application online, or request an application from the address listed. MMI provides preparatory materials that outline how to plan for the trip and what to expect. Team orientation occurs on the first day in the host country.

Needed Skills and Specific Populations: Doctors, dentists, and surgeons must be currently licensed to practice. Volunteers aged twelve to fourteen must be accompanied by a parent; youths fifteen to seventeen years old must be accompanied by a designated adult and need a notarized letter signed by both parents (or legal guardians) authorizing them to make the trip; volunteers under eighteen years of age will not be allowed in operating rooms. People aged eighteen and over are welcome to volunteer as adults. Families with children who meet the minimum age requirements listed are welcomed, as are senior volunteers; spouses may accompany medical volunteers. Volunteers with disabilities are welcomed provided they are able to travel in places that are not handicap-accessible; please contact MMI before applying.

We Keep Coming Back

By George Deering, M.D.

Medical Ministry International

Attending doctor on an October 2007 medical project
serving patients in the Galapagos, Ecuador.

She was very old and appeared very weak and tired. Her family crowded around the bed as I introduced myself and began to examine her. It was our first "working" day in Playas and somewhere in that hectic day of trying to turn from a group of friendly strangers into a medical team, I was asked if I would make a house call that evening. I said I would. I knew she was an elderly lady too weak to come to the clinic. We piled into the pickup and drove down dirt streets. When we got out of the truck we walked down a short, narrow alley, up a staircase, and into a living room where I was greeted by a family and my patient. She had a heart condition, and I was told that her meds had been changed a few weeks before, but she had been failing for several days—"A little cough, poor appetite, no energy."

She needed help to sit up—the most significant thing in her exam was her blood pressure: 80/50. I reviewed her meds and discovered that twice a day she was being given Lasix, a powerful drug that was lowering her pressure. I took her off the Lasix, advised fluids, then prayed with her and her family. I returned two days later and she was a new woman. She sat up, greeted me, kissed my cheek, and held my hand. I checked her pressure and it was 140/80.

You might wonder why MMIers "keep coming back"—I know why.

Mercy Ships

P.O. Box 2020
Garden Valley, TX 75771
(903) 939-7000
E-mail: jobs@mercyships.org
Web site: www.mercyships.org

Project Type: Administrative; Agriculture; Community Development; Construction; Education; Medical/Health

Mission Statement Excerpt: "Mercy Ships, a global charity, has operated a growing fleet of ships in developing nations since 1978. Following the example of Jesus, Mercy Ships brings hope and healing to the poor, mobilizing people and resources worldwide."

Year Founded: 1978

Number of Volunteers Last Year: Approximately 1,600

Funding Sources: Government, faith-based, and private sources

The Work They Do: Mercy Ships provides medical care, relief aid, and training for long-term sustainable change in developing nations. A global charity that serves people of all faiths, Mercy Ships is best known for its work in health care services, which are provided to patients free of charge. Their newest vessel, the *Africa Mercy,* includes six state-of-the-art operating rooms and intensive care and ward bed space for up to seventy-eight patients. On shore, mobile medical and dental teams establish field clinics in nearby communities to offer vaccination programs, dental care, and minor operations. Mercy Ships supports the training of national doctors and nurses in the countries it serves, and it provides local people with education in hygiene, nutrition, and basic health care. Mercy Ships teams also help to construct hospitals, clinics, schools, vocational training facilities, homes, and churches; they carry out agricultural projects, teaching communities how to become more productive and efficient in growing food for themselves and for the marketplace; and they test local water sources and train village representatives in how to break the waterborne disease cycle. The

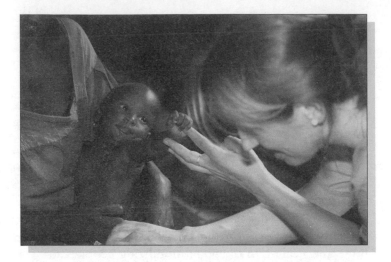

A Mercy Ships volunteer nurse takes a moment to play with a baby in Benin, West Africa, during a medical screening. Mercy Ships programs promote health and well-being by serving the urgent surgical needs of the forgotten poor and empowering developing communities. Volunteers also perform free eye, orthopedic, or maxillofacial surgeries aboard the hospital ship, or work in one of many community development projects including construction, agriculture, community health education, water and sanitation projects, and others. *Photo courtesy of Mercy Ships*

teams assist with individual and community latrine construction, and they drill and rehabilitate wells to provide safe water for consumption and irrigation.

Project Location: Most projects are located in West Africa with some in Central America or the Caribbean. Most volunteers are fed and housed on a Mercy Ships vessel.

Time Line: Available positions are listed on the Mercy Ships Web site. Volunteers commit to at least two weeks of service, which they can extend for as long as they like, even to the extent of making a career of being part of the Mercy Ships' crew. Volunteers are considered short-term if they work for two weeks to two years.

Cost: Volunteers on Mercy Ships pay an onboard living fee of $150 per week, which includes all meals and accommodations, and are responsible for paying for their own international travel expenses.

Getting Started: Prospective volunteers can download an application from the Mercy Ships Web site. Training is required for anyone wanting to serve for nine months or more and is offered at Mercy Ships' office in Texas. Volunteers who plan to serve for two years or more must attend a weeklong "Introduction to Mercy Ships," which includes an interview process.

Needed Skills and Specific Populations: Mercy Ships offers both skilled and unskilled volunteer opportunities. Medical volunteers must be experienced, fully licensed, and certified. Volunteers must be at least eighteen years old; there is no maximum age limit as long as the volunteer is healthy. Due to the limited confines of the Mercy Ships vessels, the organization generally cannot accommodate people with disabilities or families with children.

Mobility International USA (MIUSA)

P.O. Box 10767
Eugene, OR 97440
(541) 343-1284 (TTY); Fax: (541) 343-6812
E-mail: exchange@miusa.org
Web site: www.miusa.org

Project Type: Community Development; Developmental Disabilities; Human Rights; Social Justice; Women's Issues; Youth

Mission Statement Excerpt: "Empowering people with disabilities around the world, through international exchange and international development, to achieve their human rights."

Year Founded: 1981

Number of Volunteers Last Year: Approximately 50

Funding Sources: Some funding from private foundations

The Work They Do: MIUSA organizes international exchange programs for people with and without disabilities that feature volunteer work as a key component. International exchange trip activities include living with homestay families, leadership seminars, disability rights workshops, cross-cultural learning, and team-building activities such as river rafting and challenge courses. Participants develop strategies for making changes both within themselves and in their communities. MIUSA programs provide a cross-disability, cross-cultural leadership experience for participants interested in leadership and disability rights. Past volunteer projects have included working at the Tokyo Wild Bird Park and visiting schools for deaf and blind children.

Project Location: International exchange programs are held throughout the year in the United States and abroad. Past exchange locations include Azerbaijan, Russia, Japan, England, Costa Rica, Mexico, Germany, Uzbekistan, Australia, and China. Volunteers usually stay in homestays, hotels, or camp.

Time Line: MIUSA usually offers two to four exchange programs during each calendar year. Each program typically lasts two to four weeks.

Cost: Program fees vary, and most are subsidized by grants or other funding. An example of a program fee is $850 for a two-week exchange to Japan, which includes round-trip international airfare from San Jose, California, to Tokyo, Japan, accessible lodging, meals, and activities. MIUSA also offers generous partial scholarships to qualified applicants. Prospective volunteers must send in a $15 nonrefundable fee at the time of application.

Getting Started: Prospective applicants can download a four-page application from MIUSA's Web site, which may then be submitted by e-mail or postal mail. Applications also require letters of recommendation. All application materials are available in alternative formats upon request, including large print, Braille, and on diskette. Application deadlines are typically three to four months before the departure date, but late applications will be considered as space permits. Qualified applicants will be interviewed by telephone, TTY, or online via Instant Messenger. Accepted applicants will receive an orientation packet and will be put in contact with an alumnus of a similar MIUSA program in order to communicate about airline travel, accessibility, packing tips, health and safety, and any other questions or concerns the volunteer may have.

Needed Skills and Specific Populations: MIUSA requires only that volunteers show great enthusiasm for their project; there are no minimum or maximum age limits. Many families have volunteered in the past through MIUSA.

MondoChallenge

Malsor House, Gayton Road, Milton Malsor
Northampton, NN7 3AB
United Kingdom
+44 (0) 1604 858 225; Fax: +44 (0) 1604 859 323
E-mail: info@mondochallenge.org
Web site: www.mondochallenge.org

Project Type: Administrative; Community Development;
Economic Development; Education; Orphans; Rural Development; Women's Issues
Mission Statement Excerpt: "We aim to help local people by
providing education as well as business development opportunities, and so keep rural communities together and reduce
urban migration."
Year Founded: 2001
Number of Volunteers Last Year: 200
Funding Sources: None outside of program fees
The Work They Do: MondoChallenge supports vulnerable rural
communities through the generation of education and livelihood opportunities. Many volunteers help with English
teaching in schools and education centers for children and
adults of all ages. They are also encouraged to initiate
sports, music, art, drama, and agricultural activities for the
benefit of the wider community. Other volunteers work on
business development projects, such as small grants projects
that aim to provide widows living with HIV the means and
training to set up sustainable small businesses, enabling
them to support their families. Other projects include
ecotourism and care work in orphanages or children's
homes.
Project Location: MondoChallenge volunteers work in Ecuador,
Chile, Tanzania, Gambia, Senegal, India, Sri Lanka, Nepal,
and Romania. All projects are community based, and volunteers live in homestays arranged by MondoChallenge, generally in fairly basic, local conditions.

A MondoChallenge volunteer takes a moment to pose for the camera with several students from the Shree Swait Ganesh Primary School located in Chaukot (eastern Nepal) where she taught both English and helped with extracurricular activities. Yes, those are the Himalayas behind her. *Photo courtesy of MondoChallenge*

Time Line: MondoChallenge's projects are ongoing, and they are flexible on volunteer arrival and departure dates. Volunteers commit to a minimum of one month of service, with no maximum, though the average volunteer stays about three months.

Cost: MondoChallenge's program fees begin at $1,300 and increase gradually for each subsequent month. The program fee does not include international airfare or insurance, which is required of volunteers, nor does it incude room and board, which usually costs about $20 per week.

Getting Started: Prospective volunteers should e-mail MondoChallenge at the e-mail address listed; there are no deadlines for applications, though an interview is required, either in-person or by phone. Volunteers receive a one- or two-day training upon arrival in-country, which covers cultural issues and how to best contribute to the project.

MondoChallenge also offers English-teaching workshops on the weekend in the UK.

Needed Skills and Specific Populations: Volunteers do not need to have prior teaching experience, but business volunteers do need to have several years experience in a related area, such as marketing or finance. The minimum age for volunteers is eighteen, with the exception of Tanzania, where it is twenty-two. There is no maximum age, and MondoChallenge encourages senior volunteers. MondoChallenge will work to accommodate volunteers with disabilities, though this may be challenging in some rural areas. While children cannot volunteer with MondoChallenge, they may accompany their parents and are not required to pay the program fee. Families may be eligible for a 15 percent discount, and MondoChallenge will place them in appropriate accommodations and help make arrangements for children to attend classes at a nearby school.

Changing Lives: Teaching in a Sri Lankan Buddhist Temple

By Alice Eastaugh

MondoChallenge

Alice Eastaugh (aged forty-nine) volunteered for two months (Feb–March 2007) in Pilimathalawa, a small village near Kandy in Sri Lanka.

After eighteen years of language teaching in a small school in England, bringing up three daughters, and supporting an over-worked doctor husband, I began to wonder where "I" had got to in all of that. I went about my work and tasks, outwardly cheerful, but sometimes wondering what it was all about and where my enthusiasm for life had got to. I loved my students, and seeking to inspire them to learn, but often felt I was just leading them through hoops, and at times questioned the validity of teaching languages when the real need was to help the children make sense of an often rather senseless world.

When I realized that all three of my daughters were about to leave either home or the UK at the same time, I decided something had to be done to prevent me becoming a "has-been" mother with little else to look forward to except more time on my hands. So I took a leaf out of my daughters' books and started to plan an adventure. Their gap years had been action packed and full of new places. My intention was to do something rather different: to go to live in and learn from another culture, shake up my middle-class comfort zones a bit, and volunteer somewhere I could be a help. My research ideas evolved from volunteering in the Amazonian rainforest, in areas of conservation that I knew nothing about, to being a modern-day Florence Nightingale, a health worker in an AIDS epidemic or malaria-ridden swamps—to finally a more realistic proposition: teaching English in a Buddhist community in Sri Lanka. I decided to volunteer with MondoChallenge. I learnt a lot about myself and my capabilities even in the process of signing up for this volunteer teaching. My courage ran the gauntlet from feeling I could and would take on anything that was thrown at me, to needing considerable reassurance when heading off on a plane for a strange destination, with strange food and bugs, a language I didn't speak, and a host family I had not met.

This feeling of smallness, lack of control, and anxiety was to be a key reminder of how a pupil can feel at the beginning of a new course with a teacher they don't know, and I think it was a useful shake-up at this turning point for me. Of course when I arrived at Pilimathalawa, a little village just a few miles down the potholed road from the old capital of Kandy, the sense of wonder at the strangeness of it all, the myriad of sights and colors and the smells assailing me became the prevalent emotion, so much so that I forgot all sense of fear and anxiety and relaxed into the, "Well, I'm here now, no turning back, let me make of it what I can," sort of attitude.

A couple of days later it seemed the most natural thing in the world to be standing at an old-fashioned blackboard in front of a motley selection of monks, clad in orange robes and wearing broad and shy grins. It took patience and perseverance to get started with the range of classes, beginning with the Montessori preschool, through to primary school children, classes of monks, and an after-school class for young lay adults. Trying to inculcate a sense of timing where clocks were never seen, breaking through a wall of stiffness and shyness, and the fact that the toilet and the cupboard for books were kept permanently locked and the key was rarely to be found in the same place twice, provided just some of the challenges to be overcome. It certainly made a change from issues back home: discipline and differentiation, homework and assessments, report writing and communicating with reluctant parents over awkward children. The main difference was that every pupil wanted to learn, and once I got them to forget some of their shyness with me and each other, every pupil wanted to practice their English. Seeing young children playing hopscotch outside while counting up to ten and arranging plastic animals alphabetically into their "zoo pens" gave me a ridiculous amount of joy. Having been quite unable at first to get the older boys and girls to talk to each other, let alone sit at the same bench, imagine my sense of jubilation when they were holding a full-scale debate after a month, debating the relative merits of different chosen countries.

But my biggest achievement was not in what I taught them but in what I learnt, and in the sense of overwhelming innocence and joy in their daily lives. My advanced group of monks told me with great eagerness and sincerity how wonderful it was to be a monk in Sri Lanka: how it gave you a sense of dignity and reverence, how people respected you and you respected yourself, and how you really took pride in trying to live a good life, and helping other people to understand how to do this too. I thought of the bands of disaffected youth in my own country, of the drug-taking, muggings, and murders, of the old people who are afraid to go out into the street, and I wished I could explain and share some of this pride at respectable living, some of the palpable family values that are held dear in this country and make a plea that we Westerners do not forget them in our strides for individuality and freedom. I reflected on relative ideas about rich and poor and realized how much more these referred to than just monetary value. Volunteering with MondoChallenge was an amazing experience, truly life changing for all parties.

National Trust Working Holidays

Heelis, Kemble Drive
Swindon, SN2 2NA
United Kingdom
+44 (0) 844 800 3099
E-mail: working.holidays@nationaltrust.org.uk
Web site: www.nationaltrust.org.uk

Project Type: Agriculture; Historic Preservation; Natural
  Conservation (Land)
Mission Statement Excerpt: "For ever, for every one."
Year Founded: 1895
Number of Volunteers Last Year: 39,000
Funding Sources: Individual donors
The Work They Do: The National Trust carries out conserva-
  tion projects in historic homes, gardens, and countrysides.
  Volunteers assist in this mission through practical conserva-
  tion tasks such as biodiversity surveys, helping with events,
  gardening, and educational activities.
Project Location: Volunteer projects take place throughout
  England, Wales, and Northern Ireland. Accommodations are
  provided, and include a large range of options depending on
  the project and location.
Time Line: Volunteer projects take place throughout the year
  for a minimum of three days and a maximum of eleven
  days.
Cost: Program fees start at £40 and go up to £350; all program
  fees include room and board. Volunteers are responsible for
  their own expenses en route to the project, including airfare
  to the UK.
Getting Started: Prospective volunteers can book a trip through
  the National Trust's Web site listed above; volunteers are
  not required to interview before beginning their booking.
  Each project begins with a health and safety talk that
  includes an orientation to the project and any tools to be
  used.

Needed Skills and Specific Populations: No specific skills are needed to volunteer with the National Trust. Volunteers must be at least eighteen years old, and there is no upper age limit. Volunteers with disabilities should discuss this with the National Trust's booking office, as not all accommodations are accessible, but some projects may be. The National Trust does offer specific family-friendly volunteer opportunities.

Naucrates

Colle Tenne
04010 Giulianello di Cori (LT)
Italy
+39 3334306643; Fax: +39 069665018
E-mail: naucrates12@tiscali.it
Web site: www.naucrates.org

Project Type: Community Development; Natural Conservation (Land); Natural Conservation (Sea)

Mission Statement Excerpt: "We work toward conservation of nature with particular interest in endangered species and habitats."

Year Founded: 2001

Number of Volunteers Last Year: 40

Funding Sources: Naucrates receives money from some private sources.

The Work They Do: Naucrates takes on conservation, education, and scientific research projects, specifically in the areas of sea turtle survival and the protection of mangrove forests and Mediterranean wood. Volunteers help by walking the beach looking for sea turtle nests, taking weather measurements, participating in fundraisers, educating local schoolchildren, and planting new trees to restore mangrove forests and Mediterranean woods.

Project Location: Naucrates's work is mainly conducted on an island off the coast of Thailand, based at Lion Village (Pak Choke). Lodging in the local village is in homestays. Each house has toilets and a shower, and laundry is done on request by local ladies. Tap water at the village is not potable, but bottled water is always available. Electricity is available only between 6:30 P.M. and 10:00 P.M. Food is cooked by a local woman, with a vegetarian option available on request. Naucrates is in the process of developing another project that will be based in Southern Italy and that will focus on community development and habitat restoration; see their Web site for details on this new project.

Time Line: The Thailand project runs between January and April; volunteers must commit to a minimum of two weeks. Most volunteers stay for one two-week period.

Cost: The program fee is €650 for two weeks, which covers three meals a day, accommodations, and training. Travel expenses and insurance are not included.

Getting Started: Prospective volunteers can download an application from the Naucrates Web site or contact the organization to request one. Training is provided on the first day, and workshops are held throughout the stay.

Needed Skills and Specific Populations: Volunteers must be fit and able to work in a group. The minimum age for volunteers is eighteen; seniors are welcomed provided they are in good physical health. Naucrates cannot host volunteers with disabilities.

New Era Galapagos Foundation (NEGF)

780 Shotwell Street
San Francisco, CA 94110
(415) 336-4091
E-mail: volunteer@neweragalapagos.org
Web site: www.negf.org

Project Type: Administrative; Community Development; Education; Natural Conservation (Land); Natural Conservation (Sea); Youth

Mission Statement Excerpt: "To conserve the Galapagos Islands by empowering local residents through educational programs and environmental action projects."

Year Founded: 2000

Funding Sources: Private donations

The Work They Do: NEGF programs consist of educational and environmental action projects, including foreign language training and art, administration/communications, and environmental education programs. All of these empower local residents with the skills and awareness needed for the long-term conservation of the Galapagos Islands, while simultaneously providing human and social development opportunities that enable the local population to benefit from conservation. Specific projects include running a summer camp for children and teens, teaching courses in English as a Foreign Language (EFL), camping with Boy Scouts and Girl Scouts, teaching teens gardening skills, and helping with coastal cleanups. Volunteers usually work twenty to twenty-five hours per week.

Project Location: All of NEGF's projects are located on San Cristobal Island, Galapagos, Ecuador. The building in which EFL and environmental education courses take place has electricity year-round and reliable air conditioning in the summer months of December through February. Volunteers can either stay with a local host family or live in a local hotel or apartment. Volunteers live in a friendly, low-key community, surrounded by wildlife, and should not expect much in the way of nightlife.

Time Line: Projects are available from February through December, though not all projects are available year-round. All outdoor volunteer opportunities are offered from May through December. All of the projects require a three-month commitment. Exceptions are rarely made and are based solely on resource needs. Most volunteers stay for three months, though exceptions to this can be made in February and March during the children's camp.

Cost: There is no program fee. Volunteers typically pay $350 to $450 per month to live in the Galapagos, depending on housing and food arrangements. Volunteers must cover all of their own costs, including airfare. NEGF provides all volunteers a waiver for the $100 Galapagos National Park entrance fee.

Getting Started: Prospective volunteers can either fill out the online application form at the Web site listed or send a resume with a cover letter that specifies area of interest, level of Spanish, and dates available for volunteer work to the e-mail address listed. This information should arrive at NEGF no less than two months prior to the start date of the project in which they are interested. Volunteers can decide on housing arrangements after they arrive. NEGF provides a general overview of its programs and basic introductions to the volunteer program. For the summer camp, volunteers arrive a minimum of one week in advance to design and prepare the various programs. All volunteers, regardless of the programs in which they are involved, are encouraged to arrive one week before their programs start.

Needed Skills and Specific Populations: Most volunteers have previous EFL teaching experience, though exceptions are made for fluent English speakers when resources are limited. Basic Spanish (at a minimum) is preferred, but is not required for the EFL program. Volunteers who teach environmental education typically also have a background in this area or in the natural sciences, as well as a moderate level of fluency in

Spanish. All other positions require some level of fluency in Spanish. NEGF requires all volunteers to be at least twenty-one years of age and to have a positive attitude with a good sense of humor. Senior volunteers and volunteers with disabilities are encouraged to participate in NEGF's programs, and it has hosted several volunteers from each of these populations.

Oceanic Society

Fort Mason Center, Building E
San Francisco, CA 94123
(800) 326-7491 or (415) 441-1106; Fax: (415) 474-3395
E-mail: info@oceanicsociety.org
Web site: www.oceanicsociety.org

Project Type: Education; Natural Conservation (Land); Natural
  Conservation (Sea); Scientific Research
Mission Statement Excerpt: "The mission of the Oceanic Society
  is to protect marine wildlife and oceanic biodiversity
  through an integrated program of scientific research, environmental education, volunteerism, and the establishment of
  nature reserves."
Year Founded: 1969
Number of Volunteers Last Year: 258
Funding Sources: Private sources, including individual donors
  and foundations
The Work They Do: The Oceanic Society's work is focused on
  conservation. It primarily conducts conservation research
  that includes geographic information systems to help establish nature reserves. For example, in Belize, research project
  results reported in a Biosphere Reserve proposal by the
  Oceanic Society will be used for an ecologically sustainable
  management plan. The society also provides training for
  Belizean students on its projects and works closely with local
  groups and agencies. In the past, volunteers have collected
  data on dolphins, manatees, crocodiles, sea birds, sea turtles,
  and coral reefs, and they have helped to map the distribu-
  tion of various species of wildlife. They have also mapped
  habitats and conducted transects to monitor reef health.
Project Location: Most of the Oceanic Society's volunteer projects are located in Belize, Suriname, Peru, Midway, Brazil,
  and Costa Rica. Volunteers work in remote areas. They
  should be prepared to face obstacles such as heat and
  insects. All volunteer accommodations include hot water
  and electricity, and they are usually double-occupancy

cabins. Food is primarily of the local cuisine and is prepared locally.

Time Line: Volunteer projects are available year-round for a minimum of seven days and a maximum of three weeks. On average, volunteers stay for eight days.

Cost: The average program fee is $1,975, which covers all costs except airfare to the host country, non-meal refreshments, and tips for local guides.

Getting Started: Prospective volunteers should carefully review the project descriptions on the organization's Web site, complete an application form (which is also available on the Web site), and submit it with a $400 deposit. Interviews are not required. The Oceanic Society provides all volunteers a detailed research plan listing goals, objectives, and methods. It also sends, in advance of a volunteer's departure date, an outline of specific volunteer tasks and sample data sheets. Tutorials are also sometimes provided on its Web site. Once on site, formal briefings and training are provided by the researcher prior to beginning the field work. Equipment trials are run before data is collected.

Needed Skills and Specific Populations: Some projects require snorkeling abilities before beginning the volunteer assignment. There are a variety of tasks associated with each project and the Oceanic Society matches each task to the volunteer's abilities and interests. Most projects have a minimum age of sixteen, though some require volunteers to be at least eighteen years old. Some, but not all, projects accept senior volunteers. Some projects are directed at families with a minimum age of ten. Volunteers with disabilities are welcomed as locations allow.

Operation Crossroads Africa (OCA)

P.O. Box 5570
New York, NY 10027
(212) 289-1949; Fax: (212) 289-2526
E-mail: oca@igc.org
Web site: www.operationcrossroadsafrica.org

Project Type: Agriculture; Community Development; Construction; Economic Development; Education; Medical/Health; Rural Development; Women's Issues

Mission Statement Excerpt: "Make a difference for others, see the difference in yourself."

Year Founded: 1957

Number of Volunteers Last Year: Approximately 250

Funding Sources: None; OCA is self-funded.

The Work They Do: Through OCA, groups of eight to ten volunteers of diverse backgrounds work together with local people on community-initiated projects. Projects tend to be physical in nature and fall into one of five categories: community construction and development (such as constructing youth training centers, health centers, and wells); health and medical outreach; agriculture and reforestation (such as clearing land, planting seeds, and digging ditches); education and training (in which volunteers might teach ESL, help with youth recreation events, or give computer lessons); and women's development (primarily income generation and microenterprise projects).

Project Location: As its name indicates, OCA works in Africa. Specific host countries change each year, but in past years OCA has operated projects in thirty-five African nations including Ethiopia, Ghana, Kenya, Gambia, Lesotho, Malawi, Namibia, South Africa, Tanzania, Uganda, Benin, Mali, Niger, Senegal, and Togo. Volunteers live communally, often in very basic conditions and almost always in rural areas.

Time Line: All of OCA's projects run during the summer. Volunteers spend six weeks working on a volunteer project, followed by one week of travel in the host country, during which local transportation is used.

Cost: OCA's program fee is $3,800. This program fee is remarkably inclusive, in that it takes care of the volunteer's international airfare and all in-country transportation, food, accommodations, visas, and international health insurance during both the volunteer experience and the week of travel afterward.

Getting Started: A program application is available on OCA's Web site; it includes requirements of a two-page autobiographical essay and responses to five questions. Applications are due in February, and no interview is required. OCA requires volunteers to complete three days of orientation and training before departure.

Needed Skills and Specific Populations: OCA volunteers must be at least eighteen years old. Except for those volunteers who wish to work in the areas of medicine and health, no special skills are required. Racial, gender, ethnic, regional, and educational diversity are primary goals of OCA, and groups are structured to be as inclusive as possible.

Orphanage Outreach

6611 West Robert E. Lee Street
Glendale, AZ 85308
(602) 375-2900; Fax: (602) 926-1439
E-mail: volunteer@orphanage-outreach.org
Web site: www.orphanage-outreach.org

Project Type: Agriculture; Community Development; Construction; Education; Medical/Health; Orphans; Youth
Mission Statement Excerpt: "Orphanage Outreach provides opportunities to orphaned, abandoned, and disadvantaged children."
Year Founded: 1995
Number of Volunteers Last Year: 1,000
Funding Sources: Foundations, individuals, and faith-based organizations
The Work They Do: Orphanage Outreach teaches in grade schools; manages an English institute for middle school students; conducts summer camps, health fairs, and clinics; and carries out construction projects. Volunteers can teach English, tutor children in an orphanage, be counselors and teachers in the summer camp, participate in rural health clinics and health fairs, assist in the orphanage's gardens, and help with construction projects.
Project Location: Orphanage Outreach works solely in the Dominican Republic, in a small village on the north coast called Monte Cristi, home to a national park. Volunteers stay in simple, comfortable summer camp style facilities at the orphanage, with bunk beds, showers, and buffet meals.
Time Line: Volunteer projects take place year-round. Volunteers commit to a minimum of one week. Most volunteers serve one or two weeks, but they can stay as long as two years.
Cost: Program fees are $800 for a week and $1,800 for a month; a long-term volunteer's program fee is $1,000 per month. Discounts are available for groups, early registration, and families. The program fee includes all

A volunteer splashes in the ocean with a girl from the local orphanage in Monte Cristi, Dominican Republic. The orphanage is located just a mile from the beach; beach trips with the volunteers are a popular summer activity.
Photo courtesy of Tom Eklund

accommodations and meals, in-country transportation, in-country staff, and insurance. Volunteers are responsible for their own travel expenses to and from the Dominican Republic.

Getting Started: Prospective volunteers should first complete an online form, available at Orphanage Outreach's Web site, and do so at least thirty days before they want to depart. Phone interviews are only required for those planning to volunteer for a month or longer. Volunteers receive an online orientation packet, and more training in the Dominican Republic.

Needed Skills and Specific Populations: No specific skills are needed, though volunteers should be enthusiastic, flexible, and creative. Families are encouraged to volunteer, though children under age eighteen must be accompanied by a parent or temporary legal guardian. Senior volunteers are welcomed, as are volunteers with disabilities; each volunteer should discuss any specific needs with Orphanage Outreach staff prior to registering.

Pacific Crest Trail Association (PCTA)

5325 Elkhorn Boulevard PMB 256
Sacramento, CA 95842
(916) 349-2109; Fax: (916) 349-1268
E-mail: info@pcta.org
Web site: www.pcta.org

Project Type: Trail Building/Maintenance

Mission Statement Excerpt: "The mission of the Pacific Crest Trail Association (PCTA) is to protect, preserve, and promote the Pacific Crest National Scenic Trail (PCT) so as to reflect its world-class significance for the enjoyment, education, and adventure of hikers and equestrians."

Year Founded: PCTA was founded in 1977, though precursors of the group date back to the 1930s.

Number of Volunteers Last Year: The number of volunteers is not available, but last year PCTA volunteers donated more than 57,000 hours of their time.

Funding Sources: PCTA receives funding from both private donations and the federal government.

The Work They Do: PCTA volunteers carry out a wide variety of trail maintenance, construction, and reconstruction projects including brushing, blowdown removal, tread rehab and construction, and the creation of rock and log structures.

Project Location: Volunteers work along the 2,650-mile Pacific Crest Trail, which runs through the coastal ranges of Washington, Oregon, and California all the way from Canada to the United States–Mexico border. Work sites range from low-lying deserts to temperate rainforests, and from wilderness backcountry sites to easily accessible locations. Arrangements are usually made for group meals and cooking. Lodging ranges from campgrounds to backcountry tent sites.

Time Line: Projects are available year-round, though not in all locations due to weather and elevations. Volunteer projects include one-day, weekend, and weeklong commitments.

Cost: There is no program fee to volunteer with PCTA. Some projects require a $25 deposit to hold a spot in a work crew, which is refunded upon arrival. Meals are sometimes provided. PCTA volunteers' major expense is their travel to the work site.

Getting Started: Prospective volunteers should start at PCTA's Web site; volunteers are accepted throughout the year, and interviews are not required. All crews receive a safety and training orientation before work begins and project-specific training on-site. No prior experience in trail work is needed.

Needed Skills and Specific Populations: Volunteers should be capable of traveling through and living in the backcountry. There is no minimum age to volunteer, but some tasks are limited to adults. Many of PCTA's most active volunteers are seniors. PCTA welcomes volunteers with disabilities as long as they can carry out the tasks safely.

Passport in Time (PIT)

P.O. Box 15728
Rio Rancho, NM 87174
(800) 281-9176; Fax: (505) 896-1136
E-mail: volunteer@passportintime.com
Web site: www.passportintime.com

Project Type: Archaeology; Historic Preservation; Museum;
   Natural Conservation (Land); Scientific Research
Mission Statement Excerpt: "The goal of Passport in Time (PIT)
   is to preserve the nation's past with the help of the public."
Year Founded: 1988
Number of Volunteers Last Year: 1,500
Funding Sources: The U.S. Forest Service, an agency within the
   U.S. Department of Agriculture, sponsors PIT.
The Work They Do: Passport in Time (PIT) is a volunteer
   archaeology and historic preservation program on public
   lands throughout the United States. PIT volunteers work
   with professional archaeologists and historians on such
   diverse activities as archaeological survey and excavation,
   rock art restoration, archival research, historic structure
   restoration, gathering oral histories, and analysis and cura-
   tion of artifacts. What sets PIT apart from other public
   archaeology programs is that volunteers are helping professional archaeologists and historians with the daily job of
   historic preservation on public lands.
Project Location: PIT projects take place on public lands across
   the United States. Some work sites are in towns or communities, but most are in woodland areas. Some projects
   provide group meals or a camp cook and ask volunteers to
   contribute to group meals. In most cases, volunteers camp
   out near the project areas. Facilities range from
   campgrounds to bunkhouses, guard stations, and primitive
   campsites. In addition, some projects are located close to
   towns, making it possible for volunteers to stay in hotels.
   Project leaders provide prospective volunteers with a
   complete list of facilities, food, and lodging options.

Time Line: Projects take place year-round. Projects vary in length, but most are five days long. Many offer the option of staying for two five-day sessions. A few projects have a minimum time commitment of one day, and a few have longer-term options that span months, but those are exceptions to these general guidelines.

Cost: There are no program fees to volunteer with PIT. Volunteers provide their own transportation to the projects and, usually, their own meals and lodging. Out-of-pocket expenses vary widely depending on the type and length of the project and whether volunteers are camping or staying in local hotels.

Getting Started: PIT's application form is available on their Web site. For regular program updates, interested volunteers can sign up for the e-Traveler newsletter by contacting the PIT Clearinghouse. PIT volunteers receive training on-site from professional archaeologists and historians during the projects.

Needed Skills and Specific Populations: Most projects do not require specific skills; those that do note this in their project descriptions. Volunteers must be at least eighteen to participate without an adult, but many PIT projects accept children who are accompanied by an adult. The program encourages participation by families, and it is pleased with the increasing number of grandparent-and-grandchild pairs who serve on PIT projects. Senior volunteers are "absolutely" encouraged to work with PIT. Many of PIT's projects are in locations that are fully accessible to volunteers with disabilities, and the toll-free number listed includes TTY. Volunteers with special needs are encouraged to contact PIT directly to see if the projects they are interested in can accommodate their needs. International volunteers can apply to work with PIT using a tourist visa.

Peace Villages Foundation

Centro Comunitario
Lomas de Piedra Canaima via Sampai, Santa Elena de Uairen
Codigo Postal 8032, La Gran Sabana, Estado Bolivar
Venezuela
+0058 414 8704895 or +0058 289 4160718
E-mail: mail@peacevillages.org
Web site: www.peacevillages.org

Project Type: Construction; Education; Human Rights; Natural
  Conservation (Land); Professional/Technical Assistance;
  Trail Building/Maintenance; Youth
Mission Statement Excerpt: "We promote a Culture of Peace
  through enriching cross-cultural exchange and voluntary
  community service. We offer voluntary community service
  as an effective means of intercultural education and a meaningful exchange between people of all ages, races, and
  nationalities. We share the values of peace, justice, and
  tolerance, fundamentally focusing on global cooperation
  and the preservation of indigenous cultures and traditions,
  and the empowerment of young people."
Year Founded: 2001
Funding Sources: None outside of program fees
The Work They Do: Peace Villages Foundation carries out
  several kinds of projects, including operation of a mobile
  school, teaching and tutoring, working with youth, conservation and environmental projects, carpentry, a community
  radio station, therapeutic horse riding, and nonprofit
  administration. Volunteers work a minimum of four hours a
  day, four days each week.
Project Location: Volunteers work in and around Santa Elena
  and remote villages in Venezuela. Volunteers live in Peace
  Villages' guesthouse, with a host family, or in independent
  accomodations.
Time Line: Volunteers are accepted year-round for a minimum
  of one week and a maximum of one year.

Cost: Program fees vary with the length of stay and level of accommodations, ranging from €580 for one week up to almost €2,100 for three months. The program fee covers transfers from the local bus station and accommodations with a host family, in an intentional community (where people live communally, often sharing living and cooking areas and taking group responsibility for tasks such as cooking and cleaning), or in a local hotel. Volunteers who choose one of the first two options have their meals provided as a part of the program fee. Volunteers must provide their own airfare to Venezuela. A 50 percent deposit is required to secure the volunteer placement.

Getting Started: Prospective volunteers can complete an application on the Peace Villages Foundation's Web site and should also send a resume and a digital photo. Volunteers should send their application at least three months in advance of their desired arrival date. Volunteers are provided a brief, general orientation upon arrival.

Needed Skills and Specific Populations: Peace Villages Foundation accepts volunteers of all ages; volunteers under age eighteen must have a written authorization from a parent or guardian. Volunteers with certain disabilities may apply, but they will not be able to stay in the village. The ability to speak Spanish is helpful but not essential. Volunteers should be independent, flexible, and willing to take initiative.

Peacework

209 Otey Street
Blacksburg, VA 24060
(800) 272-5519; Fax: (540) 953-0300
E-mail: mail@peacework.org
Web site: www.peacework.org

Project Type: Community Development; Economic
Development; Education; Orphans; Rural Development;
Women's Issues; Youth
Mission Statement Excerpt: "Peacework is dedicated to meeting
humanitarian needs, fostering volunteerism, promoting
global understanding, and expanding personal awareness of
the world's cultures and people."
Year Founded: 1989
Number of Volunteers Last Year: Approximately 1,000
Funding Sources: Private donors
The Work They Do: Peacework arranges and manages global
volunteer service projects in collaboration with indigenous
community development organizations and educational or
service-oriented sponsors around the world. Volunteer
assignments include construction projects, teaching,
tutoring, providing medical services, providing health education, and a variety of other humanitarian and community
development efforts. Almost all of Peacework's project
arrangements are tailored for groups of volunteers, such as
those from a university or a professional service organization. In some limited cases, projects can be arranged for
individual volunteers in special disciplines such as medicine
and health care.
Project Location: Volunteer projects are located in Russia,
Vietnam, Belize, Honduras, South Africa, Ghana, the
Dominican Republic, the People's Republic of China, the
Czech and Slovak Republics, Guatemala, Nepal, Mexico,
Tobago, Guyana, Bolivia, Ukraine, Cameroon, Gabon, and
Kenya. Work sites and accommodations vary depending on
the locations, but they are provided by the host community

and are consistent with their resources. Accommodations are comfortable, safe, and usually rudimentary.

Time Line: Volunteer projects can take place at any time of year. The minimum length of time for a project is five days; each project's length is mutually agreed upon by the volunteer and the host organization. Typical projects run one to three weeks.

Cost: In general, program fees run from $1,500 to $2,500. Each program fee covers all accommodations and meals, visa expenses, and in-country travel costs, but does not include airfare to the country of service.

Getting Started: Prospective volunteers should call or e-mail Peacework's office or complete the "Getting Started" form found on its Web site. Volunteers are provided a manual as well as an on-site orientation. More extensive training and orientation is provided as requested by volunteers.

Needed Skills and Specific Populations: In general, the minimum age to volunteer with Peacework is twenty-one, though there are exceptions. Volunteer groups, for example, can include supervised children and young adults who are under age twenty-one; family projects are available. Senior volunteers are welcomed. Peacework can make full accommodations for a volunteer or group of volunteers with disabilities, and it will make recommendations regarding specific project sites, managing travel, and other details to provide for adequate services and accessibility. In some instances, entire delegations of individuals with disabilities have worked on Peacework projects; in other instances, volunteer delegations have worked with agencies and institutions that serve people with disabilities.

Por un Mejor Hoy

12 Butlerville Road
Somers, NY 10589
(777) 176-7868 (in Mexico)
E-mail: info@hoycommunity.org
Web site: www.hoycommunity.org

Project Type: Community Development; Education; Natural
    Conservation (Land); Orphans; Youth
Mission Statement Excerpt: "Por un Mejor Hoy's mission is to
    create bridges between underserved communities and inter-
    national visitors, enabling both sides to together reach
    lasting positive development."
Year Founded: 2001
Number of Volunteers Last Year: 50
Funding Sources: Individual donors
The Work They Do: Hoy works on three principal projects: the
    first is an environmental cleanup and public education
    project, Casa Atzingo, that focuses on garbage removal
    from a polluted ravine. At the second, a temporary govern-
    ment lodging facility for teens in legal custody disputes with
    their families, volunteers organize games and sports, develop
    workshops, teach English, and participate in the youth's
    social activities. Third, Hoy offers volunteer opportunities at
    an orphanage for young girls, Niñas de Eugenia, where they
    play games, draw, teach English, help with homework, or
    participate in prescheduled activities. Typically, volunteers
    visit all three organizations on different days of the week.
    Hoy also occasionally organizes specially designed trips,
    focusing on, for example, traditional healing techniques or
    rural projects. Hoy focuses on the cultural interactions
    between volunteers and the people of the host country, with
    the goal of increasing awareness of daily life in Mexico.
Project Location: Hoy's work is carried out in Cuernavaca,
    Mexico, or in the nearby towns of Temixco and Tepoztlan,
    each of which are about an hour's drive away. Working on
    the ravine cleanup project can be dirty, and the walk into

and out of the ravine can be steep. Though dirty, the ravine is its own microclimate, giving volunteers the chance to see different insects. Volunteers usually stay at Hoy's hostel, Casa Hoy, where the accommodations are dormitory-style, with hot water, a kitchen, and Wi-Fi access.

Time Line: Hoy offers weeklong volunteer opportunities, beginning on predetermined Sundays throughout the year. Volunteers must stay a minimum of one week, and are encouraged to stay for two weeks. Groups that wish to volunteer with Hoy outside of the preset schedule should contact Hoy to see if this is possible to do.

Cost: Hoy's program fee is $300 per week, which includes accommodations, breakfasts, a cultural activity, and daily transportation. Volunteers are responsible for their round-trip airfare to Mexico City, airport transfers, and meals other than breakfast.

Getting Started: Prospective volunteers should e-mail Hoy at least six weeks before the desired volunteer week. Hoy does not require interviews. An hour-long orientation is given on the first day, which covers rules, expectations, a guide to Cuernavaca, recommendations for eating and socializing, and a plan for the week.

Needed Skills and Specific Populations: Hoy does not require any special skills other than an open mind, an interest in getting to know the host culture, and a willingness to try to communicate in Spanish; a basic knowledge of Spanish is recommended, but not required. Volunteers must be at least eighteen years old, and there is no maximum age, though some seniors may not want to participate in the garbage cleanup because of the physical demands of the work. Hoy is unable, at this time, to accommodate volunteers with disabilities.

Programa Restauración de Tortugas Marinas (PRETOMA)

Apdo. 1203-1100
Tibas, San Jose
Costa Rica
+506 2241-5227; Fax: +506 2236-6017
E-mail: playas@tortugamarina.org and
voluntarios@tortugamarina.org
Web site: www.tortugamarina.org

Project Type: Community Development; Natural Conservation (Land); Natural Conservation (Sea); Scientific Research; Youth

Mission Statement Excerpt: "PRETOMA's mission is to protect, conserve, and restore the populations of sea turtles that utilize the marine environment of Costa Rica by preserving the diverse habitats and international waters upon which they depend."

Year Founded: 1997

Number of Volunteers Last Year: 100

Funding Sources: PRETOMA is, for the most part, self-funded, but it receives occasional grants from private organizations such as the National Wildlife Federation, the New England Aquarium, and the People's Trust for Endangered Species.

The Work They Do: PRETOMA focuses its energies on a multi-faceted approach to protecting the sea turtles of Costa Rica. Among many other activities, it carries out protection projects for nests and hatchlings, tracks turtles, and has a public education campaign. Volunteers assist project coordinators with these sea turtle conservation activities by walking the beach on a nightly basis looking for nesting sea turtles. When found, turtles are measured, tagged, and checked for general health conditions. Nests are then taken, monitored, and protected in a local hatchery. Turtles lay their nests on the beach after dark, so most of the project work is done during three- to six-hour shifts at night. Participants will be required to walk for the majority of these shifts, with only brief breaks at the end of each sector or when a turtle is found. The turtle nesting season coincides with the rainy season, which means that project participants should be prepared to work in the rain, of which there is a lot. Hatchery duties include monitoring for hatching baby turtles and releasing them into the ocean as well as post-hatching nest excavations to determine hatching success rates. Volunteers may also have the opportunity to take part in public education programs or to teach English at a local school.

Project Location: Volunteers work in San Miguel and Punta Banco, two small, isolated coastal communities in Costa Rica. There is electricity, water, and a couple of small markets, but the lifestyle is very simple and basic. There are several options for lodging, including stays at the station house, homestays, or private house rentals.

Time Line: Volunteers are accepted between July 15 and December 20. They can stay as briefly as one week or as long as five months.

Cost: Program fees begin at $330 for one week, and climbs to $1,750 for eight weeks; each additional week is $210. The program fee covers room and board, but not international airfare.

Getting Started: Prospective volunteers should contact PRETOMA and request a volunteer information form. Upon arrival at the project site, volunteers are greeted and given a one-hour orientation, during which project details are discussed. They are also provided a project protocol manual upon arrival.

Needed Skills and Specific Populations: Volunteers should be in good enough physical shape to walk the beaches for long periods of time at night, and they should be comfortable living in a rustic environment. There is no minimum or maximum age for applicants. Volunteers with disabilities are welcomed as long as they can perform the job duties described herein. For enrolled students, academic credit may be available for this project.

Projects Abroad

347 West 36th Street, Suite 903
New York, NY 10018
(888) 839-3535; Fax: (212) 244-7236
E-mail: info@projects-abroad.org
Web site: www.projects-abroad.org

Project Type: Community Development; Education; Human
Rights; Medical/Health; Natural Conservation (Land);
Natural Conservation (Sea); Orphans

Mission Statement Excerpt: "Projects Abroad sends volunteers
to twenty-two different developing countries to do service
projects and internships"

Year Founded: 1992

Number of Volunteers Last Year: 3,500

Funding Sources: No outside funding sources

The Work They Do: As the lengthy list of project types
mentioned indicates, Projects Abroad offers a wide range of
volunteer and internship programs including teaching,
helping in a health clinic or a hospital (including opportunities for premed students), working in orphanages, assisting
print and television journalists, doing conservation work,
taking care of animals, doing archaeological work,
providing business expertise, and coaching sports.

Project Location: Volunteer placements are available in
Argentina, Bolivia, Brazil, Cambodia, China, Costa Rica,
Ethiopia, Ghana, India, Jamaica, Mexico, Moldova,
Mongolia, Morocco, Nepal, Peru, Romania, Senegal, South
Africa, Sri Lanka, Thailand, and Togo. In most cases, volun-
teers stay with host families and have their own rooms,
although sometimes the rooms are shared with another
volunteer. The host families also provide all meals.

Time Line: Volunteers are accepted throughout the year for two
weeks up to one year. The average volunteer works for two
to three months.

Cost: Program fees vary, but range from $1,895 to $5,995
depending on where and how long the volunteer program is.

The program fee covers accommodations, food, health and travel insurance, and the twenty-four-hour support of Projects Abroad's staff.

Getting Started: Prospective volunteers can apply online via Projects Abroad's Web site, over the phone, or by requesting a brochure and completing the application form contained therein. Volunteers are sent predeparture information about what to bring and how to prepare, and they are given a one-day, in-country orientation to the area of service and to the host culture.

A volunteer provides crucial one-on-one care to a baby in an adoption center in the town of Gandhigram, located in southern India. The volunteer functioned as a nurse's assistant. She would feed the babies, clean up after them, play with them, and give them attention that they otherwise would not have had. At any given time, there were ten to twenty babies and only two to three nurses, so there was a very real need for volunteers.
Photo courtesy of Michele Krech

Needed Skills and Specific Populations: Volunteers must be at least sixteen years old, and senior volunteers are welcomed. No specific skills are required, though volunteers must be self-dependent, mobile, and able to withstand significant levels of culture shock. Projects Abroad can reasonably make accommodations for volunteers with disabilities, giving the circumstances in each specific country. Families with young children are able to volunteer with some of Projects Abroad's programs.

The Talibés of Senegal

By Michele Krech

Projects Abroad

I am a Canadian university student in global development studies and decided to fulfill my program requirements for a work-study placement with Projects Abroad in St. Louis, Senegal. My project was Care and Community and I worked at a local *talibé* centre called And Taxawu Talibé (ATT). I chose this placement because it offered me the chance to a) travel to Africa, the continent on which most of my academic and personal interest is focused; b) work with children who, despite representing our future, are often a marginalized group; and c) work in a French-speaking country where I could improve my French language skills.

Talibé is defined as a student of the Qur'an who learns from a Marabout (a religious leader), therefore living away from their parents, in order to pursue an education in Islam. The *talibés* sleep at the *daara* (the religious school/Marabout's home), generally in not very good living conditions. *Talibés* spend a great deal of time begging on the streets or working the markets, and most of the money they make they take back to the Marabout. There are questions about how much time is spent learning the Qur'an versus begging and working—however, a spiritual/Islamic education is seen as a very valuable and honorable thing. Parents desire this education for their sons and continue to send them to become *talibés*, despite the conditions they must live and work in. In response to the rather harsh life of a *talibé*, there are centers which provide basic medical care, meals, showers, and occasionally housing for *talibés*. And Taxawu Talibe (ATT) was one such center.

Working at ATT, my schedule was different from some of the other placements in St. Louis, as it varied each day. Twice a week my days started very early, arriving at work around 7:30 A.M. to prepare breakfast for over two hundred *talibés* and other children from the neighborhood. Breakfast consisted of baguettes with chocolate spread and coffee with plenty of milk and sugar. We tried to keep things as organized as possible, but it was always pretty hectic serving such a large group of hungry kids. The same was true of dinner, which consisted of egg sandwiches and juice, which I served one evening a week.

Three times a week I was in charge of facilitating showers for about twenty *talibés*. This was actually my favorite task, as it gave me time to play and interact with the kids while they were waiting for their turn in the showers. It was this core group of boys that I got to know very well and with whom I formed important relationships.

In addition to helping provide meals, showers, and basic health and hygienic care at ATT, I was also able to go on a couple trips to the beach with the children. It was really exciting to see them out of the busy city setting, laughing and playing on the beach. There were plenty of organized games and songs, as well as a picnic for everyone at the end of the day. These trips really allowed me the opportunity to have fun and bond with the kids and are some of my favorite memories from my trip.

The main challenge during my placement was the language barrier, as most of the *talibés* do not speak French. In order to cope with this situation, I learned a few key phrases in Wolof from my supervisor and coworkers, such as, "What's your name," "Wash your hands," and, "Come shower." Even though we couldn't always understand one another, by the end of my placement I found myself communicating fairly well with the *talibé* children as we realized what one another usually wanted.

Other challenges included dealing with water cuts, late bread deliverers, and a bakers' strike, but these obstacles never stopped the staff at ATT from continuing to provide *talibés* with all the regular services. These minor setbacks only made my experience all the more interesting and educational, and they could never overshadow all the positive aspects of my placement.

One thing that always made me happy during my time in St. Louis was when a *talibé* from ATT would recognize me on the street, at the market, or at a soccer game and come up to me just to say hello, shake my hand, or walk with me for a while. It was very rewarding to get to know and develop relationships with these amazing children.

My last day of work at ATT was bittersweet to say the least. I had a wonderful time with the *talibés,* as we had reached a point where we got along quite well, but I was very sad to leave. My supervisor explained to the kids that I was leaving and they all gave me high fives, handshakes, and hugs, saying, "Merci!" before I left. I certainly miss the energy and tenderness that these boys possessed and often find myself thinking about what they might be up to these days.

My placement at ATT, and my time in St. Louis in general, was certainly an educational experience. I learned a lot about the tradition of *talibés* and Marabouts that I knew nothing about prior to my trip, I learned a bit of a new language and improved on another, and I experienced many aspects of a new and different culture. I can't say enough about how amazing my experience in Senegal was and I'm looking forward to going back to visit soon.

ProWorld Service Corps (PWSC)

P.O. Box 21121
Billings, MT 59104
(877) 429-6753 or (406) 245-7348
Fax: (406) 252-3973
E-mail: info@myproworld.org
Web site: www.myproworld.org

Project Type: Administrative; Construction; Education; Human
Rights; Medical/Health; Natural Conservation (Land);
Women's Issues; Youth

Mission Statement Excerpt: "The mission of the ProWorld
Service Corps is to empower communities, promote social
and economic development, conserve the environment, and
cultivate educated compassionate global citizens."

Year Founded: 1998

The Work They Do: PWSC offers internships with nonprofit
organizations that are tailored to the individual volunteer's
skills and goals for the experience. In general, volunteer
projects are available in the areas of health care, education,
the environment, microbusiness, appropriate technology,
women's rights, construction, journalism, and the fine arts.
Examples of specific projects include constructing schools,
installing drinking water systems, providing shelter and
counseling for victims of domestic violence, teaching small-
business management skills, and supporting the educational
initiatives of local schools.

Project Location: Volunteers work in Cusco and Sacred Valley
of Peru; in tropical rainforest and inland rural communities
of Belize; in Oaxaca, Mexico; in Mysore, India; and in
Chaing Mai, Thailand. There are also programs in Brazil
and Ghana. PWSC selects project and program locations
based on multiple factors including participant safety,
community need, community interest, and quality of participant experience.

Time Line: Volunteers are accepted throughout the year for internships that last two weeks to one year. Programs start the first Saturday of every month except December.

Cost: A two-week internship costs approximately $1,895, with a $385 program fee for each additional week. Room and board with a host family, health and travel insurance, project funding and support, domestic transportation, and cultural and adventure trips are included in the program fee. Volunteers in Peru and Mexico also receive intensive Spanish language classes. Volunteers must pay for their own international airfare, as well as for individual travel outside the program.

Getting Started: Prospective volunteers can complete an online application, which is available on the PWSC Web site. Volunteers whose applications are received at least three months prior to departure are given priority for project and location placement. The deadline for applications is one month prior to departure. Each volunteer must complete an interview as a part of his or her application.

Needed Skills and Specific Populations: Volunteers must be at least eighteen years old and be in good health.

Raleigh International

Third Floor
207 Waterloo Road
London, SE1 8XD
United Kingdom
+44 (0) 207 183 1270; Fax: +44 (0) 207 504 8094
E-mail: info@raleigh.org.uk or
volunteermangers@raleigh.org.uk
Web site: www.raleighinternational.org

Project Type: Community Development; Natural Conservation
(Land); Natural Conversation (Sea); Rural Development;
Scientific Research; Youth
Mission Statement Excerpt: "Raleigh International is an educational charity that provides adventurous and challenging
expeditions for people from all backgrounds, nationalities,
and ages, especially young people. Our volunteers develop
key skills, explore the world, and make a real difference to
local communities and their environment."
Year Founded: 1984
Number of Volunteers Last Year: Approximately 1,000
Funding Sources: Foundations, government sources, and individual donors
The Work They Do: Raleigh International runs adventure and
challenge expeditions. Volunteers between the ages of seventeen and twenty-four complete sustainable community and
environmental projects, plus have the opportunity to participate in an adventure challenge. Volunteers older than that
age range are able to lead and facilitate the expeditions,
fulfilling a range of roles. These volunteer managers fulfill
roles such as project manager, medic, finance manager,
administrator, communication manager, mountain leader,
team coach, photographer, interpreter, artist, logistics
manager, and driver.
Project Location: Raleigh International has projects in
Malaysia, India, Costa Rica, and Nicaragua. Their projects

are based within national parks and rural communities, which gives volunteers greater access to remote areas and the people who live there.

Time Line: Volunteer projects run for four to ten weeks throughout the year. Volunteer managers receive training in-country, so their commitment is an additional two to three weeks.

Cost: Raleigh International's program fees for volunteers between the ages of seventeen and twenty-four range from £1,500 to £2,995. Program fees for volunteer managers range from £1,350 to £1,950. The program fees include travel and medical insurance, food and accommodation, in-country travel, specialist equipment, training, and support. Program fees do not include flights, vaccinations, or any required visas.

Getting Started: Prospective volunteers can access an online application on Raleigh International's Web site. Volunteers ages seventeen to twenty-four do not need to complete an interview, but volunteer managers need to either attend an assessment weekend in the UK or complete a telephone interview.

Needed Skills and Specific Populations: Families may volunteer together as long as everyone is at least seventeen years old, but Raleigh International cannot guarantee that each family member will be placed on the same project once they arrive in-country.

Reef Check

P.O. Box 1057
17575 Pacific Coast Highway
Pacific Palisades, CA 90272
(310) 230-2371 or (310) 230-2360; Fax: (310) 230-2376
E-mail: rcinfo@reefcheck.org
Web site: www.reefcheck.org

Project Type: Natural Conservation (Sea); Scientific Research
Mission Statement Excerpt: "Reef Check's objectives are: to educate the public about the value of reef ecosystems and the current crisis affecting marine life; to create a global network of volunteer teams trained in Reef Check's scientific methods who regularly monitor and report on reef health; to facilitate collaboration that produces ecologically sound and economically sustainable solutions; and to stimulate local community action to protect remaining pristine reefs and rehabilitate damaged reefs worldwide."
Year Founded: 1997
Number of Volunteers Last Year: More than 1,000
Funding Sources: Both governmental and private sources
The Work They Do: Reef Check is the only volunteer-based organization that measures reef health using a standard method on a global scale. Its programs focus on building a global community of reef stakeholders and helping them at the grassroots level to improve reef health. Most volunteers participate in a reef monitoring survey, either by establishing their own Reef Check team or by joining an already established team.
Project Location: Reef Check has had teams in more than ninety countries and territories around the world, and there is potential for volunteers wherever there is a coral reef. Conditions vary depending on the location and the team's setup, but volunteers should expect that their work site will be the ocean, as most Reef Check volunteers spend their days diving and actively looking at reefs. Volunteers are responsible for their own accommodations; some teams may

be associated with a particular resort or hotel that can offer a discounted package.

Time Line: Volunteers can work with Reef Check throughout the year, depending on weather conditions. Volunteer assignments are usually for a minimum of one week, but they can vary depending on the monitoring period established by the team. The average volunteer stint with Reef Check is two weeks.

Cost: There is no program fee to volunteer with Reef Check, but there may be a small fee for training or other required classes. Volunteers, therefore, are responsible for all of their own costs. Average costs for a volunteer vacation with Reef Check vary depending on location, lodging, length of stay, and dive expenses. Reef Check offers memberships starting at $25 per year, but membership is not a prerequisite to volunteering. All costs are the responsibility of the volunteer unless otherwise arranged with their team.

Getting Started: Prospective volunteers should e-mail Reef Check at the address listed. Some teams require a phone interview in advance of the volunteer's service. Reef Check offers trainings that typically last three days and include both land-based and ocean components.

Needed Skills and Specific Populations: In order to work with Reef Check, volunteers should be certified scuba divers with excellent buoyancy control. Some surveys may be able to be done via snorkel. Additional skills may be required, depending on the team. As long as the diver demonstrates the needed skills and can understand the survey protocol, there are no age or ability limits on who can volunteer with Reef Check. Families are welcome to volunteer with Reef Check, but to participate in a reef survey all members must be experienced scuba divers.

Service Civil International—International Voluntary Service (SCI-IVS)

5505 Walnut Level Road
Crozet, VA 22932
(206) 350-6585
E-mail: sciivs.placement@gmail.com
Web site: www.sci-ivs.org

Project Type: Community Development; Construction; Developmental Disabilities; Historic Preservation; Human Rights; Orphans; Trail Building/Maintenance

Mission Statement Excerpt: "Peace through deeds, not words."

Year Founded: 1920

Number of Volunteers Last Year: 50 via the U.S. branch; over 5,000 total through international branches

Funding Sources: Individual donors

The Work They Do: SCI-IVS sponsors short-term international group work camps as well as longer-term individual volunteer opportunities. Broadly speaking, their placements fall into two categories: physical (building, planting, weeding, digging, painting, gardening, cleaning, constructing) and social (working with children, the elderly, or people with special needs; taking part in art or social projects). Specific examples of work done by SCI-IVS volunteers includes rebuilding homes in New Orleans, assisting alpine farmers in Austria, restoring beaches in southern Spain, maintenance of buildings at an Ukrainian orphanage, or helping on an organic tea farm in Japan. Long-term volunteers work in one of SCI-IVS's international offices, with a partner organization, or carry out specific tasks for local grassroots organizations.

Project Location: Through its partners around the globe, SCI-IVS sponsors hundreds of volunteer camp opportunities in over fifty countries worldwide, mostly in Europe, North America, and Asia. This broad range of locations means that there are also a broad range of work sites and volunteer accommodations, all of which are detailed on SCI-IVS's

Web site. Accommodations may be in tents, dormitories, or in a community center or hostel.

Time Line: Most of SCI-IVS's camps are in March through September, with some opportunities available during the winter months. Work camps typically run two to three weeks; long-term volunteer opportunities range from three to twelve months.

Cost: SCI-IVS has an application fee of $235 for international camps and $100 for domestic camps, which includes accommodations, meals, and some insurance coverage. Some projects, especially in economically developing countries, may ask for an additional accommodations fee upon arrival. Volunteers are also responsible for the cost of their round-trip travel to the project site. Long-term volunteers receive room and board, a small stipend, and basic insurance coverage.

Getting Started: Applications may be downloaded from the SCI-IVS Web site and submitted electronically or by mail. Interviews are conducted on an as-needed basis, especially with first-time volunteers who wish to participate in African or Asian work camps. SCI-IVS does not conduct a training or orientation, but does provide some written guidance to volunteers before departure. Long-term volunteers have a separate application process.

Needed Skills and Specific Populations: No specific skills are required, except for certain camps as noted on SCI-IVS's Web site. Volunteers must be at least sixteen years old to participate in U.S. work camps; eighteen for international opportunities in economically developed countries; and twenty-one for international work camps in economically developing countries. A few work camps have upper age limits but most do not; some are specifically designed and designated as "mixed age camps." Volunteers with disabilities are welcome, but should work with an SCI-IVS placement officer to find an accessible camp. Families are also welcome, and will find some camps that are specifically designed for family participation.

Sierra Club Outings

85 Second Street, 2nd Floor
San Francisco, CA 94105
(415) 977-5522; Fax: (415) 977-5795
E-mail: national.outings@sierraclub.org
Web site: www.sierraclub.org/outings/national

Project Type: Archaeology; Historic Preservation; Natural
  Conservation (Land); Natural Conservation (Sea); Scientific
  Research; Trail Building/Maintenance
Mission Statement Excerpt: "Explore, enjoy, and protect the
  planet."
Year Founded: The Sierra Club was founded in 1892, and the
  first Sierra Club Outings were undertaken in 1901.
Number of Volunteers Last Year: Approximately 1,000
Funding Sources: None; the Sierra Club Outings organization is
  run entirely on program fees, and it does not receive any
  funds from outside organizations or from the Sierra Club
  itself.
The Work They Do: Sierra Club Outings offers a range of
  volunteer activities focused on the outdoors and
  environmental work. Volunteer opportunities include but
  are not limited to archaeological digs, animal and habitat
  projects, trail work, and invasive plant removal. All service
  trips include at least one day with no activities scheduled to
  allow volunteers to explore the surrounding wilderness
  areas. The leaders of Sierra Club Outings projects are volunteers themselves who scout, propose, plan, and run all of
  the trips. Sierra Club Outings stresses the importance of
  building a strong community as a group, so volunteers may
  feel more of a bond with their fellow participants than
  volunteers do with other organizations.
Project Location: Outings are offered throughout the United
  States and in Puerto Rico, the Virgin Islands, and Canada.
  Work sites vary from national parks and wilderness areas to
  animal sanctuaries. Accommodations are provided, usually

either through camping or in a rustic lodge, though some trips stay in bed-and-breakfasts or cabins.

Time Line: Outings are offered almost every month of the year, and most last for one week.

Cost: In general, program fees are between $350 and $600, with a few both above and below this range. The program fee includes all room and board, work equipment, and group activities. Volunteers who are eighteen or older must be members of the Sierra Club. The program fees do not cover travel costs to the volunteer sites, and volunteers typically need to bring their own camping gear.

Getting Started: Information and application forms for prospective volunteers are available on the Web site listed. Volunteers register for a specific trip online or by calling the Sierra Club. After registration, they interview by phone with the trip leader, who determines whether or not they are approved for the trip, mostly based on whether or not the volunteer has the physical capacity to safely participate in the trip. Acceptance is not competitive, and the interview is not designed to weed out prospective volunteers. Training in specific tools and methodologies is provided on-site.

Needed Skills and Specific Populations: Most work sites are moderately strenuous, but there are trips that can be undertaken by anyone in decent physical shape. Usually the minimum age for volunteers is eighteen, but this can be waived if the project leader agrees and if the minor's parent or guardian also volunteers on the project. There are also a few trips designed specifically for families with children, such as a trail-building trip near Aspen, Colorado and a family archeology trip in Dixie National Forest. The largest demographic group for Sierra Club Outings is people aged forty to seventy years old, so senior volunteers are very much welcomed. Outings also offers special-interest service trips for multigenerational families, teens, seniors, and women. Specific work sites may be able to accommodate volunteers with disabilities, depending on what disabilities are involved.

Sioux YMCA

P.O. Box 218
1 YMCA Street
Dupree, SD 57623
(605) 365-5232; Fax: (605) 365-5230
E-mail: crandall@siouxymca.org
Web site: www.siouxymca.org

Project Type: Community Development; Youth
Mission Statement Excerpt: "Our mission is to develop and
strengthen the children and families in our Reservation
communities so they can fulfill their greatest individual and
collective potential, spiritually, mentally, and physically."
Year Founded: Founded in 1879, incorporated in 1972
Number of Volunteers Last Year: 206
Funding Sources: Foundations, individual donors, and other
YMCAs
The Work They Do: The Sioux YMCA is a non-facility, multi-
program YMCA. Programs offered through the YMCA
focus on families and children, and they include an after-
school program, a game room, computer and Internet
access, special events, basketball and other sports and
fitness clinics, a teen leaders program, and summer community day camps. Most volunteer projects involve a specific
work project and youth activities. The majority of Sioux
YMCA's volunteers come in groups, but individual volunteers may also be accepted. Groups of more than twelve
people are not recommended.
Project Location: All volunteers work through the Sioux YMCA
in Dupree, South Dakota, serving communities on the
Cheyenne River Sioux Reservation. Temperatures on the
reservation vary throughout the year from 100° F to -50° F.
Individual volunteers are housed in a volunteer house or
community center; groups of volunteers are housed in a
YMCA building or in a community cernter.
Time Line: Volunteers are accepted year-round. All volunteers,
whether as part of a group or individually, must arrange the

details of their visits prior to arriving and are advised to begin this process well in advance; most groups begin the booking process one year prior to their arrival. Groups of volunteers come for one to two weeks on average. Individual volunteers should be willing to make a minimum commitment of two months or longer.

Cost: Groups of volunteers pay a program fee of $200 per group; individual volunteers do not pay a program fee unless there are additional housing costs. All travel and living expenses are the sole responsibility of the group or individual. The YMCA has limited sleeping space on cots in the building. There are cooking, shower, and toilet facilities in the public areas of the YMCA.

Getting Started: Groups of volunteers should phone or e-mail Sioux YMCA via the contact information listed. An online application is available for individual volunteers. Criminal, credit, and driving background checks are required of individuals. All groups and individuals must interview by phone with Sioux YMCA staff members before being accepted as volunteers; once accepted, drug testing is required of all volunteers. Orientation topics include Lakota culture, safety, YMCA programs, child abuse protection requirements, safe driving procedures, and other policies.

Needed Skills and Specific Populations: Volunteers must exhibit flexibility, a sense of humor, a positive attitude, and the ability to work in a remote location with limited services and extreme temperatures. The minimum age to volunteer with Sioux YMCA is sixteen, though they prefer that volunteers are over age twenty-one; there is no upper age limit for volunteers. Volunteers with disabilities are welcomed, and some of the buildings are wheelchair accessible. Volunteers must be U.S. citizens. All volunteers, regardless of age, are required to remain tobacco, alcohol, and drug free while at the Sioux YMCA. Women and men are expected to wear conservative, non-revealing clothing without advertising for beer, alcohol, drugs, tobacco, promotion of drinking or sexual activity, or other similar topics.

Students Partnership Worldwide (SPW)

1413 K Street NW, 5th Floor
Washington, DC 20005
(202) 289-0858
E-mail: info@spw-usa.org
Web site: www.spw-usa.org

Project Type: Community Development; Education; Human
Rights; Medical/Health; Natural Conservation (Land); Rural
Development; Youth

Mission Statement Excerpt: "Students Partnership Worldwide's
(SPW) mission is to mobilize young volunteers to empower
rural youth to take control over their own lives and shape
the future of their communities by delivering interactive,
youth-to-youth peer education programs."

Year Founded: 1985

Number of Volunteers Last Year: More than 1,000

Funding Sources: SPW receives some funding from international
governments, private foundations, and individuals.

The Work They Do: SPW is dedicated to making young people
central to the development process. Through SPW, young
American, European, and Australian volunteers live and
work alongside African and Asian volunteers who are
recruited by the host country. SPW's emphasis is on training
these volunteers (all aged eighteen to twenty-eight) to create
a sustainable framework for development that responds to
the needs of each community. SPW volunteers work in rural
communities, where volunteers coordinate with schools and
community leaders to identify and resolve key health or
environmental issues. Health volunteers accomplish this
goal through teaching health classes, providing skills
training, and organizing community health workshops.
Environmental volunteers introduce and encourage sustainable use of natural resources, waste management,
appropriate technologies, and income generation projects.

Project Location: Volunteers work in rural communities in
Nepal, India, Tanzania, Uganda, Zambia, and South Africa.

(SPW also administers programs in Sierra Leone and Zimbabwe, but these are run completely by national volunteers and do not accept international volunteer applications at this time.) Living conditions are very basic, as volunteers live in the same way that the community members do. Transport around the community is generally by foot. Most villages do not have running water or electricity. Volunteers live in a family's home or in pairs in one house in the village. Accommodations will be arranged in advance by SPW but will be at the discretion of the community, so volunteer lodging may be in a school, an empty house, or a local family's home. Volunteers purchase food from local shops and markets, and they are generally responsible for cooking themselves.

Time Line: Generally, volunteers to Africa depart in January, those in India depart in September, and Nepal volunteers leave in November. The shortest program is five months and the longest is twelve months, with the first month devoted to training. Holidays and time off varies by program, but volunteers can expect to have one or two days off each week (though they will generally stay in the village); long-term volunteers receive two to three weeks' midterm holiday.

Cost: SPW's program fee is $6,500, which covers a flight from the UK or United States to placement, comprehensive travel and health insurance, visas acquired by in-country staff, training, food, accommodations, in-country work-related travel expenses, and predeparture and in-country support. SPW books volunteers on twelve-month return flights, so many volunteers travel independently or in small groups after the program ends.

Getting Started: SPW's application process is selective and places in programs are limited. SPW recommends applying four to twelve months before departure to maximize choice of programs. Applications are accepted on a first-come, first-served basis. Prospective volunteers can download an information packet and an application form from the Web site, or they can contact the office to request that these materials be mailed. Applicants are interviewed by SPW, preferably in-person in Washington, D.C., though phone interviews can be arranged. All volunteers participate in a predeparture conference call, which generally lasts two-and-a-half hours and which provides an opportunity for volunteers to talk with returned volunteers and SPW staff. Once in-country, all volunteers will receive three to six weeks of training (depending on the length of the program), which will include program-specific information, training in non-formal education techniques and appropriate rural technologies, participatory rural appraisal skills, and information on language and health and safety.

Needed Skills and Specific Populations: SPW volunteers must have graduated from high school, and must be at least eighteen years old. The maximum age for volunteers is twenty-eight. People with disabilities should contact the SPW office to discuss their specific circumstances. There are no restrictions on citizenship.

Sudan Volunteer Programme (SVP)

34 Estelle Road
London, NW3 2JY
United Kingdom
+44 (0) 20 7485 8619
E-mail: david@svp-uk.com
Web site: www.svp-uk.com

Project Type: Education

Mission Statement Excerpt: "Sudan Volunteer Programme (SVP) is a charity whose object is the teaching of English in Sudan, the largest country in Africa."

Year Founded: 1997

Funding Sources: Individual donors

The Work They Do: SVP offers the opportunity to teach English to university students in Sudan. The English language is increasingly recognized in Sudan as a key component of business and development, but while many Sudanese have received formal instruction in English grammar they have had no experience of hearing a native English speaker or lack the confidence to speak the language in ordinary conversation. Most SVP volunteers work with students in universities where an informal approach has best results. Volunteers need to be available to work from 8 A.M. to 5 P.M., five days per week, but will not be assigned more than thirty hours of work per week, and no more than twenty of those hours will be spent on classroom instruction.

Project Location: Volunteers work at universities in the capital of Khartoum, in the city of Omdurman, and in the areas around these urban centers. Volunteers are housed with one other volunteer of the same sex, and are responsible for cooking for themselves.

Time Line: SVP requests that volunteers commit to a minimum of six months. SVP volunteers tend to fly to Sudan together in small groups several times each year, especially when the academic terms begin in September and January, but individuals may also travel by themselves.

Cost: Volunteers pay for their international airfare to Sudan but then are paid approximately $150 per month by their host university, which also provides accommodations. SVP also arranges for airport transfers and provides group medical insurance. Volunteers should take at least $100 for start-up costs.

Getting Started: Application forms are available on the SVP Web site. SVP provides an orientation and training upon arrival, as well as notes from past volunteers. Volunteers are also encouraged to join other volunteers in their classrooms as training.

Needed Skills and Specific Populations: SVP volunteers must be at least eighteen years old, be native speakers of English, and hold or be working toward a college degree. Volunteers should also be enthusiastic about the idea of teaching English, patient, tenacious, resilient, and have a good sense of humor. Volunteers will find that previous experience teaching, traveling, or living in discomfort will all be advantages.

Sunseed Desert Techno

Apdo. 9, 04270 Sorbas
Almeria
Spain
+(34) 950 525 770
E-mail: sunseedspain@arrakis.
Web site: www.sunseed.org.u

Project Type: Agriculture; Construction; Natural Conservation
(Land); Rural Development; Scientific Research
Mission Statement Excerpt: "Sunseed Desert Technology aims
to develop, demonstrate, and communicate accessible low-
tech methods of living sustainably in a semiarid
environment."
Year Founded: 1986
Number of Volunteers Last Year: 250
Funding Sources: The organization receives a few donations
from individuals.
The Work They Do: Sunseed Desert Technology demonstrates a
sustainable lifestyle by using and developing low-tech
methods that have the least detrimental environmental
impact as an appropriate alternative to other often less-
accessible technologies and techniques. Program areas
include appropriate technology, construction and
maintenance, dryland management, organic growing, and
education and publicity. Volunteers can work in all of
Sunseed's departments, both in research as well as in
community activities such as gardening, housework, and
building. Longer-term volunteers may undertake their own
individual projects, choosing an idea from Sunseed's Project
Pack or designing a project themselves in consultation with
the organization. Examples of past such projects include
setting up an urban garden, investigating the use of seed
pellets, constructing a thermal compost water heater,
producing a study of local ecology, and looking at erosion
control techniques.

Location: Sunseed Desert Technology is based in a small rural village located in a valley in the semiarid landscape of southeast Spain. Living and working conditions are basic and shared, but they are comfortable. Sunseed Desert Technology volunteers follow a vegetarian diet (no milk, eggs and cheese once a week).

Time Line: All of Sunseed's projects are ongoing and accept volunteers throughout the year. Volunteers can participate at two levels: part-time volunteers stay less than four weeks and work four hours per day, six days per week; full-time volunteers stay at least five weeks and work seven hours per day, five days per week.

Cost: Program fees vary by time of year and length of stay, but they range from €56 to €165 per week. Each program fee covers room and board and the materials for individual projects, but not travel to or from Spain.

Getting Started: Prospective volunteers should download the booking form found on Sunseed's Web site or contact the organization to request that one be mailed. Volunteers receive a two-hour orientation upon arrival. Training is done on the job, and work is supervised as needed.

Needed Skills and Specific Populations: Volunteers under sixteen years old must be accompanied by an adult. Volunteers aged between sixteen and eighteen years old must provide a written statement from an adult testifying to the volunteer's maturity and ability to volunteer. Senior volunteers are welcomed, but they should recognize the difficulty of the terrain at the center. While Sunseed tries to accommodate as many volunteers as possible, people with restricted mobility may have difficulty navigating the center, as it is not wheelchair accessible.

Tethys Research Institute
Viale G.B. Gadio, 2
20121, Milan
Italy
+39 0272001947 or +39 0272601446
Fax: +39 0286995011
E-mail: tethys@tethys.org
Web site: www.tethys.org

Project Type: Natural Conservation (Sea); Scientific Research

Mission Statement Excerpt: "The Tethys Research Institute is dedicated to the preservation of the marine environment. It focuses on marine animals and particularly on cetaceans inhabiting the Mediterranean Sea, and it aims to protect its biodiversity by promoting the adoption of a precautionary approach to the management of natural resources."

Year Founded: 1986

Number of Volunteers Last Year: Approximately 250

Funding Sources: Tethys is funded largely by faith-based and private sources.

The Work They Do: Tethys does scientific research to identify the threats affecting Mediterranean cetaceans, and it proposes solutions to these problems. Projects open to volunteer assistance include cetacean research in the Ligurian Sea's Pelagos Sanctuary, and dolphin research in the eastern Ionian Sea. Volunteers actively collaborate in the collection of field data on cetaceans, and they are requested to help in all project activities. These may include recording navigation data, plotting sighting positions on a navigation chart, loading data in the computer, collecting ecological and behavioral data, noting photo-identification data, and helping with the identification of individual whales and dolphins. Volunteers and researchers alike take part in cooking and cleaning shifts.

Project Location: In the Ligurian Sea, Tethys has a 21-meter (69-foot) research ship that normally stays in the harbor of Portosole, San Remo, Italy. Volunteers sleep and live onboard

309

during the research project. There are five cabins onboard, which can host sixteen people: two single beds in the bow sharing one bathroom, two four-bed cabins, and a large room for six people (two double and two single beds), each with private bathroom, shower, and hot water. The dolphin project is run out of a field station on the island of Kalamos, Greece. This field station is a comfortable house that includes a living room, a kitchen, a bathroom with hot water, and a garden with almond and olive trees. Dolphin research is carried out from large inflatable boats with fiberglass keels.

Time Line: Volunteers are accepted May through October for six days; volunteers can sign up for more than one project.

Cost: Program fees range from €600 to €890. Each program fee covers all lodging and food, though volunteers must provide for their own travel expenses. Students under the age of twenty-six are offered a discount in some programs.

Getting Started: Prospective volunteers should call or fax the Milan office at the numbers listed between 9:30 A.M. and 1:00 P.M., or 2:00 and 5:00 P.M. in the summer, Monday through Friday (please remember to adjust for time zones). They will then complete an application form and send the program fee, which will secure the reservation. Interviews are not required to volunteer with Tethys. During each project, researchers give daily lectures on cetaceans and conservation issues. Practical training is also provided during the research project.

Needed Skills and Specific Populations: Volunteers must be able to swim, and they must be at least eighteen years old, though minors accompanied by family members will be considered on a case-by-case basis. Volunteers should be able to speak enough English in order to communicate with other project participants and team members. They should be in good physical condition and able to tolerate hot weather, sun, and long periods on a boat. Anyone in good physical condition, including seniors, is welcome to volunteer. Prospective volunteers with disabilities should contact the organization's office and will be considered on a case-by-case basis.

Theodore Roosevelt Medora Foundation

P.O. Box 1696
Bismarck, ND 58502
(701) 223-4800; Fax: (701) 223-3347
E-mail: volunteer@medora.com
Web site: www.medora.com

Project Type: Administrative; Community Development;
Economic Development; Historic Preservation; Museum;
Youth

Mission Statement Excerpt: "Preserve the values and traditions
of the Old West embodied in the pioneer cattle town of
Historic Medora and the 'Bully Spirit' of Theodore
Roosevelt."

Year Founded: 1986

Number of Volunteers Last Year: 415

Funding Sources: Individual donors

The Work They Do: The historic town of Medora, North
Dakota, offers a number of historical tourist destinations
that work collectively to keep the history of the Old West
alive, and to present it to thousands of visitors each year.
Volunteers help in the preseason by helping to clean, paint,
stain, prepare flower beds, and by planting flowers. During
the heavy tourist season, volunteers work in the information
center, theater, restaurant, heritage center, campground, gift
shop, and musical stage. End-of-season volunteers help
clean up, work in food establishments, and assist with
grounds and maintenance positions.

Project Location: Medora is a small town located in North
Dakota's Badlands, near Interstate 94 and the Theodore
Roosevelt National Park. Volunteers who bring their own
camper or RV are housed in a local campground; others
find accommodations in a local hotel or a residence built
specially for volunteers, by volunteers.

Time Line: The preseason begins in mid-May and lasts about
two weeks, and volunteers work for at least five days,
beginning on a Monday. In-season volunteers are welcomed

311

between June and August, beginning on Mondays for eight days. End-of-season volunteers have eleven-day commitments in August and September.

Cost: There is no program fee. Volunteers are provided with all of their meals and lodging, and receive discounts at local retail shops, entertainment, and museums. Volunteers must provide their own transportation to Medora, and to volunteer sites that are not within walking distance.

Getting Started: Prospective volunteers can request information and an application by mail or e-mail; the foundation asks that prospective volunteers do not call for information. There are no deadlines, but volunteer positions do fill up quickly, and volunteers should submit their application by the end of January; no interview is required. The selection of volunteers is completed in March. Volunteers go through orientation on the day they arrive, usually for about eight hours, which covers basic information about Medora and on-site training for specific tasks.

Needed Skills and Specific Populations: Volunteers must be cheery and welcoming, with a positive attitude and be willing to "tackle any task with a smile!" Most of Medora's volunteers are ages fifty to eighty-five, so while there is no minimum age to volunteer, children are not encouraged to volunteer, and families with children are a rarity in the volunteer corps. Volunteers with disabilities are welcome.

Transformational Journeys

6320 Brookside Plaza #182
Kansas City, MO 64113
(816) 808-3668; Fax: (816) 363-3457 Attn: Box 182
E-mail: tjourney@sbcglobal.net
Web site: www.tjourneys.org

Project Type: Community Development; Construction; Education; Professional/Technical Assistance; Rural Development; Social Justice; Youth

Mission Statement Excerpt: "To teach people and cultures to understand and serve one another through international humanitarian travel."

Year Founded: 1997

Number of Volunteers Last Year: Approximately 125

Funding Sources: Private sources

The Work They Do: Volunteers with Transformational Journeys carry out short-term projects such as building homes, community centers, schools, and churches for economically disadvantaged communities in developing countries. Volunteers lead recreational projects, teach, build, paint, repair, and pour foundations. Some examples of projects include teaching dance or crafts to the children in a community in Brazil, erecting a multipurpose center for a Mayan village in Guatemala, building homes or small home repair in the Dominican Republic in partnership with local families, participating in the daily life activities of Haitians, and providing care and companionship for children with HIV/AIDS and other disabilities in Kenya.

Project Location: Volunteers can currently work on projects in Brazil, the Dominican Republic, Guatemala, Haiti, Kenya, and Tanzania. Work sites range from very urban environments in Brazil and Kenya, to rural Mayan villages in Guatemala's mountains, to a Caribbean seaside community in the Dominican Republic. Lodging varies by country and ranges from dormitory style accommodations, homestays, guesthouses, simple hotel rooms with shared or private bath, to a possible four-star hotel in Brazil.

Time Line: Projects follow set time lines as specified by Transformational Journey's country partners and run throughout the calendar year. Contact Transformational Journeys to find out about upcoming dates. Volunteer trips range from a minimum of nine days to a maximum of fifteen days.

Cost: Transformational Journey's program fee includes international travel costs and are priced on a per-trip basis. Because of this, program fees may fluctuate as air costs change. Estimated costs range from $1,600 to $2,750 for a ten-day program, depending on the country of service. Beyond international airfare, the program fee also covers medical travel insurance, and most in-country expenses such as hotels, transportation, and meals. Volunteers are responsible for visa fees, which can range from $40 to $100 dollars, depending on the country, obtaining their own passport, vaccinations when required, and one or two meals during excursion days.

Getting Started: Prospective volunteers should e-mail or call Transformational Journeys to request an application. Participation in an orientation session is required prior to departure, which includes instruction about culture, language, politics, religion, and sociology of the destination country. Work training is provided on-site.

Needed Skills and Specific Populations: Volunteers' ages range from young children to seniors, and families are welcome. Minors must be accompanied by a parent or guardian. Some trips require specific activity levels due to site conditions or terrain. The work projects are identified prior to trip scheduling in order to allow prospective volunteers to evaluate their ability to perform the tasks the project requires. Work training is provided on-site and therefore no special skills are required for participation on a trip. Transformational Journeys will make every effort to accommodate volunteers with disabilities. A detailed interview will assist Transformational Journeys in assessing the volunteer's specific needs for in-country requirements, which will allow their in-country partners to determine their ability to handle these accommodations.

Travellers Worldwide

7 Mulberry Close
Ferring, West Sussex, BN12 5HY
United Kingdom
+44 (0) 1903 502595; Fax: +44 (0) 1903 500364
E-mail: info@travellersworldwide.com
Web site: www.travellersworldwide.com

Project Type: Community Development; Education;
Medical/Health; Natural Conservation (Land); Natural
Conservation (Sea); Orphans; Youth

Mission Statement Excerpt: "Travellers makes a positive and
lasting impact upon the environments, communities, institutions, volunteers, and all stakeholders that we work with,
by providing placement opportunities whilst ensuring that
our own ethical standards are met."

Year Founded: 1994

Number of Volunteers Last Year: Over 1,000

Funding Sources: None outside program fees

The Work They Do: Travellers Worldwide offers over three
hundred projects around the world, primarily in the areas of
teaching, conservation, health care, and sports. Volunteers
can take part in projects ranging from coaching youth in
Cape Town, to teaching children and adults in Guatemala,
to working in conservation, sustainability, and education
efforts in the Peruvian rainforest.

Project Location: Volunteer projects are located in twenty
different countries around the world. Volunteers are usually
housed in homestays or youth hostels.

Time Line: Volunteers are welcome throughout the year, in projects ranging from one week to one year.

Cost: Program fees start at £695 for some two-week programs,
and rise, depending on the program and length of stay, to a
maximum of £2,795. Room and board is generally included
in the program fee.

Getting Started: There are no deadlines for applications, which
are accepted throughout the year and are available on Trav-

ellers Worldwide's Web site. Travellers Worldwide offers an orientation before the trip and upon arrival; one- and two-day training courses are also available for teaching projects. Prospective volunteers need to complete a phone interview as a part of the application process.

Needed Skills and Specific Populations: Volunteers must be at least seventeen years old, and there is no maximum age for volunteers. Some of Travellers Worldwide's projects are suitable for volunteers with disabilities, but this requires discussions between the volunteer and Travellers Worldwide before registering. Families are welcome, as long as all children are at least sixteen years old.

Of Puja and Pappadams: Teaching English in South India

by Erica Garrecht-Williams

Travellers Worldwide

In the winter of my gap year, I left the familiarity of home to teach English in India with Travellers Worldwide. With only a backpack on my back and hope in my heart that someone would actually be waiting there to greet me, I boarded a Chennai-bound airplane alone. I can't remember ever feeling smaller or more alone that I did then, at JFK airport walking away from my parents into the January night, into the great unknown.

I had no idea what to expect when I landed in Madurai. Even now, India remains the only place I have ever experienced genuine culture shock. The trip to the hotel was unforgettable—the traffic of rickshaws, bicycles, and ox carts competing vehemently for a piece of the road, the silky bright pinks and yellows of women's saris hanging languidly off their caramel shoulders, the sight of beggar children in doorways, the cows munching garbage piles on the side of the road, the smell of samosas frying in oil, of fresh pineapple, curries, and jasmine, of trash and red earth baking in the noonday sun—all flew past my open window, overwhelming my senses. I remember spending the first few days mainly in my hotel room, protected from the realities of where I was. But slowly, surely, I came out more and confronted my discomfort. Sooner than I ever thought, I got comfortable, and realized it was just living, getting up in the morning, eating, teaching, breathing, like anywhere else. My friends and I slowly discovered our way around, visited the temples, found where to buy the best mango juice in town, learned to navigate the best stalls at labyrinthine market, and fell into routines. It was wonderful and novel to make Madurai my home, to really learn and appreciate its daily rhythms, from the 5 A.M. wailings of the mosque call to prayer, to the cool respite of a quiet evening, full of neon light and stars.

My placement was teaching at the YWCA Matriculation Higher Secondary School. I taught an eighth standard English class (twelve- to thirteen-year-olds) and with another volunteer taught several music classes that consisted mostly of learning and practicing English songs like "Head-Shoulders-Knees-and-Toes" and the "Hokey Pokey." Teaching English was a more challenging, but more rewarding experience. I remember feeling very frustrated, especially by trying to negotiate a medium, a common ground, between two very different cultures and two very different educational systems. My students were very bright, but they hadn't been taught to think, rather to copy and memorize. They had trouble asking questions or admitting they didn't understand. It really made me think about and appreciate the privilege of my own education. But it was also exciting to see their progress, to see them learning to be a little more creative and engaged with English, and to see that I had had a part in that.

Starting to untangle India brought me closer than I ever would have expected to my fellow volunteers, as we all grappled with it together. It was strange and interesting to really understand how Indians saw us as Westerners, to feel like celebrities everywhere we went (I once got asked for my autograph at school!), to try to look at our own culture from the outside, for better or worse. And to learn about Indian people: their beautiful culture, the way they see religion as integral to daily life, their infinite generosity and patience, the challenges many of them face. It was so mind-blowing to see a way of life that is so ancient and that still hasn't been bought out by homogenous Western culture, to see how possible it is to live a life less wastefully and more fully than we do. I came home changed in more ways than I could've hoped for, more conscious of who I was, my priorities, my responsibilities as a privileged American, and more aware of the unbelievable beauty and terrible disparity that exists in the world. Four years later, none of those lessons have faded, and I can still smell the jasmine in the air.

United Action for Children (UAC)

P.O. Box 177
Muvuka, South West Province
Cameroon
+237 772-0418
E-mail: unitedactionfoc@yahoo.com
Web site: www.unitedactionforchildren.org

Project Type: Administrative; Economic Development; Education; Youth

Mission Statement Excerpt: "To create a caring and sustaining environment for children and young people through innovative programs."

Year Founded: Organization was founded in 1996; first volunteers arrived in 2001

Number of Volunteers Last Year: Approximately 15

Funding Sources: Several governmental, foundation, and private donor organizations

The Work They Do: United Action for Children (UAC) operates a number of programs for youth and their parents aimed at promoting education and skill acquisition. These programs include HIV/AIDS education, vocational training (carpentry, woodwork, painting), and computer classes. Volunteers are able to assist in the nursery school, teach skills, paint murals, help with administrative work, or become involved in local work or get involved in fundraising both locally and internationally.

Project Location: All volunteers work at UAC's project site in Buea, Cameroon. Volunteers are housed in locally rented accommodations, which are included in the project fee. Volunteers take all meals at the project director's house.

Time Line: Volunteers are accepted throughout the year, though only six volunteers are allowed at any given time. UAC prefers that volunteers stay for a minimum of three months and requires that volunteers work at least five hours each day, beginning at 8:30 A.M.

Cost: UAC's program fee is $300 for volunteers who stay less than one month; $350 for one month of volunteering; $550 for two months' work; and $150 for subsequent months. The program fee includes airport transfers, accommodations, and meals. Volunteers must pay for their own airfare to Cameroon.

Getting Started: Prospective volunteers can apply via one of UAC's international partners, as listed on their Web site. No interview is required.

Needed Skills and Specific Populations: Volunteers must be at least eighteen years old, and there is no maximum age limit for volunteers. UAC does not require that volunteers have any specialized skills.

United Planet

11 Arlington Street
Boston, MA 02116
(800) 292-2316 or (617) 267-7763; Fax: (617) 292-0712
E-mail: quest@unitedplanet.org
Web site: www.unitedplanet.org

Project Type: Community Development; Human Rights;
Medical/Health; Rural Development; Social Justice;
Women's Issues; Youth

Mission Statement Excerpt: "The mission of United Planet is to
foster cross-cultural understanding and friendship in order
to unite the world in a community beyond borders."

Year Founded: United Planet was founded in 2001, and is the
U.S. associate member of ICYE, which was formed more
than fifty years ago after World War II.

Number of Volunteers Last Year: More than 300

Funding Sources: United Planet receives donations from the
public as well as grants for specific projects.

The Work They Do: United Planet runs many kinds of volunteer programs in more than fifty countries worldwide. Some
examples of projects undertaken by United Planet volunteers
include helping with sea turtle conservation efforts in Costa
Rica; assisting in public schools in Kathmandu, Nepal;
working at health clinics in Guatemala; repairing the homes
of senior citizens in a small village in northern Iceland; and
assisting with daily activities in an orphanage in Romania.
After the volunteer experience, participants are encouraged
to share their experience in their schools and communities
at home through the United Planet Cultural Awareness
Project and on the Internet via the United Planet online
community. This passing on of knowledge is seen as critical
to United Planet's mission.

Project Location: Volunteers can work in urban and rural settings
around the world. Work sites vary widely from site to site, as
do accommodations, which may include homestays,
guesthouses, or residential accommodations at the project.

Time Line: Volunteers can work with United Planet year-round, either through one- to twelve-week short-term projects, or six-month to one-year long-term projects.

Cost: Program fees start at $1,295. Each program fee covers all meals, lodging, insurance, orientation, cultural activities, and excursions and, for some programs, in-country transportation. Longer-term commitments carry greater benefits.

A volunteer wields a wheelbarrow in Quebradas, Costa Rica, working with an environmental conservation group that serves to repair existing trails and construct new ones within a nature reserve. *Photo courtesy of Theresa Higgs, Director of International Programs, United Planet*

Getting Started: Prospective volunteers can complete an application on United Planet's Web site. United Planet requires that all prospective volunteers complete an interview so that the organization can better understand the applicant's background and motivation for volunteering.

Needed Skills and Specific Populations: No specific skills are required to volunteer with United Planet, but if a volunteer has a specialized skill such as medical or dental, computer, educational, or environmental training, the organization will try to place the volunteer in a position that utilizes this skill. United Planet encourages volunteerism by people of all ages, so there is no minimum or maximum age. This philosophy of inclusion extends to volunteers with disabilities, as United Planet does its best to include everyone. United Planet is also open to non-U.S. citizens. Many families have volunteered through United Planet, mostly in orphanages, schools, and in environmental conservation programs; United Planet offers a family discount.

Visions in Action (VIA)

2710 Ontario Road NW
Washington, DC 20009
(202) 625-7402; Fax: (202) 588-9344
E-mail: visions@visionsinaction.org
Web site: www.visionsinaction.org

Project Type: Community Development; Economic
Development; Education; Human Rights; Medical/Health;
Orphans

Mission Statement Excerpt: "Visions in Action is committed to
achieving social and economic justice in the developing
world through the participation of communities of self-
reliant, grassroots volunteers."

Year Founded: 1988

Number of Volunteers Last Year: 20

Funding Sources: VIA volunteer programs are funded by
program fees, private contributions, and in-kind donations.

The Work They Do: VIA places volunteers in short-term,
medium-term, and long-term positions with local nonprofit
development organizations, research institutes, health
clinics, community and activist groups, and the media.
Volunteers can work in one of the following positions:
Project Managers, a supervisory position for professionals
who work in the field or office helping to manage rural and
urban development projects; *Program Assistants*, volunteers
who work with a mentor or supervisor in an entry-level
position; *Community Development*, field-based positions
that entail working with community groups in low-
income neighborhoods or rural areas; *Health
Professionals*, volunteers who work in a health clinic, a
medical laboratory, or a hospital as a doctor, nurse, or clinical assistant; *Public Health Educators*, people who perform
baseline research, grassroots education, or design health
communication materials; *Researchers*, volunteers who
work as social science or natural science research assistants;
Journalists, who work as reporters, photographers, assistant

editors, or newsletter editors for newspapers, magazines, book publishers, or nonprofit organizations, or as assistant producers for radio or television stations; *Youth Group Coordinators*, volunteers who run an orphanage, counsel runaways, coach, tutor, and lead community service projects for teens and children; *Educators/Teachers,* who teach in a primary or secondary school, support enhancement program, and train teachers; and *HIV/AIDS Caregivers*, who support people living with HIV and AIDS, and advocate for drugs and care.

Project Location: VIA places volunteers in work sites in Mexico, Uganda, Tanzania, Liberia, and South Africa. Volunteers usually live together in group housing.

Time Line: VIA usually places volunteers in six- and twelve-month positions, but it also offers six-week short-term positions in Mexico and Tanzania. Volunteers in Mexico, Tanzania, and South Africa begin in January or July; volunteers in Uganda begin in September or March.

Cost: Program fees for VIA volunteer opportunities range from $2,800 for four weeks in Mexico to $5,900 for some of the organization's twelve-month programs. Each program fee covers housing, health insurance, orientation, staff support, and program administration. Long-term volunteers also receive a $50-per-month stipend to assist with daily living expenses. Airfare is not included in the program fee.

Getting Started: Prospective volunteers can download an application from VIA's Web site. The application is due three months before the project start date, and it must be submitted along with two letters of recommendation and a nonrefundable $45 application fee; a phone interview is also required. VIA's volunteer programs each begin with several weeks of orientation that include development seminars, language classes, homestays, and travel to areas around the volunteer site.

Needed Skills and Specific Populations: Volunteers must be at least twenty years old and have a college degree or equivalent experience; there is no maximum age limit for volunteers. Volunteers in Mexico must be proficient in Spanish.

Health volunteers must have completed at least two years of medical school, have a nursing or physical therapy degree, or have a background in public health. Volunteers with disabilities are welcome to volunteer with VIA.

Vitalise

Shap Road
Kendal Cumbria, LA9 6NZ
United Kingdom
+44 (0) 1539 814682; Fax: +44 (0) 1539 735567
E-mail: volunteer@vitalise.org.uk
Web site: www.vitalise.org.uk

Project Type: Developmental Disabilities; Medical/Health

Mission Statement Excerpt: "To enable disabled and visually impaired people to exercise choice and to provide vital breaks for careers and inspirational opportunities for volunteers."

Year Founded: 1963

Number of Volunteers Last Year: Approximately 5,000

Funding Sources: Various charitable organizations

The Work They Do: Vitalise works to provide disabled and visually impaired people, who are referred to as guests, the opportunity for respite and breaks in a holiday environment. Volunteers assist in this work by providing personal and social support to guests and by helping with activities and outings.

Project Location: Vitalise has five centers in the United Kingdom, which are located in London, Southampton, Nottingham, Southport, and Cornwall. These centers were built specifically to host Vitalise guests and volunteers. Accommodations are shared.

Time Line: Vitalise accepts volunteers year-round for a minimum of one week and a maximum of one year.

Cost: Vitalise does not charge any program fee and provides room and board free of charge to volunteers. Volunteers are responsible for providing their own transportation to the center.

Getting Started: Prospective volunteers must complete a booking form, provide references, and agree to a background check; no interview is necessary. Volunteers receive training in health, safety, and moving and handling guests.

Needed Skills and Specific Populations: Volunteers must be reasonably fit and have a good command of the English language. The minimum age for volunteers from the United Kingdom is sixteen; from other countries it is eighteen. Senior volunteers are welcomed, and volunteers with disabilities will be considered, depending on their individual circumstances. Families are welcome, as long as all members meet the minimum age requirements.

Volunteer Africa

P.O. Box 24, Bakewell
Derbyshire, DE45 1YP
United Kingdom
E-mail: support@volunteerafrica.org
Web site: www.volunteerafrica.org

Project Type: Community Development; Construction; Rural
Development

Mission Statement Excerpt: "Volunteer Africa has been established to give people from around the world the opportunity
to work on community-initiated projects in developing
countries."

Year Founded: 2001

Number of Volunteers Last Year: 132

Funding Sources: None; Volunteer Africa is self-funded.

The Work They Do: Volunteer Africa offers volunteer opportunities in the Tanzanian provinces of Tabora and Singida on
community-development projects. In Singida, volunteers
work in rural villages on building projects such as the
construction of school classrooms or medical clinics. In
Tabora, volunteers work with orphans and other vulnerable
children.

Project Location: Volunteers work in the Singida and Tabora
regions of Tanzania. In Singida, volunteers stay in a camp in
the village they are working in with four to twelve other
volunteers. Life is similar to local villagers; the conditions
are basic with no electricity or running water. Volunteers are
involved in daily camp duties such as fetching and purifying
water and cooking. In Tabora, volunteers stay in a shared
volunteer house of five volunteers.

Time Line: Volunteers for the Tabora Orphans Program are
accepted throughout the year; the Singida Rural Development Program operates from May to November, during the
Tanzanian dry season. Volunteers participate for four to
twelve weeks.

A volunteer takes a moment to sit with three-year-old Veronika at the job site in Mghumbu village, Tanzania. Veronkia waited at the gate every morning for the volunteers to get up so she could walk to the well with them! She was such a little sweetheart. *Photo courtesy of Kelly Christie*

Cost: Participation for four weeks costs $1,980; seven weeks costs $2,590, and the program fee for twelve weeks is $3,670. Each program fee covers food, accommodation, language training, and in-country travel, but does not include insurance or travel to Tanzania. Approximately 60 percent of the program fee goes toward direct program costs and is therefore invested in the community being served.

Getting Started: Applications are available only online or via e-mail; Volunteer Africa does not maintain a phone or fax line so as to cut down on costs. An interview is required of all prospective volunteers. Volunteers receive an extensive guide for predeparture arrangements.

Needed Skills and Specific Populations: No specific skills are required, but volunteers should be able to live with a close team for four to twelve weeks, have good communication skills, and the ability to problem-solve. Volunteers must be at least eighteen years old, and senior volunteers are welcomed. Applications from volunteers with disabilities will be screened for appropriate placements, just as any volunteer would be. Volunteer Africa has had a number of families volunteer with them.

The Last Leg: Kelly Comes Home

By Kelly Christie

Volunteer Africa

I write about how great it will be to return home from Tanzania. How I can't wait to see my family and give gifts and show photos. I try not to think about going back to school and my daily routine and leaving this place that has taught me so much. Ten o'clock comes. I get in the taxi and once again, I don't look back. I talk to the taxi driver. I use my Swahili and he uses his English and we get each other's life stories in a twenty-minute nutshell. He tells me where his family is from and he's been driving a taxi for twelve years and he doesn't have any children. I tell him about Canada and the cold and the snow and school and the sky train. He says Canada sounds so hard to believe and I say, "Man, you're telling' me!" and he's all smiles and happy eyes. I tell him I can't believe I'm leaving this place. He looks at me and says that for all the tourists he's seen in Dar (the capital of Tanzania) and all the travelers he's known, he's never had the desire to leave Tanzania. Finally, I feel like that's something that I can understand.

The night is cold and I buy a few books to read and a *chukka* (blanket) to keep me warm on the plane. The books are all about Africa, of course. As I'm waiting to board the plane, I feel like I'm holding back a huge wave of sadness. I am so different. I am not someone who is meant to stay in North America. I know that I am leaving a place that I am going to spend the rest of my life trying to return to. I wrap my *chukka* around me and pull my knees to my chest and feel smaller than when I arrived. I want to run out into the night and tear up my ticket and return to the village and live there, basking in the warmth of strangers and the satisfaction of owning nothing. I stand in line, waiting to board the flight.

I write as I'm sitting on the plane, with the whirrs and hums of pressurization and the dim overhead lights. This is it. Goodbye, Tanzania. Goodbye, Swahili on my lips, holding hands with strangers, children playing with my hair. I feel a sense of heartache and loss spread through my chest. Oh, the tragedy of leaving your great fresh paradise! The wonder I have discovered in the world. I have helped deliver babies, cuddled street children, fed starving puppies, built a school, climbed a mountain, swam the sea, felt earthquakes and tornadoes, seen poisonous snakes, and felt the fear of bees and frogs that appear in the shower as if from nowhere! I watched elephants fight and felt the rain warm on my skin and the sand hot under my feet. I felt the wind and snow atop Kilimanjaro and the air, thin in my lungs. I have thought new thoughts, seen new sights, read and written new words. This experience has truly been a journey of self-discovery. This trip is something that not even the most expensive HDTV could give you. This experience is life.

I have tested my limits and found new comfort in the mystery of this world. Whatever happens in my life, wherever the road takes me; I have done this. This summer existed and I was here. I have learned enough not to last a lifetime, but to begin one and am returning a new person to an old home. I now see that life can be whatever you want it to be. There is an entire world out there, so far removed from where we started. Time is precious, palpable, and subjective. Above all things, time is the currency of our existence. Spending it wisely, on things that truly matter, is the only way to ensure that it won't run out too fast. Lead a life worth living. Don't waste one second on unhappiness. This lesson is what I have learned in Africa.

Volunteer Bolivia

Casilla 2411
Cochabamba
Bolivia
+591-4-452-6028; Fax +591-4-452-9459
E-mail: info@volunteerbolivia.org
Web site: www.volunteerbolivia.org

Project Type: Developmental Disabilities; Education;
Medical/Health; Social Justice; Youth
Mission Statement Excerpt: "Volunteer Bolivia . . . will match
your skills and interests to local needs in order to provide
you with an unforgettable cross-cultural experience."
Year Founded: 2002
Number of Volunteers Last Year: 65
Funding Sources: Individual donors
The Work They Do: Volunteer Bolivia offers two types of placements: short-term volunteers, who work for one to five
months serving as aides to Bolivian educators, and long-
term volunteers, who serve for five or more months in an
area of their own expertise that matches the needs of
communities in Bolivia. Short-term volunteers might help
children with homework, design arts and crafts projects, or
assist in a classroom. Examples of long-term volunteer
placements include working in a health profession, physical
therapy, graphic design, teaching advanced computer skills,
or in project development and administration.
Project Location: Most volunteers work in the city of
Cochabamba, Bolivia, but Volunteer Bolivia can also place
volunteers in other parts of the country. Volunteer
placement sites have basic infrastructure, such as electricity,
and may have running water. Volunteers typically stay in
homestays with a private room and shared bath, or may
choose to rent a house or apartment.
Time Line: Volunteer Bolivia accepts volunteers throughout the
year for a minimum of one month. They do not have a
maximum time limit for volunteers.

Cost: Volunteer Bolivia's program fee for four weeks is $1,520, increasing up to $2,250 for twelve weeks, and $320 for each additional four weeks beyond the first twelve. The program fee includes airport transfers, an in-country orientation, Spanish language classes, a homestay with all meals, and the volunteer placement. Volunteers are responsible for their international airfare to Bolivia and insurance fees, as well as a visa.

Getting Started: Prospective volunteers can apply online via Volunteer Bolivia's Web site; applications are accepted throughout the year. Interviews are not required. A basic orientation is provided upon arrival.

Needed Skills and Specific Populations: Long-term volunteers must have at least intermediate Spanish skills prior to volunteering. Volunteers must be at least eighteen years old, with no maximum age. Volunteer Bolivia welcomes volunteers with disabilities, and gladly hosts families, as they have found families "to be a great addition to the program."

Acceptance and Affirmation

By Aaron Haddad

Volunteer Bolivia

I went to Bolivia last summer for four months, living with a wonderful homestay family (the Quirogas), learning Spanish intensively, and volunteering at the Centro de Apoyo Integral Comunitario (CAIC). CAIC was founded by two Spaniards and a Canadian in 1994 upon their discovering that kids were living in prisons with parents. CAIC's stated mandate is to serve as a positive alternative space for the youth aged two to eighteen either living in the neighborhood or in the women's or men's sections of the San Sebastián prison in Cochabamba or the San Pablo prison in Quillacollo. I helped with just about every service that CAIC offers. This translated into various combinations of homework support, cooking and cleaning, serving food to youth, playing sports with youth, talking with youth about their personal issues, and escorting and supervising youth on field trips.

My time in Bolivia and with CAIC was coloured by personal issues related to vulnerability and attachment. By vulnerability I refer to the anxiety that I felt as a Canadian often identified as Latin American who could barely speak and understand Spanish. Learning Spanish relieved me of my anxiety and vulnerability and allowed me to become part of the lives of the people I was living and working with. I became increasingly attached to the people in my home and especially CAIC staff and youth. I had never been in such a personally affirming environment. As an emotional, people-oriented person, I could literally and figuratively speaking touch and be touched, something that I have never really experienced in

Canada except in a few relationships I have had with specific individuals. Furthermore—and this was perhaps due to being perceived as Latin American in an actual Latin American environment where I was using Spanish fluently—for the first time in my life I did not feel like I was being chronically marginalized by other people. I felt accepted and affirmed. The summer of 2007 was without question a watershed in my life.

While in Bolivia I created a diary of poetry that allowed me to grapple with thoughts that now act as cherished *recuerdos* (memories). I close with the first and last excerpts of the diary, as I think they summarize the essence of my experience as only poetry can:

> April 26, 2007
> skying and polluting
> my way
> from the real
> to another real
> wondering,
> supposing,
> waiting,
> when I am
> going,
> going,
> gone?
> August 25, 2007

I'm leaving that which I can never leave, that which will never leave me.

Such is the physics of love.

Thanks to Voluntarios Bolivia, the Quiroga family, CAIC staff, and especially, CAIC youth—you made possible what was one of the best periods of my life and will always inform my actions. *Hasta la proxima amigos* (Until the next time friends).

Volunteers for Outdoor Colorado (VOC)

600 South Marion Parkway
Denver, CO 80209
(800) 925-2220 or (303) 715-1010; Fax: (303) 715-1212
E-mail: voc@voc.org
Web site: www.voc.org

Project Type: Natural Conservation (Land); Trail
Building/Maintenance
Mission Statement Excerpt: "Volunteers for Outdoor Colorado's
(VOC's) mission is to motivate and enable citizens to be
active stewards of Colorado's public lands."
Year Founded: 1984
Number of Volunteers Last Year: Approximately 4,000
Funding Sources: Government and private sources
The Work They Do: Each year VOC carries out more than
twenty-five projects that involve trail building, trail maintenance, habitat restoration, wetlands restoration, light
construction, and nonnative invasive plant control. Volunteers
cut and move dirt, move rocks, cut and move brush and tree
branches, dig out plants, and plant seedlings. Repeat or experienced volunteers may elect to go through a weekend-long
training process to take on leadership roles and become
involved in the project planning and operation process.
Project Location: VOC projects take place throughout
Colorado, from urban areas, to plains, to high mountains.
Work sites may be urban parks, open-space areas, or
forested mountain areas. Weather conditions are highly vari-
able in Colorado, and volunteers should be prepared for
weather conditions that range from hot and sunny to snow
showers. Some sites are open with little shade and others
are in heavily forested areas. Though some sites allow for
RV or pop-up camper use, most volunteers camp in tents,
and food is provided by VOC.
Time Line: VOC typically runs two volunteer work crews per
month from March or April through October. Most of the
VOC volunteer opportunities are weekend projects; volun-

teers arrive early Saturday morning, make lunch, split into work crews of ten to twelve, and work until about 4:00 P.M., with lunch and rest breaks. Everyone then gathers for dinner, which is cooked by a volunteer team, followed by social activities and entertainment. Sunday starts with a hot breakfast, and work continues until the project closes at 4:00 to 5:00 P.M. VOC occasionally offers single-day volunteer opportunities, as well as a five-day event each summer.

Cost: There is no program fee to volunteer with VOC, and most of the food is provided by the organization. Volunteers must provide their own transportation to the work site, tents and sleeping bags, and any personal food needs.

Getting Started: Prospective volunteers should apply via VOC's Web site or call the office at one of the numbers listed. No interview is required as a part of the registration process. Volunteers must register beforehand, preferably at least two weeks prior to the project's starting date. Any needed training is done on-site during the project. Volunteers who become leaders, though, must participate in a formal training session.

Needed Skills and Specific Populations: Volunteer crew members do not need to have prior experience or skills. VOC's minimum age for volunteers depends on the project, but it ranges from eight to sixteen years old. Senior volunteers are welcomed. Volunteers with disabilities are welcomed as long as they can perform moderate to hard physical work at altitudes as high as twelve thousand feet. Some projects may require applicants to file a brief application or verification of physical health. Families are welcome to volunteer with VOC, as long as children meet the minimum age requirements.

Volunteers for Peace (VFP)

1034 Tiffany Road
Belmont, VT 05730
(802) 259-2759; Fax: (802) 259-2922
E-mail: vfp@vfp.org
Web site: www.vfp.org

Project Type: Community Development; Construction;
Economic Development; Education; Natural Conservation
(Land); Social Justice; Youth

Mission Statement Excerpt: "Volunteers for Peace (VFP) . . .
provides programs where people from diverse backgrounds
can work together to help overcome the need, violence, and
environmental decay facing our planet."

Year Founded: 1982

Number of Volunteers Last Year: 1,211

Funding Sources: VFP receives a few small donations from
individuals.

The Work They Do: VFP provides placements for two- to three-
week service programs by recruiting volunteers and linking
them with programs. They help organize work camp
programs in the United States and internationally,
partnering with organizations in more than ninety other
countries. In the last twenty-five years, VFP has exchanged
more than twenty-five thousand volunteers in international
work camps worldwide. In previous years more than thirty-
four hundred projects have been listed annually. A typical
work camp finds ten to fifteen volunteers from five or more
countries working together for thirty to forty hours per
week. VFP's programs have a stated goal of fostering international education, voluntary service, and friendship. An
example of a work camp project recently took place in
Kenya, about four hours outside of Nairobi. There, volunteers assisted the Amkeni Women's Group with tree
planting, farm work, weaving, terracing, and brick making.

Project Location: Volunteers can work in one of one hundred
countries around the world. Work sites vary widely and

range from developed cities to very rural communities; some locations are much more rustic than others. Accommodations are usually in a house, a community center, a school, or tents. Volunteers share cooking and cleaning responsibilities as a group. Unless otherwise specified, volunteers must bring a sleeping bag.

Time Line: Most of VFP's projects take place May through September, although some are offered year-round. A list of the majority of projects is published annually in late March. Most programs last two to three weeks, though some medium-term projects are available for one to six months, and VFP offers a few long-term, six-month to two-year projects.

Cost: VFP's basic fee is $300, which covers lodging, food, and work materials. Programs in developing countries charge an additional fee upon arrival that averages $150, which is kept by the host organization. However, VFP refunds $50 to volunteers who have to pay an extra fee if the volunteer writes a work camp report. Volunteers must pay their own transportation costs.

Getting Started: Prospective volunteers usually become VFP members for an annual fee of $30, then apply via a two-page registration form, which is e-mailed to VFP's office. Once the volunteer is placed in a work project, VFP will e-mail him or her an acceptance letter and information sheet that details how to get to the project and what to bring. VFP volunteers are responsible for educating themselves about their destination country, though a basic orientation is provided upon arrival in the first days of all projects.

Needed Skills and Specific Populations: No special skills are required, though VFP stresses that volunteers need to be motivated, cooperative, flexible, and culturally sensitive. Though some projects for teens exist in France, Germany, and a handful of other countries, most programs require volunteers to be at least eighteen years old. Senior volunteers are welcomed, though they should be aware that the large majority of VFP's volunteers are in the eighteen to twenty-five age group, and some programs have maximum age limits. Volunteers with disabilities are encouraged to apply, as work camps are designed to provide everyone with an opportunity to help; VFP will make reasonable accommodations. VFP primarily places U.S. and Canadian citizens, but it will also place citizens of countries in which it does not have a partner organization. VFP has several family-friendly programs, which are published on its Web site at the end of March each year; the family placement fee is fixed at $500 regardless of the family's size.

Volunteers in Asia (VIA)

482 Galvex Street, Room 101
Stanford, CA 94305
(650) 723-3229; Fax: (650) 725-1805
E-mail: info@viaprograms.org
Web site: www.viaprograms.org

Project Type: Community Development; Developmental Disabilities; Education

Mission Statement Excerpt: "VIA is dedicated to increasing understanding between the United States and Asia through public service and programs promoting cross-cultural education."

Year Founded: 1963

Number of Volunteers Last Year: 40

The Work They Do: Through VIA, volunteers either work as an English teacher at an educational institution or as an English resource volunteer with a local nonprofit organization. VIA's short-term, summer projects include work with nonprofits in Bali, Indonesia; teaching at the University of Hue in Vietnam; a medical exchange program in China that focuses on traditional Chinese medical practices; and a service-learning program for Vietnamese-Americans.

Project Location: In addition to the short-term programs listed, VIA operates long-term, one- or two-year volunteer programs in China, Vietnam, Indonesia, Myanmar, Laos, Cambodia, and Thailand.

Time Line: The summer programs run for five and a half weeks in Vietnam and eight weeks in Indonesia. The long-term programs are for one or two years.

Cost: VIA's Vietnam summer program fee is $1,500; the Indonesia summer program fee is $2,000 for undergraduates, and $2,500 for all others. Long-term volunteers pay a program fee of $2,000, and two-year volunteers receive a readjustment allowance of $500 when they return. The short-term program fee covers cross-cultural training, visa, emergency medical and evacuation insurance, local ground transportation, and accommodations. Long-term program fees cover five weeks of training, airfare from Thailand to the country of service, visa expenses, insurance, ground transportation, a monthly living stipend, housing, and an annual conference. Over 40 percent of VIA's volunteers receive partial scholarships.

Getting Started: Prospective volunteers can access application materials and scholarship information from the VIA Web site or by contacting the office at the e-mail address or phone number listed. The application deadline is in late February. Applicants must interview with VIA, either in their California offices or with a VIA alum elsewhere in the United States. VIA emphasizes training and preparation before departure.

Needed Skills and Specific Populations: Volunteers must speak English with native fluency, have a BA or BS degree, and attend all training sessions. It is recommended that volunteers also prepare by studying TEFL methodology and the local language. Volunteers must be between the ages of eighteen and seventy-five. The summer programs are open only to undergraduate students, and the long-term programs are only open to college graduates.

Volunthai: Volunteers for Thailand

86/24 Soi Kanprapa, Prachacheun Rd.
Bahng Sue, 10800
Bangkok
Thailand
(202) 403-1540 (US)
E-mail: info@volunthai.com
Web site: www.volunthai.com

Project Type: Community Development; Education; Orphans;
Rural Development; Youth
Mission Statement Excerpt: "Volunthai is a not-for-profit volun-
teer organization that gives rural Thai students an opportu-
nity to learn English and gives foreign volunteers the
opportunity to learn a whole lot more."
Year Founded: 2001
Number of Volunteers Last Year: 100
Funding Sources: No outside sources; program fees only
The Work They Do: Volunthai offers individual volunteers and
school groups a chance to teach English in rural schools in
Thailand. Volunteers are also given the opportunity to try
extracurricular studies, meditate, and study languages.
Volunthai is a small, independent organization run by a U.S.
volunteer and his Thai family
Project Location: Volunthai operates in northeastern Thailand,
in the area between Cambodia and Laos. Volunteers are
expected to live and eat as local Thais do; this means simple
accommodations, cold showers, and primarily Thai food.
Volunteers are hosted by their school, often living with the
head English teacher's family or in a teacher's dorm on the
school's campus.
Time Line: Volunteers are welcomed year-round, with the
exception of Thailand's school holidays in September,
March, and April. Volunteers usually commit to at least one
month, and most volunteers stay for two or more.
Cost: Volunthai has a program fee of $275 for one month and
$100 for every month thereafter. This fee includes all room

and board during the homestay; volunteers are responsible for their own transportation and personal expenses outside of the room and board.

Getting Started: Applications are available by e-mail via the Web site. Volunteers can apply as little as one week before starting to teach. Volunteers are met in Bangkok for an orientation before traveling by bus to Chaiyaphum for one or two days of cultural and language training.

Needed Skills and Specific Populations: Volunteers must be flexible, open-minded, enthusiastic about Thai culture, and speak English clearly. Except in special preapproved circumstances, volunteers must be at least eighteen years old, though there is no maximum age limit. Families and nonnative speakers of English are welcome to apply.

Voluntourists Without Borders (VWB)

22/8 Moo 4, Mahidol Road, NongHoi
Amphur Muang, Chiang Mai, 50000
Thailand
+66 53 801 674
E-mail: enquiry@voluntourists-without-borders.com
Web site: www.voluntourists-without-borders.com

Project Type: Agriculture; Community Development; Construction; Economic Development; Education; Scientific Research; Trail Building/Maintenance

Mission Statement Excerpt: "The Voluntourists Without Borders Initiative aims to use the skills and funding of paying volunteers alongside the labour of the rural community to develop a sustainable ecotourism industry of world class standard, that is owned by the host community, and operated under a fixed length development contract with a private sector tour operator."

Year Founded: 2005

Number of Volunteers Last Year: 250

Funding Sources: Foundations, individuals, and corporations

The Work They Do: VWB works in collaboration with the local population of Ban Mae Lai, near Chiang Mai, Thailand, to create nature trails as a sustainable ecotourism business model. In doing so, they plan to stop the destruction of forests and watershed and increase the power of local stakeholders. Volunteers help with reforestation; agricultural education, including the introduction of more sustainable farming practices; small business development; teaching of English language and computer skills; and scientific research into the environmental and socioeconomic impacts of VWB's work in the region. VWB has a goal of having the local community take over the project in its entirety by 2015.

Project Location: Volunteers work in northern Thailand, specifically in and around the city of Chiang Mai. The first project is located in a remote area one hour from Chiang Mai near the village of Ban Huay Kaew. Located in the jungle, the

346

work on the nature trail is physically demanding. Volunteers stay in a nearby lodge with shared bunk-style accommodations, and shared bathrooms with hot running water.

Time Line: Volunteers are welcome throughout the year. Volun-tourist programs are shorter-term, generally one-half day to two days, while Volunteer Vacation programs are for six days, from Sunday to Saturday. Both programs also feature optional extensions of the volunteer's service.

Cost: VWB's program fee is $50 to $60 per day, which includes room and board, materials, and equipment. Volunteers must pay for their own transport to Chiang Mai.

Getting Started: The VWB Web page includes an application package. VWB will discuss the placement with the prospective volunteer by e-mail and phone to ensure that they have the necessary skills and attitude. Training and orientation takes place on-site in the first few days, and covers an introduction to the VWB project, as well as Thai culture and language.

Needed Skills and Specific Populations: VWB volunteers should be good communicators, hard workers, positive thinkers, creative, proactive, able to work independently and in teams, culturally aware, and committed. The project will most likely appeal to those who have a strong interest in environmental, development, and ecotourism fields. Volunteers of all ages are welcome, with no minimum or maximum age limit; children are welcome with their parents. VWB welcomes volunteers with disabilities in their Chiang Mai office or as "virtual volunteers."

Winant and Clayton Volunteers

109 East 50th Street
New York, NY 10022
(212) 378-0271
E-mail: info@winantclaytonvolunteers.org
Web site: www.winantclaytonvolunteers.org

Project Type: Community Development; Youth

Mission Statement Excerpt: "Winant and Clayton volunteers are an energetic, caring team of volunteers who provide community service in the United Kingdom and in the United States, and in the process enhance their personal development while experiencing both cultures from the 'inside.'"

Year Founded: 1948

Number of Volunteers Last Year: 24

Funding Sources: Foundations and individual donors

The Work They Do: Winant and Clayton volunteers fulfill the vision of the late John G. Winant, U.S. ambassador to Great Britain during World War II, and the late Reverend Philip "Tubby" Clayton, vicar of All Hallows Church in London and private chaplain to the Queen Mother. Following World War II, these two men envisioned teams of volunteers comprised of people from the United Kingdom, known as Claytons, and from the United States, known as Winants, who would travel to the each other's countries to volunteer and learn about life there. Winant volunteers from the United States are placed in full-time volunteer positions on projects dealing with people of all ages with a variety of needs. Specific examples of volunteer work sites include community settlement clubs for the elderly, children, immigrants, teenagers at risk; drop-in service centers for people with HIV/AIDS; psychiatric rehabilitation centers; and summer day-care programs for inner-city children. Placements range from structured to self-structured, but all require energy, enthusiasm, initiative, and flexibility. Volunteers may be placed alone or with another Winant volunteer.

Project Location: Winant volunteers serve primarily in the East

348

End of London. Housing is provided to volunteers in the form of host-family accomodations, flats, or dormitory rooms.

Time Line: Winant volunteers work full-time, five days per week, for seven weeks. This volunteer experience is then followed by two weeks of independent travel. The program begins in mid-June and ends in late August.

Cost: Winant and Clayton does not charge a program fee to participate, but volunteers must pay for their own airfare to and from London, which is arranged through Winant and Clayton. Volunteers must travel as a group from New York City. Housing is provided to volunteers at no charge. A volunteer who stays with a host family will be fed by that family; all other volunteers are provided a small stipend of approximately $70 a week for food. If a volunteer is required to use public transportation to travel to and from a work site, those travel costs will be covered. A small amount of financial aid is available.

Getting Started: Prospective volunteers can download an application from the organization's Web site or write or call the office at the address and phone number listed for information and an application. Applicants must submit applications, two references, and a nonrefundable $35 application fee by the deadline in late January. Each applicant will be interviewed, either in New York City or by a former Winant volunteer who lives near the applicant. Accepted volunteers must submit a $100 nonrefundable deposit by mid-April, with the balance due by the end of that month.

Needed Skills and Specific Populations: Winant volunteers must be at least eighteen years old and be U.S. citizens; there are no specific skills required to be a Winant volunteer, just the right attitude and the desire to work hard for a good cause. There is no upper age limit, though families are not able to volunteer through this organization.

349

Women in Progress (WIP)

P.O. Box 18323
Minneapolis, MN 55418
(800) 338-3032; Fax: (612) 781-0450
E-mail: info@womeninprogress.org
Web site: www.womeninprogress.org

Project Type: Community Development; Economic
Development; Women's Issues

Mission Statement Excerpt: "Women in Progress works to
achieve economic independence of women and alleviate
poverty at a grassroots level in Africa through the sustainable
growth of small women-owned businesses and at the
same time establishes mutual understanding among people
of diverse cultures."

Year Founded: 2003

Number of Volunteers Last Year: 45

Funding Sources: Revenue from the sales of fair trade products

The Work They Do: WIP works with small women-owned micro-
businesses that produce a line of high quality, fair trade
goods. WIP's primary program is to penetrate international
markets in order to generate increased income. WIP offers a
holistic approach to business development that enables business women to "pull it all together" with measurable income
generation through exports and hands-on, personalized business assistance. Examples of volunteer activities include intro-
ducing a woman entrepreneur to computer applications;
helping a small business create a marketing plan and execute
it through designing and creating brochures; generating new
product ideas for successful export to the United States and
Europe; or assessing business practices of cooperative
members against fair trade principles to determine whether
they will receive a fair trade certification.

Project Location: All of WIPs projects are located in Ghana.
Housing is very simple, with electricity and running water most
of the time. The house includes kitchen facilities and mosquito
netting. Volunteers generally share a bathroom and perhaps a

bedroom. Internet access is available on-site or nearby. Volunteers may also stay with a nearby host family for an additional charge.

Time Line: WIP's projects run year-round, and volunteers establish their own dates, usually between two and twenty-four weeks. WIP does encourage volunteers to coordinate their travel plans with other volunteers in order to coordinate transportation to the assigned project.

Cost: Program fees are based on the length of stay, and range from $1,025 to $2,835. The program fee includes orientation, lodging, and project-related expenses. Volunteers are responsible for their travel to Ghana, food, and in-country transportation.

A volunteer takes the measurements of a girl during one of the sizing sessions while developing new products for Global Mamas, a collective of women seamstresses in Ghana who are trying to make their products marketable not only locally but to the Western market. *Photo courtesy of Women in Progress*

Getting Started: WIP accepts volunteers year-round via a registration form on their Web site. They provide a volunteer guide prior to departure, and an informal orientation upon arrival. No interview is necessary.

Needed Skills and Specific Populations: While WIP recruits volunteers with business skills, they do not require these skills in their volunteers. Volunteers must be at least sixteen years old unless accompanied by a parent; there is no maximum age limit to volunteer with WIP. WIP would be happy to attempt to accommodate volunteers with disabilities, though it may be difficult to do so in Ghana. Families are welcome to volunteer with WIP, especially mother-daughter teams.

Professionals Working Together

By Women in Progress

Women in Progress

Project

Natalie Sturman, a recent fashion design graduate, left Ipswich, England, for Cape Coast, Ghana, to volunteer with Women in Progress (WIP). Specifically, she worked with a cooperative of seamstresses called Global Mamas. When Natalie arrived, she quickly learned about the challenges that the Global Mamas cooperative was facing in making fair trade products that meet the quality expectations of the Western markets. WIP did not have formal quality control systems in place and also needed assistance in expanding the Global Mamas clothing line to include new textile designs and garments to keep the existing customer base happy. Natalie said, "I made a point of visiting the women's residences and workshops to get first-hand insight into how they work and what the conditions are like in comparison to a design studio back in England. The one recurring thing I noticed was that most of the women had their children and family around them while they worked. One seamstress was breastfeeding while continuing to sort out pattern pieces on fabric. Good multitasking I think!"

Achievements

Natalie persevered through challenges in the product development process and accomplished the following:

- Updated Quality Control Specifications for many of the new Global Mamas products
- Facilitated two design workshops with both the seamstresses and the batikers (women who specialize in making batik fabric)
- Carried out several sizing sessions to ensure the clothing was fitting properly
- Worked closely with all of the seamstresses in pattern adjustments
- Introduced five new children's and adults' garments into the new Global Mamas wholesale catalog: women's halter dress, women's ruffle skirt, women's gypsy blouse, women's A-line dress, and a babies' top/knickers outfit
- Introduced several new textile designs used in the Global Mamas catalog

Highlights

Natalie's highlight was at the monthly roundtable meeting of the Global Mama seamstresses. She had suggested giving an award to one of the women for being hardworking, trustworthy, and on time. Natalie and other WIP staff decided to give the award to seamstress Grace Adoboe. Upon receipt of the award, Grace was thrilled to pieces! At the end of the meeting Natalie congratulated Grace on her achievement, and Grace said to Natalie, "It's because of you. I couldn't have done it without you!"

World Horizons

P.O. Box 662
Bethlehem, CT 06751
(800) 262-5874 or (203) 266-5874; Fax: (203) 266-6227
E-mail: worldhorizons@att.net
Web site: www.world-horizons.com

Project Type: Construction; Natural Conservation (Land);
Natural Conservation (Sea); Trail Building/Maintenance;
Youth

Mission Statement Excerpt: "World Horizons facilitates community service projects, promotes cross-cultural learning, and
facilitates language immersion in particular locations."

Year Founded: 1987

Number of Volunteers Last Year: Approximately 65

Funding Sources: None; World Horizons is self-supporting.

The Work They Do: World Horizons offers high school
students, college students, adults, and families the opportunity to participate in short-term international and domestic
volunteer projects. Project areas may include working with
seniors or children or working in the areas of agriculture,
the environment, construction, or painting. Examples of
past projects include environmental work in Iceland; helping
children and adults with physical and emotional disabilities
involved in therapeutic riding programs in Italy and
California; assisting teachers in schools in Fiji; organizing
children's activities and doing repairs in schools in Costa
Rica, Dominica, and Ecuador; and working with abandoned
and abused animals in Utah, New York, and India. World
Horizons was founded by a returned Peace Corps administrator who wanted to offer teens the opportunity to experience a mini Peace Corps–style project.

Project Location: World Horizons offers international projects
in Costa Rica, Dominica, the Eastern Caribbean, Ecuador,
Fiji, Iceland, India, and Italy, and domestic projects in California, New York, and Utah. In general, accommodations
tend to be basic. Students and leaders live in rented houses,

community halls, or schools. Volunteers often sleep on the floor in a sleeping bag. Volunteer groups cook for themselves and live as a family unit.

Time Line: Project start dates begin in late June and run through early August. Most projects last three weeks, with some lasting from ten days or two weeks.

Cost: The organization's all-inclusive program fees range from $2,500 to $5,300 and cover all transportation, food, accommodations, and sightseeing. Personal expenses, such as money spent on souvenirs and snacks, are the only expenses not included in the program fee.

Getting Started: Students who are interested in volunteering with World Horizons should visit the organization's Web site and download an application; interviews are not required. Orientation is given the night before the trip begins.

Needed Skills and Specific Populations: World Horizons volunteers must be thirteen to eighteen years old. The only required skill is at least one year of appropriate language training if the project takes place in a Spanish- or French-speaking country. Volunteers with disabilities would probably find World Horizons projects to be difficult. World Horizons accepts volunteers from all over the world; volunteers do not have to be U.S. citizens.

WorldTeach

Center for International Development, Harvard University
79 John F. Kennedy Street
Cambridge, MA 02138
(617) 495-5527 or (800) 4-TEACH-O; Fax: (617) 495-1599
E-mail: info@worldteach.org
Web site: www.worldteach.org

Project Type: Community Development; Economic
  Development; Education; Youth
Mission Statement Excerpt: "WorldTeach . . . provides opportunities for individuals to make a meaningful contribution to
  international education by living and working as volunteer
  teachers in developing countries."
Year Founded: 1986
Number of Volunteers Last Year: 400
Funding Sources: Some funding from private donors
The Work They Do: Volunteers teach English to students of a
  wide age range depending on the needs of the country and
  host institution. In some countries, volunteers may also
  teach math, science, computer skills, and HIV/AIDS awareness. Volunteers work as full-time teachers and are
  employed by their host schools or sponsoring institutions in
  their placement countries. Most volunteers live with host
  families or on the school campus, and they participate fully
  in the lives of their host communities.
Project Location: Volunteers can work in American Samoa,
  Bangladesh, Bulgaria, Chile, China, Costa Rica, Ecuador,
  Guyana, Kenya, the Marshall Islands, Micronesia, Namibia,
  Poland, Rwanda, Thailand, and South Africa. Host institutions may be public or private primary or secondary
  schools, public or private universities, vocational schools
  and institutions, community resource centers, local organizations, or government agencies. Placement depends on the
  needs of the host communities and the location in which
  volunteers can be of most use to their host countries. Educational resources available to volunteers depend on

placement and vary widely from country to country. Volunteers may live with local families, share houses with other local or foreign teachers, or, in some cases, have their own apartments. Volunteers in some countries live in traditional houses without running water or electricity; others have apartments with many modern amenities. Wherever volunteers are placed, they are likely to have their own furnished bedroom and access to a bathroom and kitchen or cafeteria.

Time Line: WorldTeach offers short-term, eight-week summer programs that depart in June, and long-term, ten- to twelve-month programs with varying departure dates throughout the year.

Cost: Program fees vary by location and range from $1,500 to $7,990, with the exception of the American Samoa, Micronesia, Marshall Islands, and Bangladesh programs, which have no program fees and are fully funded. Each program fee covers international round-trip airfare from a gateway city within the United States to the country of service, room and board, health insurance, emergency evacuation, visa and predeparture materials, and in-country orientation and training. Long-term teaching volunteers receive a small monthly living stipend that is usually equivalent to what local teachers earn.

Getting Started: Prospective volunteers can download an application from WorldTeach's Web site or call and request that one be sent via postal mail. All candidates must submit two letters of recommendation, and applicants for long-term teaching programs are required to interview with a WorldTeach volunteer who has completed a program. Admission to some of WorldTeach's programs, especially the fully funded programs, can be competitive. Admissions decisions are made on a rolling basis within two to three weeks of the receipt of a completed application, and final application deadlines are typically three months before the program departure date. WorldTeach provides intensive in-country orientation for every program: seven to ten days for summer programs and three to four weeks for long-term programs. Orientation includes training in the host country's language,

A volunteer teaches in front of a class of raptly attentive students In the Marshall Islands, Pacific Ocean. *Photo courtesy of WorldTeach*

instruction on teaching English as a foreign language, a teaching practicum, discussions of the host country's history and culture, informational sessions on health and safety issues, exploration of the region, and group building and social activities. Orientation is led by the in-country field director as well as by orientation assistants, who are usually current volunteers who have already begun their work.

Needed Skills and Specific Populations: Volunteers for the long-term programs must be college graduates; volunteers for the summer programs must be at least eighteen years old; and fluency in the English language is required of volunteers in all programs except those in China, where volunteers must be native English speakers. Because of WorldTeach's minimum age requirement, it is uncommon for families to volunteer with WorldTeach. Volunteers must also be responsible, caring, self-motivated individuals with a strong interest in cultural exchange and teaching. Volunteers do not have to have previous teaching experience or training. WorldTeach welcomes senior volunteers. Because WorldTeach places volunteers in challenging circumstances in developing countries and with local host families, it may not be able to accommodate volunteers with certain disabilities or serious health limitations, or those who require specialized housing arrangements.

We Will Succeed

By Torin Perez

WorldTeach

I spent the summer in Cape Town, South Africa, with
WorldTeach. The program I was involved in, Snack Sneakers,
was designed for seventh grade students from Masiphumelele,
one of the black townships. Ten volunteers total, we taught
basic entrepreneurship skills and business concepts to thirty-
five students. In an environment like Masiphumelele where
unemployment is very common, starting a business on your
own is the best path for an individual seeking success. Many
terms such as "loan" and "wholesaler" were foreign words
and working with ESL students made our assignment even
more challenging.

During the program we acted as actual bankers and
wholesalers and allowed the students to buy and sell sweets
and chips while teaching them about other facets such as public relations and marketing. We also stressed principles like
respect, commitment, punctuality, honesty, self-confidence,
persistence, responsibility, and teamwork. The children were
initially attracted to the program because money and sweets
were involved, but in the end they realized that there was a lot
more to entrepreneurship than just money and commodities.
Through team-building exercises and small classroom lessons,
they learned more about entrepreneurship than they ever
thought they could.

The name Masiphumelele means "we will succeed." Having formed during the Apartheid era, Masiphumelele still
exhibits much poverty and a general lack of resources. I hope
that what we have done here can, at least on a micro-scale,

contribute to the Masiphumelele community, helping it live up to the meaning of its name.

The morning of the last day of the Snack Sneakers program I was touched by the tribal song recitals of the children. Previously, whenever a teacher walked into the room, the noise dropped to silence. But on this day, the song continued, and as I listened, my eyes filled with tears. Something about their voices and their song raised my spirits and made me feel appreciated. But more importantly, it represented their own pride in themselves, their culture, and their country. What is most satisfying to me is that I am confident that the twenty-five children who were dedicated throughout and completed the entire two-week program are on the road to a brighter future, and I know that their hunger for better lives will lead them on to bigger and better things. My experience in South Africa is surely one that I will always remember.

World-Wide Opportunities on Organic Farms (WWOOF)—United Kingdom & Independents

P.O. Box 2154, Winslow
Buckingham, MK18 3WS
United Kingdom
+44 (0) 1296 714652
E-mail: member@wwoof.org.uk
Web site: www.wwoof.org or www.wwoof.org.uk

Project Type: Agriculture

Mission Statement Excerpt: "To get into the countryside; to help the organic movement; to get firsthand experience of organic farming and growing; to make contact with other people in the organic movement."

Year Founded: 1971

Number of Volunteers Last Year: WWOOF does not keep statistics on the number of volunteers, but the UK branch had 1,745 members last year.

Funding Sources: None; WWOOF is self-funded.

The Work They Do: WWOOF's premise is simple: volunteers help organic growers in exchange for food and accommodations. WWOOF helps link volunteers to growers, and it leaves the details for the individuals to work out for themselves. Therefore, each volunteer experience with WWOOF is unique, but volunteers can expect that they could be involved with any growing or farming-related activity on an organic farm.

Project Location: WWOOF growers are located all over the world. Living situations vary widely, as each grower provides accommodations to the WWOOF volunteer.

Time Line: With so many opportunities around the world, there is always a WWOOF grower in need of help. The start and end date, as well as the minimum and maximum amount of time the volunteer spends with the grower, are up to the volunteer and the grower to negotiate.

Cost: There is no cost to volunteer. WWOOF's membership fee is £15, for which members receive access to listings of

A volunteer learns the remarkable method of haying on an organic farm in Holland. *Photo courtesy of World-Wide Opportunities on Organic Farms (WWOOF)—United Kingdom*

grower hosts and six newsletters per year. Volunteers pay their own travel costs.

Getting Started: Applications are available on WWOOF's Web site, or prospective volunteers may contact the office and request one. Growers are responsible for providing training and orientation to volunteers.

Needed Skills and Specific Populations: WWOOF volunteers must be at least eighteen years old; senior volunteers are welcome to work with WWOOF. Volunteers with disabilities must work with individual growers to determine the feasibility of working on specific farms. Some WWOOF hosts welcome volunteers with children, but this is at their discretion; these families must arrange this directly with prospective host farms prior to arrival.

Dig for Victory

By Mark Charlton

World-Wide Opportunities on Organic Farms

For the past four to five years, I've become increasingly inter-ested in food, nutrition, and what it actually means to live a healthy and happy life. I've earned a degree, traveled for a year around the world, and worked various jobs, but just never felt fulfilled. In an urban environment, where I spend a good deal of my time, there's an implicit pressure to rush and of immediacy, which is all part of its charm, but I was also finding it exhausting. As a young person, to admit that the speed of urban life was too fast for me left me despairing about the lack of alternatives. It was either survival of the fittest or you opt out! I remembered an advertisement for WWOOF that I'd seen while traveling in New Zealand so I checked to see if you could WWOOF in the UK. How little I knew! This moment of education began an eight-month WWOOF adven-ture here on home soil.

I spent the first month or so working mostly alone, except for my week at a Buddhist retreat centre, which was a delight after the crazy pace of life beforehand. In fact, I could barely believe how beautiful my surroundings were—the friendliness of the hosts, the generosity of the Sun, and the peace of mind that accompanied it. I was moved to tears more times than I care to remember! My innocence about the geography of Eng-land (let's call it innocence for the sake of argument) made my travels all the more exciting.

My average stay was two to three weeks, although I ended up at one market garden for two months. This particular gar-den was exactly how I'd imagined WWOOFing to be in terms of how much I'd learn and the diversity of jobs—the weekly market, the preparations for the box scheme as well as planting, sowing, and making new beds. The food there was wonderful and they also had a great library. Both the food and the books lent themselves to passionate conversations. For me, all this discovery, work, and dialogue was part of the experience I had been searching for, as I wanted to try on this new kind of life and have confirmation that there is in fact life outside TV, iTunes, and Wii!

There were difficult times like when I missed friends and family, or a farm was nothing that I expected, or I just completely doubted my decision to leave my other life behind. But I think that's what life is—it's an adventure, full of surprises, good and bad. I think if everything is what we expect, then how can we be challenged and grow?

I'm now back up North and bringing nature and its inherent easy pace into my life as much as possible. I've started work at a small organic café in order to save some money for next year—I think WWOOFing is back in the cards! I have realized a lost connection with nature. I welcome it wholeheartedly into my life because alongside it comes humility, truthfulness, meaning, and a childlike appreciation—the simple pleasure of just being alive can be obscured in an urban environment with so much to think about. I've developed a massive respect for all the farmers, gardeners, seed-savers, cooks, and conservation workers who silently and often thanklessly protect our countryside, culture, heritage, and quality of life. I am positive about their voice becoming louder in society. I urge anyone and everyone to try WWOOFing and support your community and country. Dig for victory!

World-Wide Opportunities on Organic Farms (WWOOF)—USA

P.O. Box 1098
Philmont, NY 12565
(831) 425- FARM
E-mail: info@wwoofusa.org
Web site: www.wwoofusa.org

Project Type: Agriculture; Construction; Natural Conservation (Land)

Mission Statement Excerpt: "WWOOF—USA is part of a worldwide effort to link volunteers with organic farmers, promote an educational exchange, and build a global community conscious of ecological farming practices."

Year Founded: 2001

Number of Volunteers Last Year: Approximately 1,500

Funding Sources: None; self-funded through memberships

The Work They Do: WWOOF—USA provides a network of organic farms willing to host volunteers that wish to learn about sustainable agriculture through hands-on experience on the farms. Volunteers may help in the farms or gardens by planting, weeding, harvesting, and providing animal care. Other opportunities on farms may include tending medicinal plants, construction, green and alternative building, permaculture, and solar energy projects. WWOOF—USA does not provide actual placements, but rather a directory of potential host farms that volunteers can contact directly.

Project Location: WWOOF—USA lists more than 800 host farms in all fifty U.S. states, including Alaska and Hawaii. Accommodations vary by host farm.

Time Line: Volunteers are accepted throughout the year. The length of the volunteer experience is directly negotiated between the volunteer and the host farm. Some host farms request that volunteers make multi-month commitments, while others accept weekend volunteers. Most participants volunteer for four to six hours per day.

Cost: The membership fee to join WWOOF—USA is $20 for one person or $30 for two people who plan to travel together. Volunteers receive free room and board from their hosts, but they are responsible for their own travel to the farms.

Getting Started: Prospective volunteers should join WWOOF—USA and obtain the host farm directory. Volunteers can join WWOOF—USA either through the organization's Web site or by downloading, completing, and mailing in an application with a check. Any orientation or training is left up to the individual host farm.

Needed Skills and Specific Populations: Individual volunteers must be at least eighteen years old. Some host farms will accept volunteers under that age, as long as they are volunteering with a parent. Senior volunteers are welcomed. Some host farms may be able to accommodate volunteers with disabilities. In general, no previous experience or skills are needed, though some individual host farms may have their own requirements. WWOOF cannot help international volunteers with visas.

Wyoming Dinosaur Center (WDC)

110 Carter Ranch Road
P.O. Box 868
Thermopolis, WY 82443
(800) 455-DINO or (307) 864-2997; Fax: (307) 864-5762
E-mail: wdinoc@wyodino.org
Web site: www.wyodino.org

Project Type: Archaeology; Museum; Scientific Research

Mission Statement Excerpt: "To educate the public about the science of paleontology through hands-on work at an ongoing digsite, and constantly evolving museum displays."

Year Founded: 1993

Number of Volunteers Last Year: Approximately 350

Funding Sources: Foundations and individual donors

The Work They Do: WDC offers Dig-for-a-Day programs, which allow volunteers to help discover, collect, and document Jurassic period dinosaur fossils. Excavation work at the WDC's two main quarries has yielded well-preserved bones of Camarasaurus and Diplodocus dinosaurs. All activities assist in current scientific research projects, which provide valuable information concerning the environment that existed in the area more than 140 million years ago.

Project Location: The dig sites are located fifteen minutes from the WDC on Warm Springs Ranch at the northern end of Wind River Canyon in Wyoming. Volunteers usually stay at local hotels, although individuals who stay for prolonged service are often provided cheaper accomodations on an individual basis.

Time Line: As the project name indicates, this is a one-day volunteer program. When the weather allows, WDC runs the Dig-for-a-Day program from late spring through early fall, Monday through Friday. The day begins at 8:00 A.M., ends by 5:00 P.M., and includes a thirty-minute lunch break. If needed, volunteers return to the WDC on one of the hourly tour buses earlier than 5:00 P.M.

Cost: The program fee for Dig-for-a-Day volunteers is $150 per adult and $80 per child. WDC requires a $25 deposit, which is refunded if the dig is canceled because of inclement weather. Volunteers who cancel a reservation at least thirty days before the project date will receive a full refund. The program fee includes lunch, but volunteers are responsible for all other expenses, including travel, accommodations, and other meals.

Getting Started: Prospective volunteers must call the WDC at the number listed to register in advance; teams are limited to six people per day. Volunteers undergo a one-hour orientation at the start of the day that discusses the geology and paleontology of the work site as well as digging and data-collection procedures.

Needed Skills and Specific Populations: Individual volunteers must be at least eighteen years old, but children younger than that age may volunteer if accompanied by an adult. Volunteers must be able to work outdoors, walk at least a quarter-mile on uneven ground, and withstand high temperatures, although shade and water is always available. In addition, a reasonable attention span is needed for the intricate work of removing fossils from the surrounding sediments. Because the work can be physically challenging and strenuous, and because fossil collection is a serious scientific endeavor requiring care and precision, families should carefully consider whether their children are well suited for this activity. Volunteers with disasbilities can work in the museum's preparation lab, stabilizing and cleaning bones for study and display. Certain disasbilities can be accomodated in the field, although the appropriateness of this will be determined on a case-by-case basis. Volunteers who successfully master the basic skills of fieldwork may join the WDC in more delicate and critical work, and they are not charged for such participation. The WDC also offers a Kid's Dig program on select days throughout the summer for children ages eight to twelve, wherein kids hunt for fossils, participate in a dig in the dinosaur quarry, work in the molding/ casting lab, and participate in an educational scavenger hunt in the museum.

YMCA Go Global

International Branch, YMCA of Greater New York
5 West 63rd Street, 2nd Floor
New York, NY 10023
(888) 477-9622 or (212) 727-8800
E-mail: Chiu@ymcanyc.org
Web site: www.internationalymca.org

Project Type: Community Development; Youth
Mission Statement Excerpt: "The YMCA Go Global program
sends young adults from various parts of the United States
to overseas YMCAs and other educational and human
service organizations, where they work in a wide variety of
cultural and community services."
Year Founded: 2000
Number of Volunteers Last Year: 52
Funding Sources: Foundations and individual donors
The Work They Do: YMCA Go Global volunteers partner with
YMCAs in other countries to assist those organizations in
their work. Work done by volunteers may include teen leadership, health care, education, social work, community
development, and many other fields. Specific examples of
volunteer opportunities with YMCA Go Global include
serving as camp counselors in Australia and the Bahamas,
helping with social work and HIV/AIDS awareness projects
in sub-Saharan Africa, and helping with public and cultural
relations campaigns in Thailand.
Project Location: YMCA Go Global currently has volunteer
programs in Australia, China, Ecuador, Ghana, Gambia,
Hong Kong, Italy, Malta, Peru, Scotland, South Africa, South
Korea, Thailand, and Trinidad. Applicants may provide
YMCA Go Global with a list of three preferred countries,
but the organization's staff members make the final decision
on volunteer placement. Housing varies by host country, but
volunteers typically stay in cabins, apartments, with a host
family, or in other similar accommodations.

Time Line: YMCA Go Global offers two-month to two-year placements. Placements are available throughout the year.

Cost: YMCA Go Global charges a $1,000 program fee. Food, accommodations, and, in some countries, a small stipend are provided to the volunteer by their host YMCAs. Volunteers must provide their own international airfare.

Getting Started: Prospective volunteers can download an application from the YMCA Go Global Web site. Application deadlines are typically in the season before departure; for example, volunteers who wish to depart in the summer will have an application deadline in the spring. Volunteers must conduct an interview by phone or in person, and may need to attend a predeparture orientation in New York City. YMCA Go Global also offers an in-country briefing and orientation sessions upon arrival in the host country, and language lessons as necessary.

Needed Skills and Specific Populations: Volunteers must be U.S. citizens, eighteen years of age or older, with no maximum age. There is no language requirement for YMCA Go Global's placements, with the exception of volunteer sites in Latin American, which ask that volunteers have at least a moderate proficiency in Spanish. Some sites may be able to host volunteers with disabilities.

Youth International

232 Wright Avenue
Toronto, Ontario, M6R 1L3
Canada
(416) 538-0152; Fax: (416) 538-7189
E-mail: info@youthinternational.org
Web site: www.youthinternational.org

Project Type: Agriculture; Community Development; Construction; Education; Natural Conservation (Land); Orphans; Youth

Mission Statement Excerpt: "Youth International opens the doors for young people to actively explore and discover a broader perspective on the world while developing a deeper understanding of who they are and what their place is within that world."

Year Founded: 1997

Number of Volunteers Last Year: 95

Funding Sources: Mostly self-funded, with a few private donors

The Work They Do: Youth International sponsors projects that include, for the most part, physically challenging manual labor, though some teaching positions are also available. Specific examples of Youth International's projects include renovating orphanages and schools, teaching English, carrying out conservation projects in the rainforest, and helping the poor in Mother Teresa's clinics.

Project Location: Youth International has an Asia program, with projects located in Thailand, India, and Vietnam, as well as a South America program, with projects located in Bolivia, Peru, and Ecuador. About half of the accommodations are in homestays, with the rest in hostels or tents. Youth International's goal is to live and travel like the residents of the country of service; conditions are often rugged, and may lack in basic comforts and amenities.

Time Line: Youth International places volunteers from September through December and February through May. Volunteer programs last twelve weeks.

Cost: Youth International's program fee is $7,900, which covers virtually all of the volunteer's costs, including all flights, visas, all overland transportation, program activities, and food and accommodations.

Getting Started: Applications for Youth International's programs are available on its Web site, or can be mailed or e-mailed to prospective volunteers. Applications are followed up with a phone interview within one week. The three-day orientation begins in Estes Park, Colorado, or alternate locations in the United States, and is completed in-country.

Needed Skills and Specific Populations: Volunteers must have a high school diploma. Senior volunteers can work with Youth International, but the organization's efforts are focused on people aged eighteen to twenty-five. Volunteers with disabilities are welcomed, with the caveat that some program areas cannot adequately accommodate all disabilities. Families are not restricted from volunteering with Youth International, but the program does focus on volunteers within a specific age range, not families.

Introduction to Long-Term Volunteer Opportunities

Ready to go to (or at least think about) the next level?

So now you've tried a volunteer vacation, or at least you've busied yourself for many hours dreaming about one. You've chosen where in the world you want to go and what skills you want to use, squirreled away some funds, and had a wonderful adventure. A short adventure, but a wonderful adventure nonetheless.

And you want more.

That's not surprising. Many, many people who go on a volunteer vacation say that it was the single best thing that they've done, that it changed how they viewed themselves and the world, and that they made friends and discovered new passions and talents. How could you not want more?

These reactions, which we have heard time and time again from volunteers, form the basis for the following short section on long-term volunteer opportunities. Note that we don't use the term "vacation" here, and that's on purpose. You can expect that these organizations will request at least a year of your time if not longer. This is especially true of the overseas volunteer agencies, which usually ask for at least two years. Though we know of two couples that joined the Peace Corps soon after getting married and jokingly referred to their time abroad as "our two-year honeymoon," the experiences you'll have with these organizations are not just a break from your daily life: they become your daily life.

Of course, if you have done a volunteer vacation, you've also found out that it can be incredibly challenging. You'll find that these challenges are even greater in long-term volunteer experiences. Not being fluent in the local language or culture, being far from family and friends, tasting different foods, and facing the problems that others live with on a daily basis in the United States and around the world can be incredibly difficult. Everyone knows the Peace Corps' slogan, "It's the Toughest Job You'll Ever Love." It is a great slogan, and it could be applied to almost any long-term volunteer organization. But there is a temptation, as we think about these programs, to focus on, "I'm going to love my job," and forget that "this will be the toughest job I'll ever have."

So why do it, then? Why leave the comfort of your home, your family, the safety of all that you know and love, for a volunteer assignment across the country or on another continent, for what will seem like a very long amount of time?

Because it is worth it. Almost serendipitously, it is worth it. Surveys of volunteers who complete full-time, long-term volunteer experiences show that the vast majority—over 90 percent—are glad they did it and would do so again. Here are some of the main reasons that you can expect to feel the same way after your experience:

You'll get a much more in-depth knowledge of the problems people face around the world, and have a much better opportunity to help people solve their problems. Their problems become your problems, and you will become a committed activist for change both during the volunteer experience and afterward.

You'll have the opportunity to make great friends who will remain with you for the rest of your life.

You'll learn skills that will benefit you for many, many years to come. As one employer told us, "I love to hire returned overseas volunteers. They're problem solvers, dedicated, flexible, often bilingual, can work independently, and have demonstrated that they really care about the world. Who wouldn't want to hire a person like that?"

You are needed. AmeriCorps has positions that go unfilled every year. Peace Corps can't find nearly enough French speakers to send to West Africa. You have real skills, and you can make a tangible difference in the lives of others.

And in case you hadn't guessed by now, the people you help will make a difference in your life, too. We promise you this: a long-term volunteer experience will change who you are as a person. It can't help but do so. How could you uproot yourself and go somewhere completely new, take on a new job helping others, learn a new language or culture, and come back the same person? You will see the world and yourself in a different light, have different priorities, and have new doors open for you.

We know. We served as rural community development volunteers in the Peace Corps for two years in the village of Ligolio, in central Suriname (go ahead, look it up on a map—we didn't know where it was, either. Here's a hint: start with South America.). Anne pursued her graduate degree, a Master's in public health, based on her experiences in Ligolio. One of our daughters is named after the old woman who lived across the mango tree from us. And our work in the Peace Corps led to our current jobs, which led Doug to write a magazine article, which led directly to being hired to write the book you're holding in your hands.

We should mention one other benefit that long-term volunteering has over volunteer vacations: by and large, you don't have to pay for the experience. There are other people, including the government, faith-based organizations, and private donors, who think that you going off and doing this is such a great idea that they'll pay for you to do it. You're not going to make any money by being a long-term volunteer, but it probably won't cost you any money, either.

To be clear, we don't want to knock volunteer vacations—we've written this book about them, and we believe in them as firmly as a person can. But the difference between a volunteer vacation and a long-term volunteer experience is similar to the difference between going to London for a week and studying there for a full semester. Both are wonderful things to do, but a semester's worth of study is going to be a much more in-depth experience, and you come home with a very different perspective on the place.

A book could (and should) be written on the organizations that offer fully funded, long-term volunteer opportunities, but we have chosen here to just whet your appetite with descriptions of five of these organizations. We know volunteers who have participated in all of them, and we feel strongly that these organizations offer phenomenal opportunities and take good care of their volunteers. Two are international (Peace Corps and Voluntary Service Overseas); two are domestic (AmeriCorps and Teach for America); and one offers both domestic and international placements (Jesuit Volunteer Corps). As for primary funding sources, some of these programs receive money from the government (Peace Corps and AmeriCorps), one from faith-based groups (Jesuit Volunteer Corps), and two from private donors (Teach for America and Voluntary Service Overseas).

We've kept the same formatting for these organizations that was used for the volunteer vacation organizations, since by this point in the book you've probably become used to it.

We've never met someone who regretted his or her decision to take a year or two and dedicate themselves to full-time volunteer work. Who could take on a challenge like this, and say at the end, "No, that wasn't worth it. I wish I hadn't met those people, learned those skills, helped out, and grown in new and different ways that I never could have dreamed of"?

Note that we didn't say "take a year or two *off*" in the last paragraph. It's not time off. It's not a long detour from your pre-programmed road of life that eventually just returns you to the same spot in the road. After this experience, you'll be different.

And it will be worth it.

Good luck. And send us a postcard.

Doug Cutchins and Anne Geissinger

AmeriCorps

1201 New York Avenue, NW
Washington, DC 20525
(202) 606-5000; TTY (202) 565-2799
E-mail: questions@americorps.org
Web site: www.americorps.org

Project Type: Community Development; Construction; Developmental Disabilities; Medical/Health; Natural Conservation (Land); Trail Building/Maintenance; Youth

Mission Statement Excerpt: "To improve lives, strengthen communities, and foster civic engagement through service and volunteering."

Year Founded: 1994

Number of Volunteers Last Year: Almost 75,000

Funding Sources: AmeriCorps is funded by the federal government and has an annual budget of more than $500 million.

The Work They Do: AmeriCorps is a national network of hundreds of programs throughout the United States. AmeriCorps comprises three very different programs:

- AmeriCorps*VISTA (Volunteers in Service to America) volunteers work to bring individuals and communities out of poverty. VISTA volunteers serve full-time for a year in capacity-building roles in nonprofits, public agencies, and faith-based groups throughout the country, working to fight illiteracy, improve health services, create businesses, increase housing opportunities, or bridge the digital divide.

- AmeriCorps*NCCC (National Civilian Community Corps) volunteers commit to a ten-month, full-time residential program, serving in teams of ten to twelve members. NCCC volunteers work on projects in the areas of public safety, public health, and disaster relief. Teams are based at one of four campuses across the country but are sent to work on short-term projects in neighboring states.

- The third group of programs comes under the general heading of AmeriCorps. These programs are found in local and national organizations throughout the United States such as the American Red Cross, Habitat for Humanity,

Boys and Girls Clubs, and local community centers and places of worship. These volunteers engage in direct, hands-on service work.

Project Location: AmeriCorps partners with one thousand local and national groups across the United States to offer seventy-five thousand positions in many cities and towns. Volunteers are usually responsible for locating their own housing, with the exception of NCCC volunteers, who live as a group, often on decommissioned military bases.

Time Line: AmeriCorps volunteers typically commit to ten months to one year of service. Most assignments are full-time, but there are some part-time service opportunities available.

Cost: For all AmeriCorps programs, members receive a modest living allowance, and some programs provide housing. Most members find the living allowance to be adequate to cover their needs, though it is not generous. AmeriCorps volunteers may also receive an education award, which can be used to pay education costs at qualified institutions of higher education or training or to repay qualified student loans. The award currently is $4,725 for a year of full-time service, with correspondingly lesser awards for part-time and reduced part-time service. A volunteer has up to seven years after his or her term of service has ended to claim the award.

Getting Started: Prospective volunteers can complete an application on the AmeriCorps Web site. All volunteers receive training at the beginning of their service and project-specific training during their service.

Needed Skills and Specific Populations: Volunteers must be U.S. citizens, nationals, or legal permanent resident aliens of the United States, and they must be at least seventeen years old (some service opportunities require volunteers to be at least eighteen). There is no maximum age limit for most positions. (NCCC volunteers must be eighteen to twenty-four years old.) Some programs have specific skill requests in certain areas, and others look for a bachelor's degree or a few years of related volunteer or work experience.

Jesuit Volunteer Corps (JVC)

801 St. Paul Street
Baltimore, MD 21202
(410) 244-1744
E-mail: jvceast@jesuitvolunteers.org (for domestic programs);
jvi@jesuitvolunteers.org (for international programs)
Web site: www.jesuitvolunteers.org

Project Type: Community Development; Developmental Disabilities; Economic Development; Legal; Medical/Health;
  Women's Issues; Youth
Mission Statement Excerpt: "The challenge to Jesuit Volunteers
  is to integrate Christian faith by working and living among
  the poor and marginalized, by living simply and in community with other Jesuit Volunteers, and by examining the
  causes of social injustice."
Year Founded: 1956
Number of Volunteers Last Year: Approximately 250
Funding Sources: Most of JVC's funding comes from Catholic
  sources.
The Work They Do: JVC is built on four pillars: social justice,
  simple living, community, and spirituality. JVC volunteers
  live in group households with other JVC volunteers, where
  they put these ideals into action. During the day, volunteers
  go to full-time work positions. Hundreds of grassroots
  organizations across the country count on JVC volunteers to
  provide essential services to low-income people and those
  who live on the fringes of our society. Volunteers serve the
  homeless, the unemployed, refugees, people with HIV/AIDS,
  the elderly, street youth, abused women and children, the
  mentally ill, and the developmentally disabled. JVC has
  become the largest Catholic lay volunteer program in the
  country. Examples of JVC work placements include a case
  manager at a homeless shelter in Hartford, Connecticut, a
  CPR and first aid instructor in Alaska, a learning center
  counselor in San Francisco, and an English teacher in Nepal.

Project Location: JVC has houses throughout the United States, and volunteers apply to serve in a specific region of the country. International placements are available in Belize, Nicaragua, Bolivia, Peru, Tanzania, Nepal, Micronesia, and the Marshall Islands.

Time Line: Domestic JVC volunteers begin in the first week of August and serve for one year. International JVC volunteers begin in July and serve for two years. Training and orientation classes are offered at the beginning of volunteer service.

Cost: Domestic volunteers pay their way to the orientation site in the region where they will serve. JVC provides travel from the orientation site to the city in which the volunteer will work, transportation to and from retreats during the year, and transportation home at the end of the year. Placement sites pay for the volunteer's housing, utilities, a food stipend, transportation to and from work (in the form of providing the volunteer a bus pass or a bicycle, for the most part), and medical insurance. Volunteers receive a small personal stipend—about $75 a month—to spend on whatever they wish. International volunteers receive transportation to orientation and to the country of placement. International volunteers are asked to undertake fund-raising efforts before they leave, but acceptance into the program is in no way conditional on this fund-raising.

Getting Started: Prospective volunteers can download an application from JVC's Web site. The deadline for international applications is February 1. Domestic applications are accepted on a rolling basis, with priority given to those received before March 1.

Needed Skills and Specific Populations: Some job placements require specific credentials or licenses, but most JVC jobs can be done by people who have a general educational background and a willingness to learn new skills. Most of JVC's volunteers are recent college graduates.

Peace Corps

1111 20th Street NW
Washington, DC 20526
(800) 424-8580
E-mail: volunteer@peacecorps.gov
Web site: www.peacecorps.gov

Project Type: Agriculture; Community Development; Construction; Economic Development; Education; Medical/Health; Natural Conservation (Land); Professional/Technical Assistance; Rural Development; Women's Issues; Youth

Mission Statement Excerpt: "Three simple goals comprise the Peace Corps' mission: helping the people of interested countries in meeting their needs for trained men and women; helping promote a better understanding of Americans on the part of the peoples served; helping promote a better understanding of other peoples on the part of all Americans."

Year Founded: 1961

Number of Volunteers Last Year: Approximately 8,000 at any given time

Funding Sources: Peace Corps is an independent agency of the United States government and has a budget of more than $330 million.

The Work They Do: Peace Corps volunteers offer expertise and training to people in economically developing nations around the world. The range of opportunities available in the Peace Corps is vast, from traditional international volunteer positions in teaching, health, and agriculture, to opportunities for addressing more modern challenges such as HIV/AIDS, information technology, and business development in urban areas. All volunteers work in one of six sectors: education and community development, business development, environment, agriculture, health and HIV/AIDS, youth, and information technology. Specific examples of volunteer work include training high school teachers; working in an urban planning office; conducting community-based conservation programs such as sustainable use of forest or marine resources, apiculture, and honey production; teaching basic nutrition courses; and implementing computer networks for government offices.

Project Location: Peace Corps volunteers work in more than seventy countries around the world. While applicants can state a preference for placement in a specific region of the world, Peace Corps makes the final decisions regarding what work the volunteer will do and where the volunteer will be placed. As the populations of economically developing countries have shifted to urban areas in the last few decades, so too have more and more Peace Corps volunteers been placed in cities. Accommodations for volunteers vary greatly, from apartments in cities to small huts in very rural areas.

Time Line: After they have completed their eight to twelve weeks of training, Peace Corps volunteers serve for two years. Applications are processed on a rolling basis, and there are no deadlines. Applicants are well advised to apply nine to twelve months before the desired departure date.

Cost: There is no program fee to be a Peace Corps volunteer, and Peace Corps is among the most generous agencies of its type. All of the volunteer's expenses, including international airfare, medical, and dental care, are paid. Volunteers receive a living allowance to pay for accommodations and food, which allows them to live at the same standard as the local people in their community. Volunteers also receive a small vacation stipend and just over $6,000 in a readjustment allowance for completing the twenty-seven months of service. Volunteers with Perkins loans are eligible for a deduction of 15 percent of their outstanding balance for each year of Peace Corps service.

Getting Started: Prospective volunteers should complete an online application. The application itself is quite extensive and includes two essays. Applicants must also complete a one-hour interview with a recruiter and pass stringent medical and legal checks before being cleared to volunteer. Peace Corps training is done in-country and lasts eight to twelve weeks, covering cultural immersion, language, and technical training.

Needed Skills and Specific Populations: Peace Corps volunteers must be at least eighteen years old. There is no maximum age for volunteers, and 5 percent of Peace Corps volunteers are more than fifty years old; currently, the oldest volunteer is eighty. While a college degree is not required for all position, 95 percent of Peace Corps volunteers have graduated from a four-year institution and 11 percent have completed some graduate studies or have a graduate degree. Each volunteer position has both educational and experiential qualifications that an applicant must meet; some positions require that volunteers have taken one or two years of college-level French or Spanish. Only married applicants will be considered for placement together, and then only after having been married for six months. Volunteers with disabilities should not be discouraged from applying to the Peace Corps.

Teach for America (TFA)

315 West 36th Street, 7th floor
New York, NY 10018
(800) 832-1230; Fax (212) 279-2081
E-mail: admissions@teachforamerica.org
Web site: www.teachforamerica.org

Project Type: Education; Rural Development; Social Justice;
Youth

Mission Statement Excerpt: "One day, all children in this nation
will have the opportunity to attain an excellent education."

Year Founded: 1990

Number of Volunteers Last Year: Approximately 5,000

Funding Sources: TFA receives support from public and private
donors, including individuals, foundations, businesses, and
local, state, and federal governments.

The Work They Do: TFA corps members commit to teaching
for two years in one of the low-income rural and urban
communities that the organization serves throughout the
United States. TFA expects that corps members will remain
lifelong advocates for educational equality long after their
teaching experience.

Project Location: Corps members teach in one of (as of this
writing) twenty-eight regional sites, which tend to be either
very urban or very rural. Sites currently include Atlanta,
Baltimore, the Bay Area (California), Charlotte, Chicago,
Connecticut, Denver, eastern North Carolina, greater New
Orleans, Hawaii, Houston, Indianapolis, Jacksonville,
Kansas City, Las Vegas valley, Los Angeles, Memphis,
Miami and Dade County, the Mississippi Delta, Newark,
New Mexico, New York City, Greater Philadelphia-
Camden, Phoenix, South Dakota, south Louisiana, St.
Louis, and Washington, D.C. (Please note that TFA updates
this list regularly.) Applicants state their preferences for
regions, and 99 percent of corps members end up in a
region for which they indicated a preference. Corps
members find their own housing, often with other corps

members, but they are given advice on doing so by TFA. Housing during the summer training is in dormitories.

Time Line: Typically, TFA has four deadlines for applications each year, with final notification about six weeks after the deadline. Regardless of application deadline, all new corps members begin training in the summer and are in the classroom at the start of the school year.

Cost: TFA corps members are hired as regular, first-year teachers by their host school districts and are paid the same salary as other first-year teachers. Because of the wide range of locations and salaries, TFA corps members earn somewhere between $25,000 and $44,000 annually, with the higher salaries in the most expensive cities. TFA corps members are also eligible for need-based transitional grants and no-interest loans to help bridge the gap between the end of college and the beginning of teaching, or for moving expenses. TFA is also a member of AmeriCorps, so corps members can receive forbearance on any college loans and the AmeriCorps $4,725 education award for each of the two years of service.

Getting Started: TFA's written application process is done entirely online through its Web site. The most promising applicants are invited to interview by phone; after this stage, an even more select group are given a day-long interview, which includes teaching a sample lesson and participating in a group interview, an individual interview, and written exercises. Admission to TFA is highly competitive; fewer than one in five applicants are given the opportunity to become a corps member. All accepted corps members complete a very intensive, five-week training institute the summer before they begin teaching, as well as a regional orientation, and they have ongoing support throughout the TFA experience.

Needed Skills and Specific Populations: TFA applicants do not need to have a background in education or a teaching certificate. Instead, TFA seeks out people who have demonstrated past achievement, persevered in the face of challenges, strong critical thinking skills, the ability to influence and motivate others, strong organizational ability, an understanding of and desire to work relentlessly in support of TFA's vision, and respect for students and families in low-income communities. Applicants must have or be in the process of completing an undergraduate degree with a minimum GPA of 2.5; the average corps member's GPA is 3.5, and 93 percent of corps members held a leadership role on their campus. TFA also specifically recruits people of color, math and science majors, and Spanish speakers. In general, applicants must be U.S. citizens, though some opportunities may exist for international students with degrees in math and science. Though there is no age limit to join TFA, corps members are overwhelmingly recent college graduates (within five years).

Voluntary Service Overseas (VSO)

44 Eccles Street, Suite 100
Ottawa, Ontario, K1R 6S4
Canada
(888) 876-2911 or (613) 234-1364; Fax (613) 234-1444
E-mail: inquiry@vsocan.org
Web site: www.vsocan.org

Project Type: Administration; Economic Development; Education; Medical/Health

Mission Statement Excerpt: "Voluntary Service Overseas (VSO) is an international development agency that works through volunteers. We promote volunteering as a way to fight global poverty by supporting people to share their skills, creativity, and learning with people and communities around the world."

Year Founded: 1958

Number of Volunteers Last Year: 1,500

Funding Sources: Private donors and organizations

The Work They Do: VSO recruits volunteers to work full-time with overseas partner organizations. VSO's work is focused on six development goal areas: education, HIV/AIDS, disability, health and social well being, secure livelihoods, and participation and governance. In general, volunteers can work as hands-on service providers; work alongside colleagues to share skills; strengthen organizations' systems, planning, and management; or develop organizations' abilities to network and influence policy at the local, national, and international level. VSO's partners include a wide range of organizations, from government ministries to community-level groups, and from small enterprises to local, national, and international nonprofit agencies. Specific examples of volunteer work through VSO include working as a radiology assistant in Tanzania, working as an advocacy and research advisor in Rwanda, and training teachers in Kenya.

Project Location: VSO places volunteers in thirty-four countries throughout Africa, Asia, the Caribbean, and the Pacific; everywhere from Bangladesh to Zambia. VSO places volunteers based on their skill sets, so volunteers must be flexible regarding placement location. Types of accommodations vary from mud-floored rooms to urban apartments, but volunteers have their own bedrooms, as well as basic furnishings such as a bed and mattress, storage space, a table and chairs, and cooking facilities.

Time Line: VSO's opportunities are for seven months to two-years, though most opportunities are for two years. Applications are accepted throughout the year, and applicants should plan on at least a four-month placement time span between application and departure; VSO recommends volunteers apply six to nine months before their desired departure date.

Cost: VSO covers most costs of volunteering, including a training and support program; the costs of required medical examinations and immunizations, as well as health insurance; round-trip airfare to the volunteer's country of service; a predeparture grant of up to C$650 for the purchase of supplies and equipment; an in-service grant and end-of-service grant; and a modest living allowance, pegged to the local economy where the volunteer is serving. Volunteers are encouraged to assist in fund-raising, with a suggested goal of $2,000.

Getting Started: Prospective volunteers can complete an application online. Qualified applicants are invited to an assessment day in Ottawa or Vancouver, for which VSO will provide partial funding for travel expenses. VSO also requires three positive references for each volunteer. Applicants are told whether or not they have been accepted into VSO within five days of the assessment. In general, VSO seeks volunteers who are positive, demonstrate a realistic commitment to VSO, are committed to learning, are flexible and adaptable, are sensitive to the needs of others, and who are interested in immersing themselves in a culture that may be very different from what they are used to. VSO also looks for a certain degree of self-assurance, natural problem-solving abilities, and an aptitude for teamwork.

VSO offers predeparture and in-country training, including a four-day "Preparing for Change" course and a five-day "Skills for Working in Development" course, both of which take place in Ottawa. Language training and a cultural orientation are provided when volunteers and interns arrive in the country of their placement.

Needed Skills and Specific Populations: Most VSO positions require a college degree plus at least two years of professional experience. Some volunteer assignments require French language skills. Volunteers must be at least twenty-one years old. VSO welcomes applications from people with disabilities, and seeks to enable these volunteers to fully participate in VSO's volunteer assessment process. Families may be able to volunteer with VSO, but should plan on a longer application timeline.

Index by Project Cost

BTCV, 73
Casa Guatemala, 81
Catalina Island Conservancy, 83
Centre for Alternative Technology
(CAT), 88
Christian Peacemaker Teams (CPT),
106
Conservation Volunteers Australia
(CVA), 114
Dakshinayan, 129
Earthwatch Institute, 131
Eco-Center Caput Insulae—Beli
(ECCIB), 134
Ecovoluteer Program, 138
Friends of the Great Baikal Trail
(FGBT), 154
Galapagos ICE, 159
Jatun Sacha, 225
Joint Assistance Centre (JAC), 228
JustWorks, 232
National Trust Working Holidays,
260
Por un Mejor Hoy, 281
Programa Restauración de Tortugas
Marinas (PRETOMA), 283
Service Civil International—
International Voluntary Service
(SCI-IVS), 296
Sierra Club Outings, 298
United Action for Children (UAC),
320
Volunteers for Peace (VFP), 339
Volunthai: Volunteers for Thailand,
344
Voluntourists Without Borders
(VWB), 346
Wyoming Dinosaur Center, 367

$500–$999

AidCamps International, 10
Ambassadors for Children (AFC), 12
American Jewish World Service
(AJWS), 20
AmeriSpan, 23
Amizade Global Service-Learning, 32

Appalachian Mountain Club (AMC),
37
Association of International
Development and Exchange
(AIDE), 50
AVIVA, 54
Bridges for Education (BFE), 71
BTCV, 73
Caretta Research Project (CRP), 77
Caribbean Volunteer Expeditions
(CVE), 79
Christian Peacemaker Teams (CPT),
106
Concordia International Volunteers,
112
Conservation Volunteers Australia
(CVA), 114
Coral Cay Conservation (CCC), 116
Cultural Destination Nepal (CDN),
124
Earthwatch Institute, 131
Eco-Center Caput Insulae—Beli
(ECCIB), 134
Ecovoluteer Program, 138
Explorations in Travel (ET), 144
Global Citizens Network (GCN), 164
Global Crossroad, 166
Global Humanitarian Expeditions
(GHE), 173
Global Volunteer Network (GVN),
180
Global Volunteers, 184
Globe Aware, 197
Go Differently, 199
Iracambi Atlantic Rainforest Research
Center, 220
Jatun Sacha, 225
Junior Art Club, 230
La Sabranenque, 236
Landmark Volunteers, 238
Medical Ministry International
(MMI), 246
❖ Mobility International USA
(MIUSA), 252
National Trust Working Holidays, 260

Index by Project Length

Two Weeks

Three or Four Weeks

One to Two Months

Two to Six Months

Six or More Months

Index by Project Location

Australia/New Zealand

Index by Project Season

Fall (September to November)

Year-Round

Index by Project Type

Community Development

Construction

Museum

Natural Conservation (Land)

Natural Conservation (Sea)

Youth

Disability-Friendly Organizations

Family-Friendly Organizations

Senior-Friendly Organizations